Rossano:
A Valley in Flames

To
SHEILA

my beloved wife, without whose encouragement, and patience throughout the long years, Rossano would never have been written, and to little VALERIE and HUGH BRIAN, is this book affectionately dedicated.

> I have eaten your bread and salt
> I have drunk your water and wine,
> The deaths ye died I have watched beside,
> And the lives that ye led were mine.
>
> Was there aught that I did not share
> In vigil or toil or ease
> One joy or woe that I did not know,
> Dear hearts across the seas?

Rydyard Kipling
Departmental Ditties

He who tells this tale is not a partisan; he would deal equally towards all. Of strong devotion, of stout nobility, of unswerving faith and self-sacrifice, he must approve; and when these qualities are displayed in a contest of forces, the wisdom of means employed, or of ultimate views entertained, may be questioned and condemned; but the men themselves may not be.

George Meredith
Vittoria

Rossano:
A Valley in Flames

A Story of the Italian Resistance

Gordon Lett

Preface by Brian Lett
Foreword by James Holland

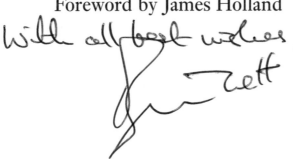

With all best wishes,

FRONTLINE BOOKS

Rossano: A Valley in Flames

This edition published in 2011 by Frontline Books,
an imprint of
Pen & Sword Books Limited,
47 Church Street, Barnsley, S. Yorkshire, S70 2AS
www.frontline-books.com

Email info@frontline-books.com or write to us at the above address.

ISBN: 978-1-84832-621-7

PUBLISHING HISTORY
Rossano: A Valley in Flames was first published in 1955 by Hodder and
Stoughton under the title *Rossano, An Adventure of the Italian Resistance*.
It was published in paperback as a Panther edition in 1956. An Italian
edition was issued in 1958. This edition includes a preface by the authors
son, Brian Lett and a foreword by James Holland.

CIP data records for this title are available from the British Library

Typeset in 11.5pt Ehrhardt
by Mac Style, Beverley, E. Yorkshire
Printed in Great Britain by CPI

Contents

Author's note from the 1971 edition

In this story the names of many of the partisans are those by which they were known in the mountains. This is rendered necessary by the fact that, for them, the political war continues.

List of Illustrations

Preface

History teaches us that, sometimes, exactly the right man finds himself in exactly the right place at the exactly the right time. That was true, I believe, from the moment of my father's arrival in the valley of Rossano in the mountains of northern Tuscany on the evening of the 30th September 1943, and throughout his stay of eighteen months.

The Italian resistance was then in its infancy. The dictator Mussolini and his Fascists had been deposed in late July, but then restored to the "throne" of Italy in mid-September by the Germans. In the interim period, many anti-fascists had exposed themselves, and now faced fierce retribution. The Italian people were experiencing both occupation by an enemy state, and civil war. The Germans had imposed harsh curfew laws upon the local Italian people, and had arrested many of the Italian military, whom they deported to labour camps in Germany.

In the mountains of Northern Tuscany, the level of poverty was extremely high, and life extremely harsh. My father described it as worse than anything that he had seen when serving with the British army in Africa and India. Many youngsters fled from the towns into the mountains to avoid conscription into the new Fascist army, causing an even greater strain upon the limited supplies of food. Justice had fled. The people were bitter and confused, and looked for leadership.

My father was in many ways different from the average British Army officer. He had been born in primitive conditions in Domara, Papua New Guinea in 1910. My grandfather was working there as an engineer, endeavouring to develop the natural resources of the country. My grandmother died as a result of the complications of childbirth. My father's first years were therefore spent living with his mother's family in Sydney, Australia, whilst his father continued to work in the spartan conditions of Papua New Guinea. At the age of eleven, my father was sent to England to complete his education, where he was cared for by members of his father's family. He was educated at Clayesmore School, in Dorset, and later at university in Dijon, France..

He took up a commission in the East Surrey Regiment in 1933. Whilst serving in India, he developed a love for the Himalayan mountains, which led him to transfer into the British Indian Army. He led two mountaineering expeditions into the remoter parts of the Himalayas. This brought him a Fellowship of the Royal Geographical Society.

My father's love of mountains undoubtedly suited him to life in the Apuan Alps, that part of the Appenine mountains where the valley of Rossano lies. He also, of course, had the benefit of ten years military experience. However, I believe that the qualities that enabled him to achieve what he did were his humanity and his humility. He understood and genuinely cared about the problems of the peasants of the Rossano valley and its surrounding areas. He was able to relate to the poorest and the most disadvantaged of its inhabitants. He shared with them much of their deprivation, suffering and hunger, and they responded by giving him a fierce and enduring loyalty.

The neighbouring Centocroci Brigade of partisans, led by "Richetto", had as their chaplain Don Luigi Canessa, known as "the fighting priest". He knew my father well. He described him as "a tall, lean man of few words; he was good, generous and charitable, a true gentleman. The only signs of his rank were the crowns of His British Majesty that he wore on his shoulders. He spoke in halting Italian, his eyes often on the ground as he searched for the precise word that he wanted."

Adrian Gallegos, the fugitive No 1 Special Force Operative, first met my father in September 1944, when he, Gallegos, was under considerable suspicion from the partisans and was thought to be a spy. He described my father as follows: "He had a fine face and my impression of him was that of a man who thought deeply, sincere and idealistic." Gallegos later described my father as the uncrowned "King of Rossano" – not by choice, but at the insistence of the local population.

In February 1945, Allied Command decided that it wanted my father back on the Allied side of the front line [then only a short distance south of Rossano] in order that he might assist in the co-ordination of the partisan elements during the "final push." This caused genuine distress amongst his partisan comrades in the Rossano area. Ermanno Gindoli, Commander of the 2nd Battalion of the Justice and Liberty Column, took the unusual step of writing personally to Allied HQ on the 22 February 1945: "In the name of that spirit of comradeship which in this hard battle unites all those fighting for freedom, and in the name of the affection which each patriot nurtures for our Major Gordon Lett, I ask that he remain with us to share the joy of the undoubted liberation and to celebrate with us the imminent victory of the Allied armies". His plea fell on stony ground, and my father was called back through the lines in March.

After the war in Italy had ended, my father returned to England. He married my mother in 1946, and they returned together to Italy, where my father was appointed British Vice Consul in Bologna. Upon their first visit together to Rossano, they slept in the former cowshed that had become the Deluchis' family home after their house was burnt down by the enemy in August 1944. My father always remained in touch with his friends in the valley.

I first visited Rossano some years later, when only a few months old, and, of course have no recollection of the visit. Our family returned to England in 1952, and as my sister and I grew up, Italy and the Valley of Rossano were often mentioned in our home. We had many Italian visitors, and there was an exciting occasion when Italian State Television, RAI, came to film us all at home. To my sister and myself, then, Rossano was just a part of the fabric of our lives. My father would travel to Italy often, but we would stay at home, at school. International travel was, of course, far more complicated in those days. I read my father's book when I was in my teens, and got to know the story well. However it was many years before I realised the full significance of what he had achieved.

My father suffered a stroke in 1972, and thereafter fought a long and courageous battle against illness. Undoubtedly, the harshness and deprivations of his time in Rossano had done long term damage to his constitution. When my father died in 1989, Mick Micallef, one of the "originals" who had been in Rossano with him, wrote to my mother describing how his health too had been adversely effected in the long term by the harsh conditions in which they had lived.

For myself and my family, my father left behind a unique inheritance. When I eventually returned to the valley of Rossano as an adult, I found a welcome of almost unbelievable warmth awaiting me. I met and was accepted into the families of numerous of my father's old partisans and helpers. The depth of their love for my father still amazes me. Even today, more than sixty years after it all happened, if I visit the houses of some of the older inhabitants of the valley carrying a copy of my father's book, they will reach forward and kiss his photograph.

This welcome is not confined to the valley of Rossano. It is widespread in the area. Many is the time that I have driven or walked into a village that I have not visited before. The streets may be quiet, and few people about. It is my habit to stop one of the older inhabitants for a chat, or to go into the local bar if there is one. At first I am regarded with suspicion, as a foreigner. But I have only to mention my father's name, and the atmosphere changes immediately. I and my companions become honoured guests in the village, and quickly a flagon of wine appears.

Many of those mentioned in the book have become my close friends in the same way that they had been my father's. Tarquinio Deluchi, Avio Braccini, and Falco Montefiori are sadly no longer with us, but Dani Bucchioni, Luciano Bracelli, and Giovanni Tognarelli, the miller's son [known to the fugitives as "the little general"] are still going strong.

My children visit the valley of Rossano often, and have done since their childhood. We have a house in the village of Chiesa. It is the old primary school, which closed as the population of the valley began to shrink, and children became too few in number to justify its existence. We often meet people whose erstwhile classrooms are now our bedrooms. The valley has proved for us to be a great place for eighteenth and twenty-first birthday parties. The local people are always delighted to see us, and don't seem to mind how much noise the youngsters make.

So what of the Rossano valley today? Many friends who visit say that it seems untouched by the passage of the years, and that nothing seems to have changed since the war. That is not true. Gone is the grinding poverty, and also, sadly, much of the younger population.

After the war, the houses of the village of Chiesa were eventually replaced or rebuilt with the support of a United Nations fund. The world of agriculture moved forward, and the old labour-intensive methods of farming became obsolete. The tiny terraced fields, impossible for a tractor, were turned to pasture, and most of the youngsters went to the cities to look for work. The population of the valley fell from over two thousand to about four hundred, most of them old. Happily, state pensions and welfare now ensure that abject poverty is a thing of the past.

What remains is the ethos of caring for one's fellow human being, however strange or objectionable he might be. Antonio Deluchi, Tarquinio's son and my greatest friend in the valley, looked me in the eye not long ago, and said: "Brian, to have money is not necessary in this valley. If there is no money, there will still, always, be food for anyone who needs to eat." In that way, the Rossano valley has not changed since my father's time.

September 2011
Brian Lett

Foreword

Some years ago, I heard about a terrible tragedy that took place in the war, in the autumn of 1944, on a mountain called Monte Sole. Despite having been studying the war for some time, I had never heard of this place, or Marzabotto, the nearest town, or that the 772 people that were killed there represented the single largest civilian massacre in the West outside the death camps - worse than Oradour in France and even Lidice in Czechoslovakia. Ashamed by my ignorance, I decided to learn more.

Monte Sole is only some twenty miles or so south of Bologna. The great city itself lies on the edge of the northern plains and the Po River Valley, and the long chain of jagged and seemingly impregnable peaks that make up the Apennines, loom to the south, and it was only a short drive before I was heading down the Reno Valley, the mountains towering either side of me. Past the small town of Marzabotto, I crossed the river and began climbing up the narrow winding road that led,eventually, to a high mountain plain, a hidden place of rough fields, small oaks and chestnuts, overlooked by the mountain peaks.

Dotted around, however, were the ruins, the remains of what had once been a thriving mountain community of villages, hamlets and farmsteads. I passed one destroyed church, then paused by a tiny walled cemetery. An old man was placing a wreath on the iron gate just as I arrived. Inside, bullet marks still dented the crosses and wall behind. It was in here that some two hundred elderly men, women and children were pushed in, lined up, and shot by troops of the 16th Waffen-SS Panzer Grenadier Division.

Even now, large parts of the Apennines are largely unknown to foreign travellers. It is to the great cities - Florence, Rome, Venice - and to the rolling countryside of Tuscany that we flock in such numbers. Monte Sole is a place of haunting beauty - wild, forgotten, still isolated - just as are the mountains to the west of Pontremoli in the Ligurian Apennines, where Gordon Lett, an escaped prisoner of war, found himself for the last year and a half of the war, fighting a desperate battle against the Fascists and Nazi occupiers, and struggling with his new-found Italian comrades-in-arms to survive the incredible deprivations that so beset the vast majority of Italians in that terrible last eighteen months of the war.

Despite the civil war that was taking place, despite the vast numbers of villages and towns that were utterly destroyed by the typhoon of war as it slowly rolled north up the leg of Italy, and despite the considerable impact the various and disparate partisan bands made towards the Allied cause, there has been woefully little mention of any of these aspects in the retelling of the Italian campaign by British and American historians. Look up the word 'partisan' in the index and you will invariably not find it listed. Ironically, our version of the war in Italy has been partisan in the extreme, largely told through the prism of our own nation's experience.

This narrow view of the Italian campaign was due, in part, to the fact that in the years following the end of the War, many of the archives that now flourish around the world were nothing like so accessible. Travel was considerably more expensive, there was no such thing as digital photography, and, most importantly, many of the documents that now have open public access were firmly locked away. British accounts tended to be written by former servicemen, who held a broadly similar attitude towards the Italians whose country they were now slogging their way through: that the Italians should never have declared war against Britain in the first place, and that, frankly, they had it coming. There was a level of contempt directed towards the Italians, who were seen as having sought armistice terms as soon as their fortunes took a turn for the worse. Italians were seen as cowardly, and any Allied soldier was always going to put his own interests and those of his comrades first. If that meant destroying villages and civilians getting killed, then so be it.

I remember one former Guardsman telling me with no small amount of amusement how they had reached a small town north of Rome and had raided a shop. Although British troops were given enough rations to keep the hunger at bay, the spoils of war - loot - were considered just desserts and so he the Guardsman demanded that the Italian hand over what food he had. The Italian denied he had any. 'I know you're lying,' said the Guardsman. 'Either you give it to me, or I'll take it from you anyway.' The Italian's protests turned to pleas as the British soldiers found the cellar and a number of foodstuffs. Needless to say, they took the lot. Another soldier told me how they spent a night on a farm and discovered a small field of potatoes. 'Please be careful of my crop,' the signora asked. 'We were,' the soldier told me. 'We picked, peeled, boiled and ate them very carefully.'

What neither of these British soldiers would probably have appreciated was that the Italians were starving. The shop-keeper would have been carefully hoarding and rationing his food reserves. Taking them away would have meant ruin. Infrastructure in the south had been largely destroyed, while it was not much better in the German occupied north. In the cities, there was almost no electricity and little if no running water, while what trains and vehicles there were had been requisitioned by the military. There was simply no means of transporting food from one place to another. On top of that, in the south, inflation was astronomical, while in the north, workers were paid a pittance. The US Fifth Army Surgeon General reckoned that in the Allied-controlled south, half the 'available' women in Italy had some form of venereal disease. It was a staggering statistic; women usually only resort to prostitution when there is absolutely no other choice.

Of course, most Allied – and indeed, German – troops had very little understanding or knowledge of the Italian people and their culture. To the Allies, the Italians were just 'Eyeties,' shifty, overly emotional types, not to be trusted. To the Germans, they were a former ally who had stabbed them in the back. Neither Allies nor Germans appreciated that the Italian people had, largely, always been reluctant combatants. It is striking how often both Allied and German troops, once billeted with Italians, came to see them as naturally warm, open-hearted individuals, rather than a contemptible mass. It was during such lulls in the fighting that lifelong friendships were often formed.

Nor did they realize that Italy, still a very young country, was really more of a geographical concept than a nation state. Fascism had only very loosely bound the country together as one. Italy might have been one of the most homogenous countries in Europe, with 99.61% of the population Roman Catholic, but it other respects it was extremely diverse. Before the *Risorgimento* of 1870, it had been made up of a patchwork of city and sovereign states. Even under Mussolini, most Italians had felt a far greater sense of local and regional, rather than national, identity and loyalty. There were an incredible number of regional dialects, for example, more so than in any other European country. A Neapolitan arriving at the mountain village of Rossano would have found the people there as hard to understand as Gordon Lett and his fellow escaped POWs did.

Outside the big cities, communities were primitive, and often extremely isolated, especially in the Apennines. There had been no agricultural or industrial revolution in Italy; farming practices and living conditions had hardly changed at all in hundreds of years. Most farmers worked as impoverished peasants, known as *contadini*, share-croppers for big land-owners, or *padroni*, who, naturally enough, benefitted far more than the contadini. Few of these country folk were educated or could read or write, while living conditions were basic in the extreme, as Gordon Lett so vividly describes. There were no metalled roads, almost no motorised vehicles even before the war before petrol and cars became so scarce; no mountain village would have had either electricity or running water and only limited sanitation. Most contadini lived in houses that doubled up as barns: the animals would be in stalls on ground floor, while the family lived above making the most, in winter, of the warmth – and the stench - of the beasts rising up from below.

Religion played an important part; going to church was a way of life, but then so too did the weather, superstitions, myth and folklore. The local witch, or *strega*, a kind of wise-woman, was frequently a notable figure in any community. This was a tight-knit, insular world - a world in which showing hospitality to strangers was a culturally accepted norm and in which most people had a marked distrust of any organized and central authority.

And it was into this world that Gordon Lett and his fellow escapees stumbled in the autumn of 1943. When Italy signed the armistice on 9th September, the gates of the numerous prisoner-of-war camps dotted throughout Italy were suddenly opened and the largest mass prison-break the world has ever seen began as some half a million Allied troops swarmed out into the Italian countryside. Unfortunately, however, for the escapees, unless the camp had been in the south, within a day or so these men discovered they were on the run in German-occupied territory. Some headed south, others headed to the Alps and to neutral Switzerland. Others still, such as Gordon Lett and his fellows, headed to the coast, hoping that the Allies would make a landing and outflank the German troops streaming to the front to the south of Rome.

All, however, were utterly dependent on the help of local Italians, who most ex-POWs found, rather to their surprise, were only too willing to help. The attitude of the contadini in the Rossano Valley was typical: they were fed up with the war, despised the Germans - or *Tedeschi* - and the neo-Fascists that were now running a puppet-Italian government in the occupied north, and recognized that trained Allied soldiers could help them with their embryonic attempts at resistance.

If helping escaped POWs was instinctive, beginning armed resistance was not. There is no doubt that most Italians wished they could keep their heads down and simply prayed the war would go away. Some, in the cities, could manage this - just - but German revenge on their treacherous former ally was so punitive, it was hard for many to just sit back and take it. Germany was bleeding the north dry - of its money, of its natural resources, of its food, and of its manpower. Volunteers could join SS police units, while others were pressed into forced labour. In addition, Mussolini was allowed to form new divisions from conscripted young men born in the years 1923, 1924, and 1925. The young men of the north had to report to conscripting offices on pain of death. The choice was a simple one: either they accepted and were conscripted, or they fled to the hills and mountains and joined the growing number of partisan bands as outlaws.

The problem for the wider rural communities was that the cores of these emerging partisan bands were usually made up of locals. Ties of kinship and community meant they were honour-bound to support them. Since these partisans were now outside the law, they had to be protected and fed, but this help came at a price: by supporting partisans they were considered as guilty of treason as the partisans themselves.

Life was hard enough for the contadini even in peacetime. Disease and the vagaries of weather meant that at any moment they could face ruin. The burden of supporting partisan bands, with its extra strain on their meagre resources, and coupled with the menacing threat of execution by German and Fascist forces if caught or even vaguely suspected, was intense. For the partisans themselves - most of whom were frightened young men, often completely severed from their families - life was tough and brutal. Italian winters can be severe, as they were both in 1943-44 and 1944-45, yet most had only threadbare clothing, a rarely a proper place to sleep or regular food. Disease was rife, while the partisan command could be both capricious and harsh. Inevitably, the lure of wages and better conditions proved too tempting for some. Betrayal was common, mistrust ever-present.

This was where men such as Gordon Lett were a Godsend. While the contadini of the Rossano Valley initially saved him and his fellows, he was in turn able to use his authority and training as an officer - as well as his innate intelligence and good sense - to help organize the partisans into an effective fighting force. It was noticeable that the most effective partisan bands were those who either had a core of former Allied POWs amongst their number, or those which were first contacted by American OSS and British SOE agents, who were, in turn, working with the clandestine resistance government, the CLNAI, or Northern Italian Committee of National Liberation. These men could help organize much-needed air drops of arms, ammunition and other supplies, such as boots and clothing. The threat of turning off this tap - even though it was extremely limited - often ensured that many partisan bands maintained some sense of cohesion.

That the efforts of the partisans in the Italian campaign has been often at best derided and at worst, completely ignored, is a travesty. It is true that few were properly trained, that they were lightly armed, and that in terms of discipline and firepower they could offer little. But one only has to look at the recent examples of Iraq and, especially, Afghanistan, to realize that resistors - or insurgents - require little of either to become a major problem to an occupying force. The Germans in Italy were having a hard enough time defending the overwhelming firepower of the Allies along the frontline without having to deal with an insurgency to their rear. Allied troops could be given leave from the front to enjoy the bars and sights of Florence and Rome, but a German soldier left the front constantly worrying that he would be ambushed or shot at. They could never relax. By September 1944, Field Marshal Kesselring, the German commander in Italy, reckoned partisans had been responsible for 30,000 German casualties - equivalent to two full-strength divisions. At a time when Kesselring could rarely call on more than two dozen *half*-strength divisions, this statistic alone proves what a contribution they were making. Nor does it take into account the intelligence work the partisans were providing. In June 1944, for example, partisans captured a complete map of the Gothic Line, with all the German defences along it, which was passed to the Allies before their assault began.

In the years following the war, a number of memoirs were written by former POWs and Allied agents who lived and fought alongside the partisans and amongst these rural communities. Perhaps the best known is Eric Newby's *Love and War in the Apennines,* yet Newby escaped to Switzerland long before the war ended and was barely involved in partisan operations. Another is *Carlino* by Stuart Hood, a fine book, but one in which the author always remained somehow remote from his surroundings. There are others, not least Roy Farran's account of clandestine operations behind enemy lines at the end of the war. None, however, have the immediacy of Gordon Lett's *Rossano,* nor the vivid portrayal of and empathy for the people he finds himself living and fighting amongst. His admiration is genuine and obvious, and touching too. Equally vivid are his descriptions of the landscape, the harshness of the conditions and the ever-present danger. Quite simply, to my mind, there is no finer account of the partisan war by an English writer.

Newby's memoir has remained in print, but the rest of all wallowed out of print for many, many years, and largely forgotten. In the case of *Rossano,* this has been a travesty, which, thankfully, is now being righted. It should be a required text for anyone wishing to understand the War in Italy that so blighted that country between September 1943 and May 1945. With luck, its re-release will help change our myopic view of that campaign.

September 2011
James Holland

Introduction

On escaping from prison some of us decided to make our way to the Mediterranean coast rather than to the north to cross the Swiss Frontier, or south to cross the Allied lines, for we believed that there might be an Allied landing from the sea.

Prisoners of war knew nothing at all about the Italian people, having been incarcerated in such camps as Bari, Chieti and Veano. We had only come into contact with those who acted as our gaolers under the control of the Nazi Gestapo. For fifteen months I had listened to news and commentaries blaring from loud speakers erected on high poles throughout the camp compounds and they continually poured out hymns of hate against the "Anglo-American Bandits". The Allied Forces were accused of atrocities towards Italian soldiers, and of the deliberate murder of women and children and the bombing of churches by the R.A.F. Newspapers sent into the camp for our "education" contained endless horror stories. On the 23rd of August 1942, for example, they advertised reports of the raid on Dieppe. It was described as the failure of the opening of the 2nd Front in Europe. On the front pages was the reproduction of an order, supposed to have been found by the German garrison, ruling that all prisoners captured by the Canadian Forces at Dieppe must be chained together and if necessary shot. This kind of venom continued until the overthrow of Mussolini on the 25th of July 1943.

On the 8th of September the Italian Commandant of prison camp No. 29 at Veano switched on the B.B.C. radio programme from London for us to hear. A commentator stated his opinion that the Germans would establish a line of defence in Italy stretching from Genoa on the west coast to somewhere on the Adriatic near Ravenna. Camp 29 lay well south of that line, but there were no signs of evacuation by German forces. From our prison on the top of a hill we could see considerable activity by Nazi planes above the Piacenza aerodrome.

The Commandant informed us that all telephone communication with Rome had been cut and he advised us to scatter into the hills. Thus it was that we were pitched into the unknown, conscious that not long before there had been an outburst on the Fascist radio which described the Italian people as anxious to cut the throats of all "Anglo-Saxons" they encountered in revenge for a naval bombardment against the port of Genoa.

After trudging through the foothills for some hours we came to a little village named Gussafame and saw a group of villagers waiting for us. I expected the worst. The villagers ran forward and surrounded us. Vividly I remember a young woman in a red dress who thrust a piece of bread into my hand. In a few moments others brought a fiasco of wine and bunches of grapes. They produced articles of clothing so that I and my two companions could discard our army uniforms which bore tell-tale coloured patches marking us as prisoners. The villagers of Gussafame were reluctant to let us go on our way and warned of German patrols searching towns and villages in the valley below. They directed us to a path leading into the mountains. On that day, although we did not know it at the time, the same thing was happening to hundreds of escaping prisoners all over northern Italy.

At the end of September I reached the Valley of Rossano in the Comune of Zeri in Massa-Carrara province, which was to become my base throughout the war of liberation.

I stopped there because the situation on the southern battle front seemed to be fluid and it was the general opinion among the population that there might be an Allied landing at any time on the coast somewhere between Livorno and Genoa.

In post war literature insufficient credit has been given to the courage of the civilian population, and especially to the contadini, once they realised that the war had not ended on the 8th of September. Without that courage the national Resistance Movement could never have been born.

During the first month, like other ex-prisoners, I intended to rejoin the British Army once we knew more about its position in the south. This I would have done had it not been that towards the end of October 1943 a young Lieutenant of Alpini came to see me. He had escaped from Pisa. Edoardo Basevi represented the newly constituted Committee of Liberation of Genoa and he had been sent into Apuania to discover whether the Resistance could be organised on a national scale. Geographically the Valley of Rossano was a promising area for the purpose and a further asset was the character of its population that numbered more than a thousand souls living in seven small villages. Their sentiments were at that time purely defensive. As early as September 1943 they were already conducting a passive disobedience campaign against the Carabinieri police to prevent them arresting youngsters who had been called up for service in the Fascist army, and from requisitioning their agricultural products demanded by the Government as a contribution to the State.

Escaped prisoners of war were regarded as being in the same category as those eligible for Army service. It was largely due to this factor that the entire population evolved into a Resistance force and throughout the period of the War of Liberation their opposition to the enemy had very little to do with the ideology of any political party.

The spirit of resistance was active in the valley by the time Edoardo arrived. And so the idea emerged that I should build up an International Battalion recruited from ex-prisoners who wanted to repay the people who were giving us shelter by helping them to defend themselves; this force would be in close liaison with the Committee of Liberation in Genoa and through that Committee would establish communication with the Allied Command.

I have been accused, since the publication of my book "Rossano" in 1955, of hostility towards some of the partisan brigades formed by the Communist and Socialist parties. This is not true. I have always had the greatest admiration for the Partisans, but not always for some of their individual leaders. In Zeri and its neighbouring Comunes, Resistance existed long before the political element. It was only after the beginning of 1944 that it began to make an impression, but it is an indisputable fact that political parties of all colours made a great and lasting contribution to the Resistance Movement. There had to be leaders for the youth of the country to follow and those leaders were anxious to ensure that the Government in post-war Italy would be very different to that which had dragged them into war. Nevertheless it cannot be denied that ideological differences between some of the political parties, which at times verged on open warfare, damaged the reputation of the Resistance as a whole in liberated Italy.

It is not for any foreigner to criticise the action of Italian politicians, although we can have our opinions. In particular no Englishman has the right to criticise. We in England, having been free of a nemico in casa for the last thousand years, cannot begin to understand the differences of temperament and outlook, the subconscious fear of dictatorship or foreign invasion, that exists among the citizens of those countries such as Italy and France who have seen their territory occupied by a foreign power three times in three successive generations.

Prisoners of war continued to reach Rossano and find shelter until they moved on towards the Allied lines. By May 1944 an organisation known as "A" Force had been established on the island of Corsica. Its purpose was to send especially trained Italian agents on to the Italian mainland to collect escaped British prisoners and evacuate them from the coast of the Cinque Terre between La Spezia and Sestri Levante. It was through an "A" Force mission with the code name of "London", which reached me on the 1st of

May, that the existence of my "International Battalion" was signalled to the chief of No. 1 Special Force, Commander Gerry Holdsworth, whose headquarters had recently arrived in southern Italy.

The International Battalion began at the end of October 1943 as a small group of British and Polish fugitives. The Poles were sent to us by a member of the Genoa Liberation Committee after they had escaped from ships in the port requisitioned by the Nazis. Soon other nationalities joined us. It is impossible to give an accurate figure for the Battalion's strength. Although the arms with which we had been provided in November consisted of only half a dozen antiquated Italian rifles and a few of their "Red Devil" hand grenades, the whole population of the Rossano Valley considered themselves as belonging to the Battalion. In critical moments when the Police were searching for recruits for the Army our ranks were swelled by all the youngsters of sixteen years old and upwards. Eventually most of them learnt to use weapons dropped to us by parachute and they played their part magnificently. But more valuable than anything else was the food and shelter provided by the older generations.

The War Office in London had ordered that British prisoners-of-war were not to remain behind in Italy unless they were on special duty. Our Internationals consisted of Poles, French, Danes, Dutch, Yugoslavs and Russians, many of whom had escaped from ships in the port of Genoa and the Todt forced labour of organisations in Italy. By May 1944 the weapon situation had improved and the International Battalion numbered about 130 combatants organised on the old Volunteer system. The soldiers lived at home but could be rallied at short notice in the event of a crisis, "home", in the case of the international personnel, being various cascinas scattered throughout the chestnut forests of the Valley. Our unit badge consisted of a miniature Union Jack and Italian flag sewn on the right shoulder of shirt or jacket.

The International Battalion had begun to make itself known as an operational unit by the time that Special Force headquarters got to hear of it. We had carried out successful ambushes of Nazi and Fascist patrols on roads leading to Pontremoli, and had expelled a number of Fascist sympathisers from neighbouring valleys where they had tried to intimidate supporters of the Resistance. On the 15th June 1944 we disarmed the Fascist garrison at the Teglia Dam that provides electric current for the Magra Valley. Rumours began to circulate among the enemy of a large British force that had been dropped into the mountains by parachute.

A. Force Mission "London" decided that our base would be a suitable rallying point for all escaped prisoners they might discover in the mountainous regions south of Genoa and the Po Valley. The International

Battalion was given the responsibility of allotting safe houses and providing guides for them to the sea coast.

In June 1944 the enemy began to take a greater interest in what became known as the 4th Partisan Zone because it lay directly behind the area to the south of the Magra Valley where the complex of Gothic Line fortifications were under construction. There had already been a number of minor rastrellamentos which we had survived with few casualties and our intelligence sources warned us of more to come.

By that time the Resistance forces had grown considerably, with bases outside the Valley of Rossano. To the north were the "Beretta" Divisions of Guglielmo and Gino Cacchioli above Borgo Taro. To the west and south-west on the slopes of Monte Gottero and in the Comune of Zignago were the "Justice and Liberty" Brigades, to the south in the Comune of Calice, the Brigades commanded by a young Army Lieutenant Dani Bucchioni, and to the east, above the City of Pontremoli, an outpost located in the village of Arzelato under the command of Nereo Giumelli, known as "Falco". The nearest danger point was the city of Pontremoli for it housed a German and Fascist garrison which was dependent on the district headquarters at Massa, and was ruled by a Fascist Vice-Prefect.

On the other side of the Magra Valley, directly behind the Gothic Line, Resistance Forces were established in the mountains north of the cities of Massa and Carrara, to the west of Monte Tondo, and in the Fivizzano area. My fellow ex-prisoner of war from Veano, Major Tony Oldham, was operating with a Partisan brigade. His theatre of activities was more dangerous than mine but an effective courier service was gradually being created direct with units of the American 5th Army.

Special Force Mission "Blundell"

As a result of the reports sent from "A" Force Mission "London", on the 27th of July 1944, I learnt from Special Force Headquarters that I had been appointed to control a military mission with the code name of "Blundell", and two Italian radio operators named Alfonso and Bianchi arrived in Rossano that day with their transmitting sets. This meant that the International Battalion had now come under direct Allied Command.

In addition to assisting with the collection and evacuation of prisoners of war we had four other duties to perform. They were:-

a) The gathering of information through Partisan intelligence sources about enemy movements within the 4th Operative Zone, and any other information that might be of value to the Allied Command.
b) Encouragement and guidance where required to partisan units in activities aimed at sabotaging the enemy war effort and undermining the

morale of Nazi and Fascist troops, and particularly in carrying out attacks on lines of communication or nerve centres of which details were sent to us by Allied intelligence headquarters.

c) To obtain reinforcements of weapons, clothing, and supplies for those Partisan Brigades which Special Force officers felt could be relied upon to make the best use of them.

d) To act as a liaison link between Allies and Partisans when forces such as the Special Air Service or Marine Commandos were sent into enemy occupied territory to carry out an operation requiring special knowledge, and which might be too difficult for the Partisans to carry out alone.

Alfonso and Bianchi carried out their tasks with great courage until the end of the war; the fact that they survived was largely due to the protection given them by the "Beretta" Brigades of the Cacchioli brothers in the Taro Valley. They particularly owed a debt to one of the Brigade Commanders, Federico Salvestri better known as "Richetto", who was a Maresciallo of Carabinieri when the partisan war began.

The month of July represented a milestone in the progress towards better organisation of the national Resistance Forces. The Partisan higher Military Command in Milan headed by General Raffaele Cadorna decided that a unified military headquarters must be established in the various Partisan Regions to co-ordinate the activities of Brigades and encourage a degree of military training among Commanders. This was essential in order that they could make the best use of the weapons, equipment, and supplies that were descending on them with increasing frequency from Allied aeroplanes. The newly formed C.L.N. in La Spezia, which had been created to control the 4th Partisan Zone, sent Colonel Mario Fontana into the mountains to establish his headquarters in the Comune of Zeri. He was an infantry officer with long and distinguished service. We first met shortly before the "Blundell" wireless operators reached me. He was fully aware of the difficult task ahead of him. He asked me to attach the International Battalion to his headquarters in the village of Adelana and to provide a radio link with Special Forces in the south. We were also to help with the security problem and supply special couriers to maintain communications between the scattered Partisan units under his command.

This arrangement had only just begun to work when early in August the area was subjected to the most severe rastrellamento of the whole war and the entire Partisan system of defence was demolished. Brigades broke up and scattered to countless safe areas outside the Comune of Zeri. In September the International Battalion returned to the Rossano Valley and in due course Colonel Fontana set up his command in the Comune of Zignago where I rejoined him.

The reaction of the Partisans to this rastrellamento provided a classic example of the resilience of the Resistance Movement. Large units were forced to break up into small and compact groups of men under chosen leaders. They had to keep on the move to avoid capture in the same way that we prisoners-of-war had done when escaping from our prison camps. After the initial shock of being forced to run for their lives it gradually dawned on the Partisans that, with effective weapons and the superior knowledge that they possessed of the terrain, the speed with which they could move from one place to another was a weapon that they could use to inflict damage on the enemy.

The post-war wisdom of writers on guerrilla tactics from Mao Tse Tung to Che Guevara was not inspired by any particular genius on their part. The principles laid down in their much-advertised text books were learnt from experience by us as Partisans in Italy, and were universally adopted by the end of the year 1944.

A serious weakness of the Resistance organisation was the lack of a rapid means of communication between formations combined with a reluctance, generally for political reasons, to act under the orders of a central command. This was a cause of friction until the end, but perhaps it is not regarded as so serious a fault in the view of the historian as it was to those of us who were commanding in the field.

During the second half of 1944 contact with the Allied Forces in the south increased, and there was a continual stream of couriers through the Gothic Line or parachuted into the 4th Zone from British and American planes. Unfortunately liaison was not very good with the vital area of Garfagnana south of the Magra Valley; Major Tony Oldham was also involved in the Partisan war having acquired a radio transmitting set and two Italian operators by accident in the month of July. The pilot who was flying them to the north dropped them in the wrong place.

The journeys of special couriers sometimes created friction between "A" Force and me. Partisans were considered a dangerous addition to parties of escaping prisoners because if the group was captured there was a possibility that all would be shot. This precaution was justified, but there were occasions when we received information on persons of such importance that the risk had to be taken.

On the 13th November General Alexander, as he then was, issued his proclamation warning the Partisans that the Allied attack on the Gothic Line had come to a standstill and would not be resumed until the new year.

The enemy redoubled their efforts to render the Partisan brigades harmless with a series of widespread rastrellamentos aimed at making safe their lines of communication along the Gothic Line, and to the north. They invaded the 6th Partisan Zone, between the 4th Zone and Genoa, swept through the Province of Parma and, using a battalion of S.S. to commit the most fiendish atrocities of the whole war, they made a determined effort to gain complete control of the valleys south of the River Magra. In that area the Partisan Brigades felt the full blast of an enemy attack on the valley of the Serchio in December which forced the American 92nd Negro Division to retreat. Major Oldham and his Partisans crossed into Allied territory to escape annihilation.

In my opinion writers on the Italian Resistance have not given sufficient importance to the fact that the Partisans were fighting for survival throughout the whole period of the war. Individual commanders had to make sudden decisions without the help of a higher command and often without knowledge of what was happening in adjoining areas. Some of those decisions were brilliant, others disastrous. Life as a Resistance fighter was tough. When Partisans were not engaged in operations at the request of Allied intelligence they were on the alert for attempts by the enemy to infiltrate their territory, and for enemy agents sent to collect information or to assassinate Partisan leaders.

By the middle of December we in the 4th Partisan Zone were left in no doubt that the enemy were preparing for a combined attack on us from all directions. Our friends in the cities warned of the gathering storm, of Nazi and Fascist troops concentrating at strategic points on the coast road from Genoa and in the Magra Valley, as well as beyond the Cisa Pass. The C.L.N. in Milan and Special Force Headquarters in the south were aware of the threat and it was with some relief that I received a message by radio shortly before Christmas stating that a squadron of the Special Air Service was to be dropped into Rossano. Their tasks would be to attack any roving enemy patrols in the area and to disrupt communications on the coast road, the Via Aurelia known as "Route 1", and in the Magra Valley. These actions were to be conducted where possible in co-operation with Partisan volunteers.

Operation "Gallia"

The squadron of S.A.S. led by Captain (now Lieut: Colonel) Walker Brown was dropped into Rossano on the 27th of December 1944 to carry out what was known as "Operation Gallia". They were to remain with us until the 11th of February. There is no doubt that the arrival of the parachutists was of great encouragement to the Partisans, for their armament included a British 3" H.B. mortar and several Vickers machine guns. There were thirty-three men altogether and both types of weapon were used with considerable success. Heavy equipment and ammunition was transported to the assembly areas before each attack on mules led by their Rossano owners. At the end the total S.A.S. casualties were six, all of whom had formed part of a section captured during the first few days by an enemy patrol. It was not until after the war that we learnt they had not been shot in La Spezia prison as we feared but had been taken to Germany, and survived the war.

A number of attacks were carried out, particularly on Route 1, and it was not until the 20th of January 1945 that the enemy was able to raise sufficient forces to counter-attack. The inevitable rastrellamento began at midnight on the 19th whilst the parachutists were engaged in an ambush against an enemy convoy in the Magra Valley. We had a valuable ally in the thick snow that covered the mountains. Mongol ski troops were employed against us, and in addition to the garrisons of the Massa and Parma military commands, the 285th German Grenadier Battalion was sent from Genoa as additional reinforcement. The crisis lasted for five hard days. It provided a classic example of the vital contribution that the unarmed population could make towards the Resistance against an enemy invading force.

A "secret weapon" which we all possessed was our knowledge of almost every metre of the territory in which Partisans had been operating for the past sixteen months. The enemy were unwelcome strangers in a strange land. They had already burnt out most of the villages and massacred some of the population the previous August and they needed what shelter remained and the help of the villagers to achieve their task of finding the British parachutists whose numbers, owing to rumour, they believed to be well over a hundred. This time elderly men and women remained in their houses. When the enemy patrols arrived they gave the impression that they were prepared to co-operate with them. The more agile volunteered as "guides" and proceeded to take them by the longest routes to the most distant mountain gorges and caves. The "guide" generally rode on a mule while the soldiers trudged through the snow behind him. They would reach their destination as it grew dark, and then the "guide" would vanish and the invading force was left to find its way back to base as best it could. The result was that on the sixth day such confusion prevailed among the scattered patrols that they were withdrawn from the area. On the way they burnt more houses in the area of Calice, but several groups were ambushed by Partisans prewarned by the villagers. This resulted in a number of Germans and Fascists being captured, and led to an exchange of prisoners under the supervision of the Bishop of Pontremoli by which the lives were saved of Partisans condemned to death in Pontremoli prison. The enemy never again attempted to over run the 4th Partisan Zone.

This event stands out in my experience as a typical example of the support that Partisans were given by the population all over northern Italy. Resistance could not have been victorious without it.

The parachutists continued their operations when the rastrellamento ended and they were given valuable support from some of the Partisan brigades, especially those of Lieut. Bucchioni and "Richetto". They left Calice on the 11th of February to return to their Allied base across the Gothic Line and Dani Bucchioni provided them with guides to cross the River Magra.

On the 15th of March 1945, Major Henderson of No. 1 Special Force having been sent in to relieve me, I departed from the Valley of Rossano to cross the Gothic Line accompanied by my Adjutant, Lieutenant Braccini and other Partisans. We were about the last group to travel along the route used so often by all nationalities. Dani Bucchioni's brigade provided us with guides for part of the way. My purpose in leaving was to discover what Allied plans might be, as little information had reached us from the battle front for some time. We crossed the Gothic Line on the outskirts of the town of Barga, then occupied by an American Negro battalion.

In due course I was instructed to return to the 4th Operative Zone. By the time I reached Castelnuovo Magra on the 20th of April it was clear that the enemy opposition was weakening. The Partisans under their leader Walter of the Moncini brigade had occupied the city of Sarzana. They indicated a crossing over the river. I entered La Spezia that evening with one partisan as guard and the driver of my Special Force jeep. We discovered that we were the only Allied representatives in the city.

On the 21st of April a Combat Platoon of the American 92nd Infantry Division arrived and I was attached to their headquarters as Liaison Officer for Partisan affairs.

The 4th Operative Zone Partisans came down from the mountains on the 23rd of April after a final battle at La Foce on Route 1 in which several were killed. Led by Colonel Mario Fontana they entered La Spezia in triumph.

Observations

Having witnessed every stage of the wartime Resistance in Italy it is my impression that subsequent historians have not given emphasis to the essentially national character of the Italian Resistance. It was not confined to any one class of society or any one political party. Members of the Italian Armed Forces worked with my International Battalion throughout, and they had a magnificent record for courage and endurance —officers such as Major Adriano Oliva, now a retired General, Colonel Mario Fontana who commanded the 4th Partisan Zone and died after the Liberation, Lieutenants of the Air Force Otello Braccini and Aldo Berti and Army Lieutenants Dani Bucchioni and Gambarotta all of whom are still serving with the rank of Lieut. Colonel, and the Lieutenant of Alpini Edoardo Basevi who left the Army after the war.

There were priests who joined the Partisans or collaborated with us to the full, such as Monsignor Giovanni Sismondo, Bishop of Pontremoli, the priests in the mountain villages of Montereggio, Torpiana and Albareto outside the Rossano Valley, and Don Guiligotti of Adelana and Don Grigoletti of Colloretta in the Comune of Zeri, both of whom were brutally murdered by the Nazis in the rastrellamento of August 1944 because they had given refuge to Partisans and escaping prisoners-of-war, including myself. Nor is it correct to maintain, as some ill-informed commentators still do, that the Partisans were all rebellious factory workers or peasants.

In the International Battalion from 1943 to 1945 we had representatives of all classes either living in the woods as combatants or acting as agents to bring important news from the towns about enemy movements. I recall to mind a barrister, two doctors, a lawyer, an ex Consul-General of the Diplomatic Corps, several fishermen from a trawler that had been requisitioned by the Fascists in the port of La Spezia, an Arab merchant seaman from Eritrea, a couple of artists, a musician, shop-keepers and café owners some of whom owned cafes or shops in London and Scotland, a butcher, a theological student, a dentist who managed to keep open his surgery in Pontremoli most of the time, a Professor from the University of Genoa, students from universities as far distant as Bologna, carpenters, two railway station masters, several railway employees, a Maresciallo and two Brigadieri of Carabinieri as well as several Carabinieri policemen. Many were farmers, and the sons and daughters of families in Rossano and the adjoining valleys.

Again, in my opinion, writers about the Italian Resistance, and especially outside Italy, often overlook the essential differences in the background to the Italian Resistance compared with that in other countries of Europe.

For instance, there was never at any time the prospect of creating a "Secret Army" on the Belgian or Dutch pattern. The war was conducted by small and compact groups, and this policy was encouraged by Special Force advisers. Events proved that it was the right policy because whenever Partisan brigades tried to adapt themselves to conventional methods of warfare and created large military formations to defend an area, they were soundly defeated. Clear examples of this are provided by the last stand of the Partisans in Garfagnana on the Gothic Line in December 1944, and the epic defence of the Republic of Domodossola.

Conclusion

In my opinion the War of Liberation from 1943 to 1945 remains a glorious page in the long and colourful history of Italy. Young Italians should be proud of it.

For hundreds of years past generations have defended their country, their homes, and their possessions against foreign mercenaries and invaders. If ever Italy should again be threatened, the Spirit of Resistance will blossom forth once more among the sons and daughters of the Partisans.

It is their natural heritage.

November 1971
Gordon Lett

Foreword

(by Freya Stark)

When Major Lett asked me to write a foreword for this book, I did something which I have never done before: I accepted before I had seen the manuscript.

For some years since the end of the war, I had been wishing to read a story of the Italian partisans and peasants fairly told. I had come back to Italy in '45, when the glow of their exploits was still warm upon them, and before the politicians, "with ugly wrack", had covered them all over. I had visited La Spezia, and had been entertained by Colonel Fontana and such of the rest of the partisan bands as still survived: and had been a witness of the respect and trust, and of something added – a warmth of true devotion – with which Major Lett was regarded. The qualities that produced this – qualities of unselfish leadership, and comfortingly English – the author naturally does not describe: but without them, the epic of the Valley could never have been lived nor its history written.

It is, in its modest way, an epic: fate and wickedness take a hand, and the simple charities that remain true to themselves and become heroic. The story of the peasants was repeated through the northern Appenine and all round the Alpine valleys; the casualties were far heavier than most people in Britain realise; and there was no thought of reward. As far as I can tell, Major Lett's account is as fair as any human document can be, in its light and in its shadow – the perpetual shadow of Italian history, by which the least political of peoples is twisted by ideas it has never believed in to acts it disdains.

Major Lett's story makes this dualism clear. But it does far more. In a setting of poverty, hardship and suffering, it lets the best of human qualities shine out – compassion, faithfulness and love – in a simple way that moves us the more deeply, in a world of pastoral remoteness where the differences of nations are less important than the gentleness or the cruelty which unites or divides them – a world which one leaves reluctantly, thankful, in spite of all, for the general goodness of mankind.

Prologue

One day a venerable Franciscan friar was toiling along a road high up in the mountains of Apuania in Northern Italy. He had travelled far, and his ultimate destination was a monastery in the city of Pontremoli, which he could see spread out in the valley below. Rounding a bend in the road, he came upon a memorial built on the rocks at one side. He stopped, and shading his eyes with a gnarled hand against the glaring sunlight, he read the inscription engraved on the marble tablet.

"To the people of Rossano, Arzelato, and Casa Gaggioli who throughout the war from September 1943 until the Liberation, assisted with lodging and food the following Allied military personnel and escaped prisoners:–

British Empire	281
Americans	18
Poles	32
Yugoslavs	9
Dutch	4
French .	2
Belgians	3
Russians	25
British Military Mission	16
British Parachutists	50

as a sign of gratitude, and in recognition of all that this partisan population has suffered for the ideal of Liberty.   G.L."

A strange inscription indeed! The holy man muttered a blessing and continued on his way. What turbulent events lay behind the simple wording on that tablet?

It is a long story.

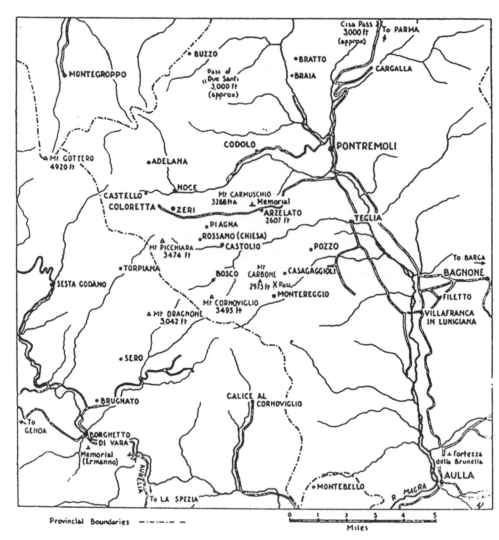

Map of the Rossano Valley in the Northern Appenine mountains, and the surrounding 4th Partisan Zone. From this area, the city of Piacenza lies to the North, Florence to the Southeast, La Spezia to the South, and Genoa to the West.

Part I

Fugitives

Chapter One

We Come to the Valley

This story really begins on the fifteenth of October 1943. It was a bright morning, and I remember feeling the hot sun on my face when I first opened my eyes, wrenched back from a dream in which, dressed in white tie and tails, I was dancing with my fiancee to the strains of the Blue Danube. We were in a beautiful ballroom somewhere in England. So real was it all that I could smell the perfume of her hair as her head rested on my shoulder. It took me a little while to adjust myself to the hard reality of my present existence.

I lay buried among crisp, warm chestnut leaves piled almost to the rafters of the small barn in which I had passed the night. Sunbeams filtering through cracks in the tiled roof threw into clear relief the dusty cobwebs and stout wooden beams of the ceiling. Underneath lived the cattle and sheep, and their constant munching, with an occasional tinkle from the bells suspended round their necks, gave a comforting illusion of general peace and goodwill.

With me were Sergeant 'Bob' Blackmore, a fellow-Australian from Queensland, and Rifleman 'Mick' Miscallef of the 2nd Rifle Brigade. Both, like myself, had been captured near Tobruk. When P.G. 29 our prisoner-of-war camp near Veano, had been abandoned by its Italian guards after the attempted Armistice of the 8th of September 1943, our Camp Commander had told us to scatter into the hills, each officer taking with him at least one of the other ranks who had been imprisoned with us.

Our experiences in various prison camps had taught us something about our Italian hosts, and our opinions of the country and its people were consequently, though understandably, far from flattering. I began to revise my opinions the day before our departure, when a young Bersegliere sentry, Gianni Pancrioli, ran considerable risk to himself and his relations by telling me of the terms of the Armistice as announced by Marshal Badoglio on the Italian radio. An hour before my departure, Gianni came into my room at the prison and insisted on giving me forty Lire and the address of his home in

Parma, suggesting that I should make for that city to find shelter. It was a friendly gesture, and the last that I had expected. Neither of us could foresee the upheaval that was to take place in Italy before we would meet again.

Bob, Mick and I passed through the open gates as in a dream, knowing that we were about to throw ourselves upon the mercy of ordinary Italian citizens, of whom we knew nothing. The sentry boxes were empty. On one of them the last occupant had scribbled in chalk the slogan Viva gli Inglesi. Outside was the country road which wound its tortuous way up to the camp from Ponte dell'Olio. Our Italian commandant, leaving in a car bound for the South, waved as he passed us. The war had taken a strange turn.

We had three courses of action to choose from – to make for the Italian coast and await the Allied invasion which would probably take place at Genoa or Leghorn; to cross the frontier into Switzerland, or go South to meet our advancing troops. I chose the first course, pinning my faith on an early landing from the sea.

So we had left the road and followed a narrow track leading to the woods. According to the map I had made in camp, a trek along the crest of the hills should lead us to the main range of the Apennines, and once we had crossed that, we should be within sight of the naval base of Spezia and the sea. A month of travelling brought us to this point – a month walking through endless forests of chestnut trees. The weather had been warm and fine at first, so we slept in the open. Although we had occasionally spent a day or two working in the fields of some farmer, we studiously avoided contact with the mountain peasants; we had no idea how they might feel towards us. But at last, when the Red Cross stores we had brought with us were exhausted, desperation made us approach a humble, isolated cottage to beg for food.

The place was poorer in appearance than any we had yet seen. At first there was no response to our knock on the battered wooden door, but just as we were about to continue on our way, we heard shuffling footsteps. An old woman opened the door a little and peered into my face. She mumbled a remark in a dialect difficult to understand. Then two younger peasants emerged from the gloom inside. For a moment all three stared at us in silence. Then the man spoke:

"Siete Inglesi?"

"Yes, we are English," I replied. "We have escaped from the prison camp at Veano."

They showed no surprise.

"Welcome to our house," said the peasant. "Come inside."

He led us to a high-backed wooden bench, beside a fire that smouldered on a stone hearth in the middle of the room. There was no chimney and the smoke escaped as best it could through the doorway, for the small windows were closed and barred. We were given a piece of coarse bread and cheese, and a glass of sour wine.

Our journey to the sea coast had been easier after that. We made our way from one peasant family to another, guided by their advice as to the safest paths to follow through the woods. Sometimes the youngest son would be deputed to take us part of the way; sometimes it would be the old grandfather who was our guide, leaning on his walking stick and talking volubly of the last war, when he had fought beside the English. I marvelled at the friendliness of these people, and at the poverty in which they lived. They did not speak much about the war and seemed to regard it as one more unavoidable evil in a life of hardship. Many of them had sons killed or taken prisoner. I noticed that, while they assumed that the war would end one day, they did not let it dominate their lives; they were fully occupied with the business of trying to scrape a living out of the soil.

One day after three weeks of trailing up and down the thickly wooded mountain slopes, we struck a well-made metal road, which appeared to follow more or less the direction that we wanted. The hospitality we had met with had created a certain carelessness in our approach to villages that lay in our path. The road led to a larger village than usual, but we were about to walk merrily through it when Fate intervened.

It was, as usual, a sunny day, and before us there was an uninterrupted view of the road and the end of the village high street. Just before we emerged from the shelter of the woods, Mick noticed a uniformed figure walking from the village towards us. It was a matter of seconds before we had dispersed amongst the trees at the roadside The Carabiniere policeman passed on his way, and we came to our senses and realised that it would be wiser to skirt the village. This took some time, as there was a deep river bed to negotiate, but at length we reached the road on the other side. Then it was that we met our first priest. Shortly after we had regained the road, he suddenly emerged from a side track, and began to walk towards us and the village. Surprise at meeting each other was mutual. He was dressed in a long black habit, and held a book in his right hand. After I had gone through the usual formula as to who we were, he stared at us intently, his brown eyes half closed. Then silently he turned round, and motioned to us to accompany him. He led us off the road, along a path through the woods, until we reached the top of the ridge of hills. Only then he spoke.

"Go down there," he said, pointing before him, "You will be safe. They are good people, although their lives are hard, and their possessions few." He wished us farewell, and, regardless of the fact that we were, comparatively speaking, heathens, blessed us with the sign of the cross. Then he hurried back the way he had come. Poor Don Quiligotti was to pay dearly for his Christian act.

From where we stood, the ground fell away and was lost in a deep canyon clothed in thick-leaved chestnut forests. On the far side a sky-line of rugged peaks formed a wall to the South-West. At each end of this panorama a mountain blocked entry from the outside world. Several villages could be seen perched precariously on the tops of small hills, and between them terraced fields of grain lay spread out among the trees. Far down in the canyon a river sang its song as it wound its way between boulders and fallen tree-trunks to the plains and the sea fifty miles away. Except for this, a strange silence hung over the scene, and no birds sang. Thus it was that we came to the Valley.

* * *

On this fine autumn morning a little over a week later, a door suddenly opened in the stall below. I stood up, and ploughed my way through dry leaves to the door of the loft.

Outside, our host's daughter sat knitting on a rock, watching the sheep that strayed contentedly across the landscape. When she saw me she jumped to her feet and ran forward clasping a white cloth in which was wrapped our breakfast of chestnut bread, a bottle of milk, and an apple. With a little air of ceremony she presented it to me; this was a daily rite.

I extracted my share, and then while she resumed her knitting, sat down beside her and began to eat.

The Valley was looking at its best this morning. A stranger might have said that the evils of war did not touch it, and that its inhabitants were completely carefree. It was not until one had come to know the people as we had done that one could see the fear that haunted them – fear that some German or Fascist patrol might arrive at any moment to steal their goods, and impress their menfolk into the enforced labour camps; fear of the Carabinieri patrols which, officially operating under the new Republic, paid occasional visits to the Valley to collect taxes, or to look for deserters from Mussolini's army.

The hopes that had been so high in the prison camp at Veano had long since faded. The Allies had not landed at Leghorn as had been expected, and obviously had no intention of doing so. Meanwhile, German resistance in Southern Italy had stiffened, and the heavy hand of the Hun had fallen on all those who had shown unduly great relief at the prospect of the end of the war. All communications were under jurisdiction of the Nazi-Fascists, and we had been obliged to accept the fact that it would be useless to go South until our Armies were on the move again. A few newspapers had reached the

Valley. They boastfully proclaimed the re-capture of Allied prisoners who had escaped from the camps, and described their subsequent transfer to Germany. One exultant editor announced that more than eighty per cent of those who had escaped had been retaken. There was nothing for it, therefore, but to remain in the Valley and await events.

Since the first day of our arrival the peasant family who owned this cascina had taken it upon themselves to look after the three of us. Giuseppe, the old father, had given me the name of Luigi, and adopted me as his son. The mother of the family quickly took upon herself the task of mending the tattered clothes which we had exchanged for our conspicuous uniform since we left Veano. Then there was the eldest son, Richetto, and his brother Tarquinio, who had instructed us in the mysterious art of tilling the soil with the mediaeval tool called a "Zappa" – a kind of hoe, with a handle too short to use it standing upright, so that the inexperienced suffered acutely from backache before ten minutes had passed. And lastly, in this hospitable family, there was the daughter, Dina, who brought our breakfast each morning. Her complexion was fair for an Italian, and she had that poise and dignity of movement so characteristic of these women in the hills who are in the habit of carrying bundles or jugs of water balanced on their heads. Dina was a determined young lady with a will of her own; she gave the impression that she would not deal kindly with the enemy when the time came.

So the days had passed, and our small British party almost began to think of ourselves as members of this Italian peasant family in the hills. Other English ex-prisoners had drifted into the Valley, and they met with the same warmhearted comradeship. They were readily accepted by their new-found friends; all became adopted by individual farmers, and all settled down to learn this new way of living, where the earth and all it produced was the vital factor that controlled one's existence; where a good meal and a night of undisturbed sleep was worth more than anything else that the world had to offer. Sometimes it was almost possible to forget the fear that hung over the Valley like a great invisible cloud. Yet subconsciously all knew that a day of reckoning would come.

I finished my breakfast and folded up the napkin in which it had been carried. It was only then that I realised that Dina had been watching me for some time. She smiled when I looked at her

"You are very thoughtful this morning, Maggiore," she said "Are you thinking of England?"

"No," I answered, "I was thinking of the valley. It is very dangerous for you to look after the English as you do. If the Germans come, they will probably burn your house."

"Then you will build us another. In any case our houses are old and dirty – there are no houses in the world so dirty as ours."

Calmly and gracefully she walked towards the barn, where Giuseppe was watching their two cows placidly cropping the grass nearby. Bob and Mick emerged from the loft, and attacked their breakfast.

How I longed for a cigarette! It was over a month now since any of us had tasted tobacco, except for the occasional rank cigar which we were given on festive occasions from the village store. It was strange to think how once one had smoked a pipeful of tobacco without a thought of where the next was coming from.

I was roused from these reveries by Mick. Through a mouthful of bread and cheese, he shouted,

"There's a party coming up the hill, sir."

From the cascina in which we had passed the night, a track fell away and zig-zagged down the mountain slope until it was lost in the inevitable chestnut woods. Five people were to be seen climbing up it. The leader I recognised as Tarquinio, our host's son – the others were four British ex-prisoners, a sailor and three soldiers, who had passed the night in one of the villages. Presently Tarquinio spotted me.

"Ho, Luigi!"

I waved in reply.

A few minutes later they reached the cascina, where the father, Giuseppe, and Dina had joined us.

"Luigi," said Tarquinio breathlessly, "you had better hide. A patrol of Carabinieri is in the Valley, searching for the English. I have brought these up with me."

"How many Carabinieri are there?"

"About twenty with the Brigadiere. My aunt heard them talking in her house. They have had orders from the Germans in Pontremoli to find the English who are in the hills and take them to prison. If they find you, the Brigadiere will be promoted, and will receive a reward of money and rations."

The old father swore loudly, and spat on the ground.

"Vigliacchi! That Brigadiere would sell his own mother!"

The rest of the party sat down on the grass where they were. Such alarms had been frequent since our arrival, and we had soon realised that it was best to leave the details of escape to our protectors. More often than not the excitement died down; it would turn out to be due to the wild babbling of some peasant woman who had returned from a shopping expedition to the nearest market town of Pontremoli, at the head of the river Magra, four hours' walk away. But this time the situation looked more serious.

After a short consultation, aided by gesticulations from Tarquinio and cries of "Mamma mia" from a deeply incensed Dina, Giuseppe gave his verdict. "It would be wiser, my sons, to go higher up, into a cave that is hidden by the big rock which you see up there."

The old man was pointing at a grey patch slightly below the summit of the mountain. It was a rock lodged between two small trees, and appeared to have no path leading up to it.

"Va bene, Babbo," I said.

"Stay there until dusk. My daughter will then come to tell you if it is safe to return to the Valley. She will bring food for your supper."

Tarquinio went ahead, and the rest of us followed in silence along a barely discernible goat track that curled up through boulders and thorn bushes towards the summit of the mountain. The sun was quite hot and we began to sweat. Presently we turned off the track and scrambled up a rocky slope with the help of our hands and knees. Half an hour later we arrived panting at the entrance to the refuge.

It consisted of a crevice in the mountain side, caused by some geological freak. Its top instead of being open to the sky, was filled in with large slabs of rock, and the outer face of this unconventional roof was now covered with a growth of coarse grass and moss. At its mouth was the great grey rock that Giuseppe had pointed out from below. The cave, known locally as "the cave of the Wolves," was so narrow that only two men could stand abreast at its entrance. Tarquinio and I took up positions behind the rock, whilst the others went inside.

From where we crouched we had a magnificent view of the landscape below, of the cascina, and the white sheep dotted about its surrounding terraced fields. We could see Dina, who had resumed her knitting again, sitting at the place where I had had breakfast. Giuseppe, meanwhile, had moved a little way down the path, and was making a pretence of hoeing a field in which he hoped one day to grow potatoes. Except for the occasional tinkle of the sheep bells, the usual deep silence hung over the scene, contrasting strangely with the blue sky and bright sunshine.

"We will be quite safe here," said Tarquinio, "It is now about ten o'clock, and the Carabinieri all like to be back in their barracks by four in the afternoon, so that they can go out with their girl friends in the evening. Besides, it is too hot for them to come as far as this."

"I hope you're right," I said doubtfully.

The possibility of the Carabinieri coming up to the cave was far from happy. We could not retreat from it without being seen, and had no arms with which to defend ourselves. I found myself for the first time sympathising with the fox in the English hunting field when the hounds are on the scent, a comparison that came nearer home as the months went by.

The hours dragged on. At last the shadows began to lengthen on the slopes below us. Giuseppe was still working in his field. Dina had disappeared, apparently to collect our food, for we did not see her again until the evening, winding her way up towards the cave, a bulky white bundle balanced on her head, while she continued to knit as she walked.

She reached us just as dusk was falling, and we could hear Giuseppe mustering the sheep. She put the bundle down by the rock.

"The 'vigliacchi' have gone back to their barracks in the next valley. The Brigadiere was very angry because he could not find any English, and the men with him drank far too much wine in each of the villages, so that they did not want to search any more. They might come back to-morrow. Therefore I have brought you sufficient food for to-night and to-morrow morning."

"But they can't sleep here," said Tarquinio.

"No, I will take them to another cascina," replied the girl, "that of Salvatore. It is not quite so comfortable as ours, as the roof has holes in it, but there is plenty of soft hay to sleep on."

Our forlorn little band shuffled out of the cave, Mick the rifleman leading the way. For them the day had passed like very many others. They had picked up in the village a pack of playing cards of the type used by the local inhabitants, and having learnt the meaning of the quaint illustrations on them, had invented a game of 'poker' of their own, and spent the time gambling with fictitious millions.

The new cascina was not far away, and well hidden from the path that led up from the Valley across Monte Picchiara. There had been no rain for some time and the hay was dry. We settled into it and then began to eat our supper of cold chestnut bread and cheese. Tarquinio took a final look at our new refuge.

"I'll come back early to-morrow, Luigi," he said, "and will bring some fresh milk. If there is any alarm in the night, go back to the cave. I do not think they will come back to-morrow."

"All right, Tarquinio. Give my love to Mamma. Thanks for the supper, Dina."

"Prego," she replied conventionally, "Buona notte e buon riposo."

The brother and sister walked away through the dusk, and we threw ourselves down on the hay. Suddenly the silence was broken by one of the soldiers.

"I wish we were armed, sir," he said, "you could do wonders in these hills, with a few rifles and hand grenades."

"Can't we get any from some of the locals?" said Bob. "There must be plenty of Italian rifles knocking about, because half the army deserted with their weapons."

"With a few rifles," joined in Mick, "we could settle these Carabs easily, and take their boots. Mine are worn out. Do you think we'll ever be able to do anything, sir?"

"I expect we'll get some news before long. The time will come soon for us to make them run instead. Our people are sure to be making plans to help us, because they know by now that we are scattered about in these mountains."

The sailor laughed. "They know all right! The other night the B.B.C. said there were thousands of British ex-prisoners in the hills in the North, all armed. Like Hell we're armed! I suppose they said that to frighten the Jerries! I bet Kesselring won't lose any sleep over it."

They relapsed into silence. In the woods outside an owl hooted. Suddenly it was night and the clear sky was lit by stars. Another day was over - one more day nearer to that freedom and normal life which must come in time. News in the Valley was scanty, for there were only two radio sets and the B.B.C. broadcasts were being regularly disrupted by the enemy. On rare occasions we heard the commentaries given by Colonel Stevens, "Candidus," or "L'Uomo Qualunque." They brought immeasurable consolation, but it was not often safe enough for us to go down.

I shut my eyes, and tried to forget my surroundings. It was surprising how easily one's mind became a blank.

Chapter Two

Alarms and Excursions

By the end of November it was clear that the Allied plan of campaign in the south had misfired. The enemy were quick to realise this, and the establishment of the new Fascist Social Republic with its consequent increase in the German garrison made movement difficult for us. The public were constantly exhorted to betray fugitives from the prison camps; increasingly large bribes were offered. At first it was a sum of 5,000 Lire to any Italian who brought about the capture of an Allied fugitive dead or alive; towards the end of November, two months' rations of food and tobacco were added. In December a decree was published threatening anybody who helped us with shooting in the back as a traitor The enemy began a series of reprisals to cow the population into subjection; the Press circulated reports of prisoners recaptured and a rumour spread that any wearing civilian clothes at the time would be shot as spies. By the end of the year few of us possessed the uniforms with which we had been issued in prison by the International Red Cross; International Law as we knew it ceased to exist.

The policing of the mountain districts remained largely the responsibility of the Carabinieri, who were under the orders of the nearest Fascist or German command. The rank and file of these police were sympathetic towards the fugitives for, in a way, they were fugitives themselves. Their families lived mainly in liberated Italy or in the occupied cities and their only hope of survival at first was to continue in the service. A very few of their leaders were fanatical "Republicans", and it was these few who temporarily dishonoured the name of the Carabinieri who, before the war, were a force esteemed by all nations of the world.

Not long after we took refuge in the Valley I had good reason to be grateful to the Carabinieri. It was towards the end of November and the Rossanesi were busy in the forests, collecting chestnuts which were to be dried and ground into flour. We had all joined various families to help with this harvesting which went on every day of the week.

War prisoners who have evaded from concentration camps

Foreigners who are wandering in the impervious regions of Italy

REMEMBER !

The Italian Army has been thoroughly reorganised and you will soon discover what a frightful fate is hanging on your heads.

Should you be caught while in possession of arms, or should you have joined a gang of "partisans", you will be considered franc-tireurs and as such you will be tried in accordance with the laws of war.

Why, then, will you still put up with hunger, defy danger and suffer all sort of discomforts? Why should you prolong your suffering for the sak of what is a hopeless cause?

Surrender to the Italian Military Authorities who will treat you as well as they did formerly and will again recognize you as war prisoners.

Only following this course will you be able to avoid being condemned and to hope to see again your Fatherland and the dear ones who are anxiously awaiting your return home.

A pamphlet scattered in the mountains of Apuania, from Fascist aeroplanes, during November 1943. It was written in four languages – English, Italian, French, and Polish.

One afternoon we were hard at work, intent on probing among the fallen leaves. Suddenly I realised that somebody must have given the alarm, for on straightening my aching back I found that the younger generation had disappeared, and only the old ladies and greybeards remained in my vicinity. Before I could follow suit old Babbo, who was nearest me, whispered that it was too late, and told me to go on working.

Hardly had he given the warning when two Carabinieri appeared, their rifles carried at the ready. As they approached I could feel that they were watching me with more than casual interest. One of them wore a Corporal's stripes. He asked Babbo and the old ladies where the youngsters had got to; the answers varied in ingenuity and the Corporal did not press the point. Then he addressed me. I feigned deafness and continued a frantic search for chestnuts.

"You, come here," he shouted.

There was nothing for it but to comply, in the hope that I could pull off a deaf-mute act.

The Corporal asked me a few questions and when I continued to look stupid motioned to me to follow him. We walked off, the other Carabinieri behind me.

By this time I knew the countryside well, for there was scarcely a path that we had not traversed in our wanderings. My one chance of escape was to jump off the track at the right moment and hope that the resulting rifle shots would miss their target. Just as I was visualising in my mind the right place to make the attempt, the Corporal halted and turned round.

We had come some distance from the chestnut gatherers and were screened from view by clumps of evergreen bushes. The policemen slung their rifles on their shoulders, and grinned at me.

"We know who you are," said the Corporal. "You're an escaped Englishman; you'd better make a bolt for it while nobody is looking. We've been sent up here to collect all the eighteen-year-olds for military service and there was nothing about English prisoners in our orders for to-day."

"Thanks," I said, and wasted no time about my departure. "Good luck," they shouted, as I half scrambled, half fell, into the river bed below.

The youth of the country were in a sorry state of confusion. They had laid down their arms in September, for the Armistice had seemed like the beginning of a saner period in their lives. Its failure drove them to look for other means of escape, to avoid at all costs being herded once again into armed masses and forced to fight against those people whom they instinctively liked more than the German "Master Race". So began a mass migration into the hills to escape the press gangs hunting them in the plains. Then came stories from Piedmont of gallant actions and isolated victories by army units that had managed to hold out, and had in fact initiated on their own a war of Liberation. This was an inspiration to many, and not only the younger generation, as something genuine; something that had risen phoenix-like from the flames and ruins of their shattered fatherland.

North of the river Po the resistance movement drew its leaders from all classes. The City of Genoa early became one of the most active centres and by December the nucleus of a Committee of Liberation had been formed that sent its agents into the mountains to discover areas where resistance could be organised against the common enemy. Those pioneers were brave men, and many of them were to perish before they could see the result of their labours. The youth of Italy badly needed leaders at that time – once they had found one, they served him with fanatical loyalty through thick and thin, regardless of his nationality or political ambitions. The Committee in

Genoa had many problems to tackle single-handed, for it could not count on support on a grand scale from other areas. Italy's new Allies knew little of conditions inside the country following the Armistice and did not understand the demoralising influence on the nation of twenty years of Fascism. Only those whose homeland had been occupied by the enemy realised to what extent the armed few could force their will upon the unarmed many.

Except for moral encouragement through the B.B.C., help from the outside world was non-existent. The Genoa organisation had established contact through Switzerland with the Army Commands in England and North Africa, but this produced no immediate results. There had been a general expectation that the Allies would send arms and equipment at once, and to the fugitives from the prison camps the situation became increasingly irksome, for we knew it would have been in our power to wreak untold havoc upon the enemy and thereby influence the whole resistance movement in northern Italy. But the help that was so urgently needed was not forthcoming, so there was nothing for it but to wait hopefully upon the future.

Although the people of the Valley were alarmed by the increasing threats made against them, they remained solidly united in their efforts to resist. Taxes remained unpaid, and in spite of manifestos sent out by the Fascist authorities in the city of Pontremoli, they refused to send any of the produce of their fields to the State depositories. There was little enough to send, but the peasants kept what there was and preferred to give it to the needy fugitives.

By the end of the year 1943, these circumstances had combined to create an atmosphere of foreboding among the mountain people. Their inherent suspicion of the city dweller, and particularly of the wealthy Fascist classes who lived securely in their villas in the plains, was accentuated to such a degree that refugee families who fled to the hills for safety found themselves coldly received. The hillmen knew that there were spies among them who would report to the "Republicans" on their standard of loyalty towards the new Government, and later events proved their suspicion to be well founded.

Christmas drew near, and the people of the Valley prepared to make merry as best they could – to forget for a while the fear that hung over them, growing more oppressive day by day.

Chapter Three

The First Day of Christmas

It was Christmas Eve 1943. The weather was cold but snow had not yet fallen; instead there were frequent storms of rain and a strong North wind swept the heights below the summit of Monte Picchiara, making the tiles rattle on the roof of the old cascina in which we had now lived for more than a month.

A wood fire smouldered on a stone hearth in one corner and the room was filled with smoke that tried to escape through the solitary iron-barred window and was blown back by the gale. Dry leaves covered the floor. In another corner were a few china bowls and a bronze basin half filled with water. A pile of dirty blankets near the rickety wooden door completed the furnishing.

A sudden burst of wind sent the acrid smoke curling round the room again.

Three Poles had joined our small colony. Mick had found them the previous day toiling across Monte Pichiara led by an Italian guide. They had come on foot all the way from Genoa, having escaped from one of the German "Todt" forced labour organisations, with the help of an agent in the resistance movement. Their presence was the more welcome in that they had each arrived armed with a revolver.

Tarquinio broke the silence.

"To-morrow, Luigi, you must come to my house. There are to be two days of 'festa', and the Carabinieri will not worry us before the New Year."

"But don't you think that might be dangerous for your family?"

"There is only one person who might be a spy in our village and we will keep a special watch on him. I have a friend who lives near the barracks in Coloretta and he will send us a message if the police show signs of moving our way. As long as you don't all collect together in one house it will be safe."

Mick spoke from the darkness.

"It will be almost like going to London, sir. It's a pity we can't go to the pictures."

"You might like to try going to Pontremoli. There are two cinemas there, and the Fascists would give you a warm welcome."

"I bet they would. I've never been considered worth as much as 5,000 Lire in my life before, not to mention two months' tobacco. I wonder if they let you have pipe tobacco, or must it be their awful popolari cigarettes?"

"I hope we shall never know the answer to that," I said.

Tarquinio went outside to collect wood for the fire. It was very dark and the sky was heavy with rain clouds which had descended so low that they covered the top of the mountain. Unpleasant as it was to endure, the weather provided a safeguard against enemy activity by night. Only two winding tracks led up to the cascina and these were difficult for the uninitiated to follow in the dark. Any unwelcome visitors would have to use lanterns to find their way.

The farmer returned carrying a bundle of logs which he threw down beside the hearth.

"That should be enough for to-night," he said, "I will go home now and tell them in the village that you are coming down to-morrow. Good night, Luigi."

"Good night, Tarquinio, and a pleasant journey home. I'm glad it's you and not me in this wind."

We were all sick to death of inaction. Little had happened during the past month, either on the battle front in the South, or on the resistance front in the North. An agent of the Liberation Committee in Genoa had at last paid me a visit, with a view to the raising of an "International Brigade" to act as a rallying unit for the whole of the Liguria area. This was an Italian Army Colonel who used the alias of "Balbi". He was not young, for he had rendered distinguished service to his country during the first World War, and three times had been awarded the Italian equivalent of the D.S.O. He was short and thick-set, with slightly greying hair. There was a twinkle in his eye that registered a vivid sense of humour constantly bubbling beneath the surface. Colonel Balbi was a born and very cheerful optimist and, as we were to learn as time went on, an unfailing source of encouragement to those around him.

We now possessed between us a few old Italian rifles, some Italian "Red Devil" hand grenades, and a quantity of red and white signalling strips. These stores had been contributed by the population. In addition, we had a reserve of flour, tinned meat, and potatoes, all hidden in the roof of the cascina. Our clothing was scanty and it was a blessing that the mountain slopes were sufficiently well covered for us to obtain firewood.

We realised well enough that it was not the fault of the Genoa organisation that progress was so slow; the real trouble was the increasing attention the

enemy were paying to the threat of armed rebellion all over the country.
They had had more than a taste of it already in the mountains north of the
River Po. The city of Genoa had fallen under suspicion, and the leaders of
the underground organisation had their work cut out avoiding arrest.

But all things are relative, and we looked forward to Christmas in the
Valley as an experience so delectable that for the time being the future paled
into insignificance.

*   *   *

Next morning Tarquinio arrived early at the cascina. We hid the few articles
that had been used the previous night, and having made sure that there was
nothing which might be seen by any stranger passing that way, Tarquinio
locked the door and we set off for the Valley. With the addition of the Poles
we numbered nine in all.

The summit of Monte Picchiara was still hidden in clouds, but the cold
wind of the past few days had blown itself out and rain fell steadily. Water
poured down the slopes in countless torrents that seethed between rocky
banks overhung by gnarled chestnut trees. Two hours later we crossed the
last stone bridge and entered the village of Valle.

Water dripped from the slate roofs, and the place looked grey and cold.
The houses, built of stone from the local quarries, had small barred windows
and little light penetrated the smoke-grimed panes. Poverty was the natural
heritage of the inhabitants of these villages, a poverty shared with their
livestock, for each house had its stalls built underneath the rooms where the
family lived, and these housed cattle, sheep and goats. No-one was astir in
the only street, which forced its way, as if in protest, between the high walls
of the buildings. A few disconsolate chickens wandered aimlessly about
pecking at the mud.

Tarquinio knocked on the door of a house in the middle of the village.

"Domenico, are you at home?"

There was the sound of shuffling feet.

"Who's there?"

"Io, Tarquinio."

A key turned in the lock.

"Come in and make yourself at home."

We crowded into the smoke-filled room. Our new host insisted on our
sitting by the fire while he poured out a glass of wine. His wife offered us
freshly baked chestnut bread. Two grubby children, one a small boy of about
eight years of age, the other a toddler of three, stared at the strange gathering

with wide eyes, hiding themselves the while in the darkest corner of the room.

"Poveri ragazzi," said the woman. "Che bruta vita!"

Tarquinio and Domenico carried on a conversation between them in the local dialect. After a while they reached some conclusion, for Domenico addressed me.

"Signor Maggiore, we will look after three of your friends if they would like to stay. We have two beds in the house, and there is enough to eat." Tarquinio then suggested that we should go on to the next billet, and we went out into the street.

By this time our presence had become common knowledge. As we continued our journey, Tarquinio leading the way, I noticed many faces at the windows watching us with interest. Bob saw them too and waved cheerfully at the more attractive damsels. His action met with responsive smiles. A few children, more curious than their parents, dared to run out of their houses into the rain to inspect the strangers more closely. The path wound up a slope past a ruined chapel where Tarquinio stopped the column for a moment to talk to his fiancée, Amelia. She stood in the dark doorway of a nearby house, a tall, fair-haired girl with striking blue eyes. Her air of quiet dignity gave an impression of strength and determination. She and her brother Silvio were to become two of our most ardent supporters.

We next came to the village of Peretola, where the procedure was repeated. The three Poles remained in the care of another family who, like that of Domenico, appeared to be relations of Tarquinio, and Mick, Bob, and I were taken to his own home.

Tarquinio lived in Chiesa, so named for the simple but adequate reason that it contained the largest church in the Valley. The church and the vicarage were on the edge of the village, and the rough stone path wound its way between them and terminated in a metal road that skirted the houses and disappeared among the trees on the hillside above. I asked Tarquinio where the road went to.

"It leads down to Pontremoli." He waved an arm in the direction of the valley of the river Magra. At its head was the city: a sinister place which in the opinion of the people of the mountains was the root of all evil.

"In that case, why do you want us to stay in your house?"

"Why not?" was the answer. "If there is any danger we will be warned. It is good for the others to realise that we, at least, are not afraid."

"Bravo, Tarquinio!" said Mick.

There was no answer to that argument. We set off again along a path diverging from the road, and climbed up into the heart of the village. As we reached Tarquinio's house the clock in the church tower struck twelve. Dina opened the door. A rough wooden staircase led up to the first floor and at the top of it stood Giuseppe and his wife.

"Welcome, welcome!" he said. "We are very pleased to see you all."

The old lady showed us up another flight of stairs to a small attic-like room whose furniture consisted of an iron stove and two wooden benches with high backs lining the walls.

"Sit down," said Mamma. "I will bring you some wine, and then we will have lunch." With which she bustled downstairs again.

We stretched our damp legs in front of the stove. Below we could hear Tarquinio speaking to his sister, for the floor consisted only of wooden planks with numerous gaps between. There was one small window in the room overlooking the path leading to the house. Directly opposite was a ruined building with only half a roof; beyond it was the road leading to the dreaded city.

"This is too good to be true," I said.

"Ah well," replied Bob. "We need not worry. Tarquinio says that nothing will make the Carabinieri come out to look for us during the Christmas holiday. He knows them pretty well; they are not a bad lot except for the Brigadiere, and the population here have got him sufficiently under their eye to know in time whether he is likely to start any trouble."

We heard footsteps on the stairs, and Tarquinio came in carrying a flask of wine and glasses.

"Scusa, Luigi," he said. "I have been talking to Dina." He filled the glasses and passed them round.

A gust of wind battered against the outside wall of the house and slithered over the roof. The rain continued, and we could hear it splashing in the puddles outside. There was a local belief that if the wind blew strongly at midday it would last for at least forty-eight hours. I hoped it would die down before we had to return to the cascina on Monte Picchiara.

Tarquinio spoke.

"Luigi, what do you think of those Poles who arrived the other day?"

"I think they are genuine enough – Why?"

"We've got to be careful – they may be spies sent to catch us out."

"They are not spies. Remember they came armed with revolvers and have slept with us for two nights. They could have killed us easily if they had wanted to. Besides, they were sent to us by the Liberation Committee in Genoa."

"Talking of spies," said Mick, "What about the spy that you said lives in this village?"

Tarquinio got up and walked over to the grimy window. Then he beckoned to us.

"You see the old man in the overcoat over there? He was once a famous painter but he lost all his money, and he now lives in one of the rooms of that ruined house. The villagers give him all his food."

"Why do you think he is a spy?"

"Because he talks too much to the Carabinieri. The other day he went to their barracks in the next valley to see the Brigadiere, and came back with some money that he soon spent buying wine in my Aunt's house."

The object of all this was a tall, distinguished looking old man with an artist's beard. He was dressed in ragged clothes partly hidden by a brown overcoat covering his thin frame. As he shuffled along the path we could see that his boots were held together by pieces of string. He passed out of sight under the window.

"He's going to get another drink," said Tarquinio. "That means he has got some more money; I wonder what he has told the police this time?"

Lunch was a lengthy affair, the biggest meal we had eaten for a long time. There was soup, pasta asciutta and meat. The meat was an unusual delicacy, and Mamma unblushingly explained its presence on the menu with a sad story about the demise of her sister's cow. It had wandered into a neighbour's field the day before, and ate so much that it suddenly burst. This sounded like something from the Chronicles of Baron Münchhausen, and we learnt the truth later. The people of Chiesa decided that Christmas should be celebrated in proper fashion, and so they had killed the cow, thus contravening the laws of the new Republic – which, however, could not prevent the mounting toll of "accidental" death among the more edible livestock.

After the meal Giuseppe produced from his pocket two "Toscana" cigars which he solemnly cut into the requisite lengths and distributed between us. We had by now become addicts of the Toscana which, looking back on it, can only mean that our constitutions had become abnormally tough. We passed the afternoon contentedly sitting round the stove.

That evening there was another vast meal. Once it was dark and there was no fear of our being observed, it was decided that we should visit the hostelry where Tarquinio's Aunt, owner of the late lamented cow, awaited us for a further celebration. It seemed too that there was a stranger anxious to make our acquaintance. At mention of the stranger Giuseppe protested loudly, declaring that to talk to him would be unsafe, but Tarquinio insisted.

The wind was cold and damp in the narrow street, and the night was starless. Little rivulets of rainwater trickled between the cobbles and filled the dark puddles. The hostelry was only a few yards away. Tarquinio preceded us up the narrow steps on to the terrace. While we concealed ourselves in the shadows, he tapped gently on the door. There was a whispered conversation.

"It's all right," he said, "There are not many people here, but don't talk as you go in, and walk quietly."

Hardly were we seated round a rickety wooden table when Auntie appeared and Tarquinio asked her to bring in his friend. I heard her protest. Tarquinio would not give way and seeing that further argument was useless she gave us a warning look, shrugged her shoulders, and left the room.

"Your Aunt doesn't seem very pleased," I said.

"That's nothing. She comes from Genoa and is always afraid of something Her house there was destroyed by bombs and that's why she and my Uncle have come here."

"R.A.F. bombs?" asked Mick.

"Yes," replied Tarquinio, "but they don't blame you for that; it happened in the big bombardment of November last year. They had all been expecting it anyway."

The stranger sat down at the table and was introduced while Auntie, who had followed him into the room, fluttered in the background obviously uneasy about the whole affair. I decided to be cautious. His name was Mario; he had been wounded serving with the Italian Army in Yugoslavia and invalided out before the Armistice. To prove this he showed us a wound in his leg still not completely healed, and various documents that he extracted from his pockets.

At first our conversation was harmless enough. After a while the newcomer began to ask questions about other ex-prisoners in the Valley. We avoided direct answers as politely as we could. Tarquinio, however, had begun to feel the effects of the day's drinking, and it was clear to all three of us that he would give something away sooner or later. For a while we discussed our different prison camps. In order to draw Mario on, I emphasised how much I disliked the Fascists and those who collaborated with the Republic. Mario appeared to agree. Then quite suddenly he remarked:

"It must be very cold on Monte Picchiara."

I was ready for that one.

"I suppose it must be. Have you been up there recently?"

"No, I don't travel about much, because of my leg."

At this point Auntie could stand it no longer, and went outside. Tarquinio helped himself to more wine and hiccoughed happily.

"I shall probably come up on the mountain in a few days," continued our guest, "as I have to go over the other side to the village of Torpiana on business. I'll bring you up some cigarettes."

"What makes you think we live up there?" asked Mick.

Mario laughed. "Everybody knows that," he said. "Besides, it's about the safest place to be in this area. The Carabinieri say there are a lot of escaped prisoners up there, all of them armed."

A relentless Fate had ordained that Tarquinio should hear that remark.

"Ah," he interposed thickly. "We'll show them when they come! We've got some arms, and some bombs. Porco Dio, we'll show them! Tell that Brigadiere – "

The door of the room burst open to admit Giuseppe. The old man was in a rage. He took one look at Mario, and put his hand roughly on his son's shoulder.

"Come to bed," he said.

To our relief, Tarquinio staggered to his feet and departed as quietly as a lamb.

Mick and Bob looked at me, wondering what to do next. The problem was solved by Mario, who emptied his glass and then shook hands with us.

"I must be getting back," he said. "Good-night."

"Have you got far to go?"

"Not very far. I live in the next valley," and, with a nod, he left us.

"That means that he must live somewhere near the Carabinieri barracks said Mick.

Auntie came back again, looking extremely worried.

"My husband says you must sleep here to-night; it will be safer. Tarquinio was a fool to introduce you to that person."

"Why, Auntie?" asked Mick. "He seems to be anti-Fascist."

"That's what he says. I don't know who he is but they say that he was a Fascist Secretary until a little while ago. He has a wireless set and the Carabinieri are always in his house listening to it. You can take it from me the Brigadiere will know all about this to-morrow."

"Then we had better sleep somewhere else," said Bob.

"No, you will be safer here because nobody will come here to-night; they all think that you have gone back to the mountain. Besides, there are plenty of people in this village – there will be ample warning if the police come anywhere near it and you can easily escape into the woods."

"What about the others?"

"They will be safe enough," said the good lady, gathering up the empty glasses with an indignant sweep of her arm. "Nobody can reach them without first passing this way." With that the matter was settled.

Auntie led us along a narrow passage to the room where we were to sleep. It contained a large double bed covered with an eiderdown and looked indescribably luxurious after the months that we had spent on dry leaves and straw.

"Sleep well, and don't worry," said our hostess. "You will have plenty of warning if anybody comes and then you can escape through a trapdoor in the next room, and out into the lane beneath this window that leads directly to the woods." She drew aside the curtain so that we could see the direction. With a final "Buona notte" she departed.

"Well nothing will keep me awake with a real bed to sleep in."

"Nor me," said Mick. "Though it will be a bit of a squash."

"Speak for yourself," said Bob.

Chapter Four

The Hunt is Up

Morning brought no fresh alarms.

The weather continued cloudy and boisterous, and rain fell steadily. This made our hosts urge us to spend the day with them and we gladly accepted any excuse not to return to that draughty mountain.

Tarquinio put in an appearance late in the afternoon. In view of the state he had been in the night before, this was hardly surprising. He had been in the next valley on the look out for trouble as a result of Mario's visit. So far as he knew, the suspect had not been near the police since his return.

That evening there was to be a dance in each village and we were invited to Castolio, which we had not yet seen. We set out as dusk was falling.

Castolio, like most of the villages of the Valley, was made up of a group of houses perched on the top of a steep spur jutting out from the northern mountain ridge. Its position was such that it offered the quickest and safest means of escape in the event of a surprise raid, for the fugitives could disappear in a matter of minutes in the deep gully below it.

We found on arrival that all our fellow refugees had been brought there to partake in the Festa. The Poles had been quick to make friends, and the initial suspicion caused by their arrival had melted away. In the new village the prerogative of looking after us fell upon the miller, Luigi Tognerelli, a man of thirty or so who lived in a house on the edge of the wooded slope.

Luigi was a merry soul, tall and wiry, with an irrepressible sense of humour. He had been working that day, and when he welcomed us was still covered from head to foot in flour dust. We were presented to his wife, and then his four offspring were introduced one by one.

There were many people at the dance from all over the Valley, for the presence of the escaped prisoners was an added attraction. The principal "orchestra,' had been engaged for the occasion, and consisted of a concertina, a violin that had never been known to play in tune, and a 'cello. The last was a truly remarkable instrument. It possessed only one string, on which the 'cellist vigorously played one note throughout the evening, and a large hole had been cut in its base in which reposed a fiasco of wine to refresh the players at increasingly frequent intervals.

The method of dancing was unusual, but we soon got the general idea. The young girls lined the walls, watched over jealously by awe-inspiring matrons. When the music began there would be a rush of menfolk, who would each grab a girl and drag her on to the floor. The dance over, she would be returned to the particular patch of wall from which she had been taken, and not a word would be spoken by either partner throughout the operation. The dances consisted of a curious form of jig peculiar to the Rossanesi.

Having done my best for the greater part of the evening, I retired at length to recover my breath. The fun was fast and furious, and that evening the war seemed very far from the Valley. The villagers had forgotten it for a while and were happy with the simple joy of living.

News had reached me that day that Colonel Balbi had successfully avoided arrest. Through him I had already met another agent, one Edoardo, who had been trying to procure firearms, and was due to arrive in the Valley again that night. Edoardo was a Lieutenant in a regiment of Alpini mountain troops. Thirty years of age, of slim build, with black hair and a fresh complexion, his brown eyes burned with an intentness that belied the calmness of his bearing, and the low pitched, slow manner of his speech. Like all those in his regiment, he was an ardent patriot who felt it his duty to give his life for his king and country. He had taken to the hills with his wife and four-year old daughter, and lived in the village of Torpiana, beyond the confines of the Valley.

It was well after midnight when the dance ended. Mick and I were taken back to Luigi's house where we found that two mattresses had been prepared on the wooden benches beside the kitchen stove. The miller was careful to point out the quickest escape route in case of an alarm. He then left us with assurances that he would return at dawn. It was essential that we should go back to Monte Picchiara the next morning. Loyal as the villagers were, there were undoubtedly some among them who talked too much, and it was impossible to prevent the children from spreading the news of our presence abroad.

* * *

December the 27th dawned with a clear sky and a cold wind that made the chestnut leaves dance madly in spirals across the muddy fields. Edoardo arrived as the first rays of sunshine were lighting up the tops of the trees. Luigi took us to a room on the first floor of his house and Mick stood guard on the terrace outside it. When we were seated, the Alpini Lieutenant began his report.

"The organisation in Genoa thought you might need some funds, and I have brought 4,000 Lire for the present."

"Thanks," I said. "That will be useful."

He then went on to describe the arrangements being made to organise resistance on a large scale in the area. A great deal of material was available in towns near the coast, and the intention was to send it up to Monte Picchiara as soon as possible. It consisted of rifles, ammunition, machine guns, grenades, signalling equipment, and a wireless transmitting set that had belonged to a battalion of Italian Army troops before the Armistice. Agents of the resistance movement in the city of La Spezia had made preparations to transfer it to the partisans.

"Until we have the men organised, this equipment can be hidden. Do you think your fellows could look after it?"

"It might be possible," I said. "But some of the villagers will have to be taken into our confidence, for we depend on them to bring us our food every day."

Edoardo did not like the idea of that. He had little faith in the peasantry when extreme secrecy was necessary. I suggested that we might first recruit our force, and then issue each man with his own rifle and ammunition for safe custody.

We discussed that point for a while. To distribute the arms would mean an end to security, for the family of every man who possessed a rifle would be sure to boast of the fact. In the end we agreed to postpone a decision until the first batch of war material arrived, and we knew how many men were available to whom it could be safely distributed.

I told Edoardo about the Poles.

"Colonel Balbi told me that they were on their way," he said.

"There should be some more arriving soon. There are about two hundred in the hills south of Genoa, and most of them have escaped with German uniforms. Unfortunately the route is particularly dangerous at the moment and we are short of reliable guides. The Colonel will be at Torpiana to-morrow and would like to talk to you, if you can come over."

I explained that we would be back at the cascina at midday, and I could therefore go down to the village in the evening. " I suppose there is no news from London yet, through Switzerland?"

"I don't think so, but Balbi will know. We are relying a great deal on the Allies sending us help soon. The partisans north of Turin are ready for offensive action on a grand scale."

We were interrupted by the sound of voices on the terrace. The door was pushed open, and Mick entered followed by a red-faced youngster who had obviously been running.

"The Carabs are after us, sir. We'd better clear out."

Edoardo, sensing danger, asked what was the matter. The peasant lad explained volubly in Italian.

"The Carabinieri have been up to the cascina and they have found all the arms. They surrounded it at dawn this morning and then made an attack. There are about forty of them, including a squad of Militia who have come from Massa and they were led by the Brigadiere and a spy from the next valley. They are now in Chiesa and have loaded on to mules all the things that they found up there. They are starting a rastrellamento of the whole Valley, and will be here soon. There is no time to lose."

At that moment Luigi appeared. His wife was behind him, two small children clinging to her skirt.

"We had better clear out," he said calmly. "We can go to the Mill, for they won't dare to follow us down there. Porco – " and he gave vent to his feelings with a string of oaths.

As we left the house I spoke to his wife.

"I'm sorry, Signora – I'm afraid it might be dangerous for you if they come here."

She smiled at me, and then looked on the ground.

"That's all right, Maggiore, I know how to deal with them. It will not be the first time."

Luigi hurried us down into the woods. By this time the alarm had spread through the village and figures were to be seen running in all directions, mostly the younger men who knew that if they were caught they would be taken away to fight in the Republican armies. Left behind in the village, the women and the old folk set to work to erase all traces of the refugees. They at least were safe enough, as they could not be used in the firing line.

Tarquinio arrived as we began the descent towards the Mill. "They were in my Aunt's house, Maggiore," he reported, "drinking wine they have no intention of paying for. The Brigadiere was very angry because he had not caught you. My Aunt talked to one of the men who said he was glad. He had been ordered to open the door of the cascina and was frightened because they were sure that the English were inside waiting to open fire. He would certainly have been killed and several more with him. The Brigadiere and the commander of the Militia detachment were hidden behind some rocks on the slopes above."

"Have you any idea who the spy was?"

"No, not at the moment. When they were on their way up they met Salvatore returning from Torpiana with a mule carrying wine that he had bought there. They made him unload the mule and hand it over to them, and then they tried to make him show them the way. He started out, and escaped when he got the opportunity – it was still dark – and gave us the warning. He says he thinks he knows who the spy is because he saw a man talking to the soldiers when they were unloading his mule, and he thinks that he recognised the voice.,'

"What about your friend Mario?"

"The man my father was so angry about? No, I'm sure he was not the one, because I've known him for a long time."

"He asked a good many questions," said Mick. "Besides, your Aunt said that he was once a Fascist secretary of sorts."

"That doesn't mean anything. If he was going to betray you he certainly would not have come to my Aunt's house. The whole village knows that he was there. Besides, he has a younger brother whom he is hiding so that he won't be taken away for military service."

By this time we were below the village, Luigi and Edoardo leading the way. I was relieved to see that the leafless trees were not the only vegetation – they were now supplemented by thick evergreen bushes that would provide good cover if we had to hide. It was some consolation to know that so far none of the other ex-prisoners had been caught. Several of them had started out soon after daylight and must have been halfway up Monte Pichiara when the patrol entered the Valley.

Tarquinio went on with his story.

"My Aunt told me they had a lot to say about the stores they found. One thing that puzzled them was an empty tin with an English label on it, and they came to the conclusion that you received supplies from England by aeroplane. They thought the signalling flags were for sending messages to British planes when they passed over."

"They weren't far wrong there," I said. "They would have been used for that if only some aeroplanes had come our way. How were they armed?"

"The Carabinieri had their usual rifles. The Militia had automatic rifles and grenades."

The column halted and we held a council of war. Tarquinio decided to return to Chiesa and keep an eye on things there. Edoardo had to get back to Torpiana at all costs to report to the Colonel. One of the refugees from Castolio, Giovanni, volunteered to guide him by way of the mountain range to the south west. They set off after I had agreed to join them that evening when we had discovered what had happened to the rest of our colleagues.

The Mill was small and built of grey stone beside a stream, the water of which turned the wooden paddles that operated the grindstones inside it. Nobody could approach the building unseen, but the Militia, if they came this way, could open fire on it from the heights above. Luigi decided to remain inside so as to give the impression that he was about his normal work, while Mick and I hid on the far side of the stream to await events. We went on, and hid ourselves in a thicket half way up the opposite mountain slope.

The morning changed to afternoon. The sun came out for a while and warmed us where we lay shivering among the damp leaves. We heard several bursts of rifle fire from the direction of Chiesa, and wondered what they meant. Time passed slowly and it was not until dusk that we saw a small figure walking down the path from Castolio. It was Luigi's eldest son. Not long afterwards the miller came out and called us to join him.

We got to our feet, stiff and cold.

"Thank God that's over," I said. "I hope Luigi's got a big fire down there."

"Oh, what couldn't I do to a good cup of tea in a NAAFI canteen," groaned Mick. "If I get home, I'm never going to go near any woods again, and if anyone suggests a picnic on Bank Holiday, there'll be a murder."

"Cheer up, Mick. If we're not surrounded, we've got a long walk to do to-night."

"Ah well – 'Join the Army and see the world' – We're certainly doing that!"

Ten minutes later we were inside the Mill. The door was locked behind us, and for a while our full attention was given to the thawing of frozen limbs in front of the iron stove. The small messenger from Castolio sat placidly chewing at a piece of dry bread and watching us.

The news that he had brought was not as good as we had hoped. Tarquinio had sent a written message to the effect that the unwelcome visitors had left a squad of five armed Militia in Chiesa as a permanent detachment, in case we returned. The population was in a state of great alarm; the soldiers had spent the day looting, and had boasted that every eligible male would be deported from the Valley during the next few days.

The other fugitives had been taken to hiding places in the forest and provided they stayed there they would come to no harm, for the patrols could not search every cascina in the woods surrounding the Valley. They were relying on informers who would lead them to the various hiding places.

Luigi's wife had sent us a basket of food. While we ate it he told us that two Carabinieri had been to his house. They had not caused any trouble, or asked too many questions. As they left, one of them had whispered to his wife: "Tell the English that we don't want to do them any harm, Signora. We have to obey orders."

It was quite dark by now; the wind had dropped, and in its place we could hear the water gurgling in the stream outside and the whining of the millstones as they continued to grind the wheat and dried chestnuts. It was time to start on our night march. Luigi's younger brother was to act as our guide.

The village of Torpiana lay in a deep valley one hour's walk beyond the summit of Monte Picchiara. Slowly we threaded our way along muddy paths skirting the villages, and then began the steep climb up the mountainside. I hoped that Edoardo had arrived safely, to warn all concerned. The events of the day had been depressing enough – we had lost the few firearms that we possessed and our reserve of rations. What was worse, the people of the Valley had been terrorised, and those who had protected us so nobly throughout the past months faced the danger of becoming the victims of reprisals by the Militia.

The future now depended on what news Colonel Balbi had to give us.

Part II

The International Battalion

Chapter Five

The Sanctuary

Monte Dragnone stands sentinel over the mountainous Commune of Zignago in the province of La Spezia. It rises steeply to a height of about 3,000 feet, and the top consists of a rocky terrace a hundred yards in length. On this platform in days gone by the faithful of the Comune built a church which they named the "Sanctuary of the Madonna". Inspired by the panorama, a wealthy priest later built a dwelling attached to the church, where he would retire for long periods of the year. Every September there is a pilgrimage to the Sanctuary, and a Festa is held to mark the occasion in the villages below.

There is a magnificent view from the church, for the mountain dominates the area between it and the sea coast. In the clear sunny days of spring, the old priest in his self-imposed exile could look out across the sea to where the island of Corsica lay rugged and black against the horizon. To the north he could see the snow-covered peaks of the Alps stretching away beyond the port of Genoa to the frontiers of Switzerland. To the south was the broad sweep of the coast where lies Livorno. Only to the east is the view blocked by the outer bastions of Monte Picchiara.

Following the death of its master, the house had remained empty until January of the year 1944. Then came the fugitives from the Valley.

The Sanctuary had been suggested as a hiding place by Don Battista Ravini, the village priest of Torpiana, a sturdy, rugged countryman who somewhat incongruously wore a pair of spectacles with black steel rims, and beneath the skirt of whose black habit a strong pair of farmer's muddy boots was usually to be seen. He was well adapted to sharing the toils and tribulations of his parishioners. He and Edoardo had worked out the plan between them the night Mick and I reached Torpiana.

Colonel Balbi was there, as optimistic as ever. He told me that the Committee was still without orders from the Allies, but they did know that one of my letters had reached London, containing details of the formation that we hoped to organise. It could only be a matter of time before help of some kind arrived and we could begin to hit back at our persecutors. Partisan formations in the north had already begun to attack the enemy lines of communication. The effectiveness of these attacks was proved by the fact that, on the Axis radio and in the Press, the term "Anglo–Saxon bandits" was now replaced by the one word "Rebels".

Life in the Sanctuary was not pleasant. Edoardo did all he could to see that we were provided with adequate food and warmth, and a squad of faithful retainers from Torpiana brought us supplies loaded on mules by night. There was sufficient wood in the building to burn in the two iron stoves. By day we were obliged to remain indoors, for the church was in full view of the surrounding countryside and the sight of human beings up there in winter would arouse curiosity. Edoardo had organised a screen of informers who lived in the villages at the foot of the mountain, so that there was little chance of our being attacked at night without previous warning. We took our exercise at night when some of the party would go out in search of fuel, and the others would undertake the long and arduous march to meet the ration convoy.

The month of January 1944 passed slowly by – a month of strong gales, frost, and driving snow that seeped under the tiles of the roof and drenched anew the musty walls of the rooms in which we tried to sleep. News of the outside world reached us from the Valley. We heard of the landing at Anzio, and our hopes were raised.

Luigi the miller came up one night and told us of the growing activities of partisans in the plains of Emilia. Colonel Lowry Corry, M.C., who had been with me in Chieti and Veano prison camps, had found his way there and was wisely leading a lone existence. Luigi had taken him under his wing. One day a party of Carabinieri suddenly appeared and surrounded the mill. They had come to collect the Colonel.

Luigi, finding himself threatened by the Brigadiere flourishing a rifle, grinned at him and asked him what he was frightened of. The Brigadiere, noted for his red complexion, went a still deeper red and demanded admission to the Mill. Luigi heartily complied and in doing so managed to upset a bag of flour over him and his rifle. Luigi, contrite, explained that accidents will happen, and gave him a glass of wine. Meanwhile the Colonel had been hidden in the undergrowth outside, and that night was taken across Monte Picchiara to Edoardo, who was now looking after him.

Our friends in the Valley had heard a wireless commentary given by "Candidus" from the B.B.C., in which the partisans were urged to begin sabotage activities, and this did much to counteract the ill-effects of visits by the police. There had been several deserters from the barracks in Pontremoli, and there was talk of an armed partisan band in the region of the Cisa Pass that commands the main road from La Spezia to Parma. When he left us, the miller insisted that we should return to the Valley when it was safe to do so. Our friends, he said, would not let us go away – we belonged to the Rossanesi and to no-one else.

Edoardo and his wife made frequent visits to the Sanctuary. Maria Rita shared to the full the cause for which her husband was fighting. She was pretty, of small and dainty stature, and essentially feminine – one of those women who manage to convey a natural air of graciousness whatever the circumstances. She was devoted to their small daughter Paola, and had abandoned a sumptuous villa in Genoa to become a partisan. To see her sitting on a dirty wooden bench talking to us, after having toiled for three hours along the dark and rocky paths from Torpiana, made me look upon her as a worthy descendant of those "daughters of Italy" so vividly described in George Meredith's "Vittoria", who had helped to liberate their country from the Austrian yoke. Her visits meant a great deal to us, and in her honour we renamed the sanctuary the "Fortezza Maria Rita".

As time passed, it became apparent that a new influence was beginning to assert itself upon the resistance movement. Knowing nothing of the political confusion in Italy – the natural result of twenty-two years of dictatorship – we were puzzled by the vehemence which our visitors displayed when they discussed various political parties, and it was some time before I realised the full significance of this. Funds were necessary to support the partisan forces, and became increasingly necessary as the movement grew. Several of the big banking houses in Genoa had contributed, and the money was handed over to the various resistance Committees. The lack of the necessary military directive meant that the Committees began to develop a strong political bias, and the various party influences ultimately spread to the partisans, a misfortune the full extent of which was to be realised later. The enemy, quick to seize every chance of preventing unity of action, took full advantage of the opportunities provided by this weakness.

Political influence spread rapidly, and was closely connected with events in the south. By the end of the month, although the Anzio landing had come to a standstill, the people of occupied Italy felt that liberation was at hand, and that it could not be more than a few months before the Allied armies swept north to drive the Germans back behind their own frontiers. With Liberation would come political freedom and the people would be called upon to elect their chosen Government. Amateur politicians, ambitious to stand for parliament, began to think of votes and set to work to gather recruits from all classes in the hope of persuading them to support their respective parties when the time came. They acted independently of the liberation Committees in the cities, and their actions had little to do with official policy. As communications with Genoa deteriorated, these political opportunists became all-powerful. On the other hand, the youth of the country, hunted, hungry, and for the most part lacking in military training, fell easy victims to the temptation of free food, clothing, and a small measure of security in return for a vote to be given at some future date.

During the last week of January I went down with an attack of mountain fever. Edoardo took me to his house in Torpiana and put me to bed; the house was shared with Doctor Fenati, a young barrister who had somehow managed to extricate himself from the Italian armed forces in Yugoslavia, and had been in hiding there since September. For a week I was nursed by Maria Rita and Edoardo. There was no hospital anywhere near the village and although for a while I was past caring, they took it in turns to watch ceaselessly by my bedside. The crisis had scarcely passed, when we received news that the Militia in Sesta Godano, the nearest market town, had discovered my whereabouts and were on their way to get me.

Edoardo was prepared. He had taken over a small house elsewhere in the village, where he proposed to live with his family under an assumed name. It was decided that I should be hidden there at dusk. In due course Carletto a lad of the village, came into the bedroom with a large sack in the bottom of which he had put some potatoes. I was lifted into this and, hoisting the sack of "vegetables" on his shoulders, he walked through the main street to the new dwelling. We passed few people on the way, and caused no comment.

Next morning a patrol of Militia arrived and went straight to the house of Doctor Fenati. Having searched it and found nothing of value, they withdrew to the local hostelry to drink, and then returned to their barracks. Carletto was courting the inn-keeper's daughter, and he learnt from her that the patrol had been attracted to Torpiana by the chatter of a woman from the village overheard in the market town three days previously.

In the new "hospital" precautions were redoubled. Edoardo's small daughter Paola had been taught not to talk to the other children about the mysterious stranger, and entered eagerly into the game of "keeping watch". She would sit for hours at the window that overlooked the village street, running to warn her mother whenever anybody passed whom she did not know. In the sitting room which possessed the only door leading on to the street, Edoardo had placed his gramophone on a wooden chest directly under my bedroom. There were few records available, but among them was the first movement of Tchaikovsky's Pianoforte Concerto in B Minor, and this was chosen as the warning signal. When I heard the opening bars I knew that a stranger had come to the house and was in the room below. If the music stopped suddenly, it told me that the visitor was suspicious, and I must prepare to climb into a small attic under the tiles – if the record played to the end, it meant that all was well. The maid-servant knew how to hide the bedclothes and make the room look as if it had never been occupied. Fortunately a real crisis never arose, although it seemed that the music was bound to stop one day, and I came to know every note of the first record by heart. There was little protection in the attic, and no way out of it except through the trapdoor in the ceiling of the dark passage outside, and all would depend on how well traces of my presence in the bedroom were hidden. If the enemy set fire to the house and I was discovered, Edoardo and his family would be shot, as they well knew.

They also possessed a radio through which we were able to keep in touch with events in the outside world. At regular intervals two of the fugitives from the "Fortezza Maria Rita" would come down by night. We would bend over the set to hear the news bulletins in English, hurriedly making notes to send up the mountain for the others. How many times, listening in the North African desert to programmes from London before the fall of Tobruk, had I heard the commentators describe clandestine gatherings of the oppressed people of Europe behind drawn curtains and locked doors. Then I had thought the reports exaggerated, now they seemed insipid in comparison with what was happening nightly in the village of Torpiana.

On the first day of my convalescence I was introduced to a young lieutenant of a Tank Regiment, who had arrived from the province of Parma. Franco was a Sardinian, of small, wiry build, with a pale complexion and wavy black hair. He was twenty-two, but did not look more than seventeen. The son of a General, he certainly lived up to the reputation of his forbears for toughness. He overflowed with nervous energy and had the courage of a Roman gladiator. On the day of the Armistice, he had fought a lively action against the Germans and then retired into the hills with a small squad of his men. They had drifted back to their homes while he, following the advice of the Genoa Committee, found his way to Torpiana. A few firearms had been collected again. We had between us four rifles and an Italian Breda light automatic, which we kept on Monte Dragnone in case we had to beat off any inquisitive patrols that might alight upon us without warning. A further ten rifles and assorted bombs had been hidden by Edoardo, and Franco decided to use these to form a band of his own.

There were other visitors to Edoardo's house, mostly couriers from Genoa or La Spezia. All brought news of increased supervision by the German S.S. and a growing anxiety on the part of the enemy to discover the roots of the resistance movement which they realised was slowly gaining in strength. Large numbers of working men had been deported to Germany with promises of high pay and liberal rations; in spite of the promises, the victims had to be forced to board the trains, and travelled under armed guard all the way. The Germans had begun to build a cement wall all along the coast of Liguria and beyond Genoa into France as a precaution against the dreaded invasion of Europe. For this labourers were impressed from the coastal towns, and paid 1,000 Lire a day of the money the Germans were printing all over Italy.

Meanwhile I was gradually regaining my strength. Accompanied by Edoardo or Carletto I would take exercise in the forest after dark, or pay visits to other partisan families. I was not the only patient. Several of the others had become ill, among them Bob, and they were brought down to the "hospital" and cared for until they were fit to return to the mountain.

One evening I found Don Ravini awaiting me in the little sitting room The priest was agitated and paced up and down muttering to himself, his hobnailed boots scraping on the stone floor. Maria Rita hastened to explain.

It appeared that one of our informers who lived at the foot of Monte Dragnone had discovered we had been denounced to the Republican Militia in the town of Borghetto on the coast road. The agent – a girl whom we knew as "Dolores", niece of an Italian Admiral who was highly esteemed in the province – had talked to the traitor, and he had said that the proper place for prisoners of war was a concentration camp. Don Ravini was in a quandary, for the man was said to be a priest, and he felt deeply hurt by such an act from one of his own calling.

We held a council of war. It was clear that the "Fortezza Maria Rita" would have to be evacuated as soon as possible. A message was despatched to "Dolores" asking her to keep watch and Edoardo went up to the church to warn the inmates to evacuate the place the next night.

The move went according to plan. Two mules from the Valley were sent to carry the heavy kit, accompanied by Tarquinio and Luigi the miller. Carletto led the way to the new hiding place, a spacious cascina owned by his uncle, not far above Torpiana. They reached it just before dawn, and threw themselves down to sleep in the hay, while their new host tilling the fields outside acted as sentry.

Don Ravini sent a message to his Bishop in La Spezia with a full report of the affair. In a few days a reply was received. The Bishop ordered that a special service should be held in the Sanctuary on a certain date, at which he wished all the population to be present. Don Ravini himself was to perform the ceremony.

I sent the news into the Valley, and there was an enthusiastic response – the Rossanesi promised to be there in full strength, more from curiosity, it was to be feared, than from religious fervour. The ceremony took place three days later, and report had it that never had such a crowd been seen on the summit of Monte Dragnone before. The congregation inspected the house

– in fact they took more interest in that than in the service – and some even insisted on exploring the roof to see if the "partisans" were still in hiding there.

Convinced that the place was empty, they returned to their homes and duly spread the news.

The Bishop had been very astute. It was impossible to keep the presence of the fugitives hidden from the population and fantastic stories began to circulate of seven hundred armed men living on the mountain, and convoys of animals loaded with all the equipment of war winding along the mountain paths throughout the winter nights. These rumours must have been widespread, for they explained the appearance one day of a fighter 'plane that circled low over the mountain top, barely skimming the roof of the house from which we were watching it. In the course of time they reached the ears of the Republican Militia, whose commander, duly alarmed, decided that his force was too weak in numbers to deal with the matter, so he sent for help from the Fascist stronghold of Massa. Before the necessary reinforcements could arrive the place had been evacuated, and the Fascists heard of the ceremony at the church. The result was that they took no further interest in it. The Huns remembered nearly a year later, and razed the house to the ground with carefully aimed mortar fire. The Sanctuary was slightly damaged, but still stands to this day as a sombre reminder of the event.

Chapter Six

Armed with Hatred

In due course I took up residence in the cascina above Torpiana. The men were glad to be in new surroundings where there was not the same need to keep hidden by day. We were left in peace for a week, and then danger threatened again. In the middle of February, an event took place that gave a long needed incentive to the resistance movement.

It was the season of "Carnevale" which fell unusually early that year. The Fascist Government had strictly forbidden dancing on festive occasions, and the population of Torpiana, considering themselves "rebels" decided to hold a dance. It took place in the Inn, and towards eleven o'clock that evening, when the merriment was at its height, a squad of Militia descended on the village and surrounded the building. Some of the menfolk escaped by jumping out of the windows. Others were arrested. Guarding their prisoners carefully, the representatives of the "Little Republic" proceeded to march them away to Sesta Godano.

Now the path from Torpiana is narrow and impossible to follow at night without lights, as it winds through thick pine woods. The column set out in single file, the prisoners with their hands tied behind them, the Militia carrying automatic rifles slung on their shoulders and using electric torches with which to find their way. They could not reach their destination for at least two hours and, to one who knew the country well, there were ample opportunities for an ambush on the way.

One of those who had escaped from the dance hall appreciated the advantages of the situation. Renaldo Benelli, born and bred in Torpiana, was something of an outlaw by profession. He had scarcely found his feet again after his drop from the windowsill, when he bethought him of his rifle hidden in a house nearby. He ran to get it, and departed again on the path for Sesta Godano, collecting Carletto as he went. Together they hurried through the woods until they reached a convenient bend from which they knew that they could cover the approaching column. They then sat down behind a rock to listen.

They did not have long to wait. First they heard voices in the distance, then the scrape of nailed boots against stone. A torch shone through the trees and in its rays they could make out the dim figures of the prisoners stumbling between their cursing guards. The light disappeared at a point where the path dipped down to cross a stream and reappeared again quite close to them. Suddenly Renaldo fired.

The resulting confusion was highly gratifying. The Militia, believing themselves to be surrounded by a large force of the dreaded "rebels", fell flat on their faces where they were. The torches went out and the harassed commander began to shout incoherent orders to his troops. They were far too concerned with their own safety to take any notice of him. Renaldo stood up and yelled at the top of his voice:

"Run for it boys, they can't stop you!"

The prisoners needed no further encouragement.

Having achieved their object, the two partisans made their way back to the village as speedily as possible and reached it in time to check the arrival of those whom they had rescued.

Next morning, morale ran high. I heard a full and picturesque account of the event from Carletto, and some of those who had been captured came in to give their version. It was a victory to be proud of – one that was bound to bring an unpleasant reaction, but nevertheless a victory. Edoardo and Maria Rita were delighted, although they knew that it would make their position more precarious than ever.

The alarm was given early next day. According to plan, the menfolk scattered to the woods. The women had already hidden their valuables, and went about their daily work cleaning their houses, or taking their livestock to graze as best they could in the snow. There was an unexpected development, in that every man in the village who possessed a firearm came to the cascina to "join the English". As most of them were youngsters who had never fired a rifle in their lives, we did not feel as flattered as we should have done, but at last the screens were down, and we could count on the wholehearted support of all the population. Edoardo and Renaldo brought news that a force of about forty armed Militia was closing in from the north, having made a detour in the hope of taking us by surprise. We moved to the shrub-covered mountainside that overlooked the village from the south, and waited under cover for them to arrive. There could be no question of our doing anything but defend ourselves; apart from the fact that there were only a few rounds of ammunition for each weapon, an attack by us could only result in still further reprisals against the unarmed inhabitants. Orders were given that nobody was to open fire unless he was in danger of being captured.

Before entering the village the commander of the enemy patrol placed pickets on all the tracks leading into it and then proceeded to carry out a house to house search. From the hillside we could see the pickets, and we derived a certain satisfaction from watching them stamping their feet and breathing on their hands as they stood ankle deep in snow. Nobody was allowed to enter or leave Torpiana. Early in the afternoon two shots rang out; a small boy had attempted to run into the woods. He was not hit, but badly frightened; that incident did more than anything else to rouse the anger of the population, and it was never forgotten.

Eventually the Militia withdrew, this time making sure that they would reach their barracks before dark. Unable to find those whom they were seeking, they had taken several hostages from the village, including Doctor Fenati. Most of the hostages were the fathers of youngsters who had been called up for national service, and who spent the day in our company. There had been considerable looting, but Edoardo's house was untouched, and his wife and little Paola were safe.

And so the affair ended. Its most important effect from our point of view was to eliminate once and for all the need for secrecy with regard to our movements. It was not long before news of the incident spread throughout the mountains and fugitives from other villages began to collect in Torpiana, which won the reputation of being the most important partisan village in the area. The "Republican" representatives in Sesta Godano tried fruitlessly to stem the flow by sending armed patrols into the surrounding countryside, but they were met with a sullen hostility that caused them to give up the contest and fall back on their barracks, to await the decision of their German masters as to the best way of dealing with the situation. At the end of February Edoardo, Franco and I had rosy dreams of creating so strong an organisation in those mountains that it would become the central command of the resistance movement, fully supported by the legitimate Italian Government; the Allies would then give us all the help we required to drive the Germans out of northern Italy. Given the necessary equipment, the men could be trained for the task, and another glorious page would be added to the history of their country. More letters were sent through Switzerland giving details of our plans, while we set about training our recruits.

Our ambitions might have been realised, but for the fact that the political influence suddenly took control, and completely changed the future course of events.

The Action Party – "Partito d'Azione" – came into being well before the armistice of 1943. Its doctrine lay halfway between Socialism as we know it, and the old republican visions of Mazzini. Its founders were men of honour and great integrity, revered by the Italian masses; they too had endured persecution under the Fascist regime for their political faith. Colonel Balbi was one of these.

Its ideals – embodied in its slogan "Justice and Liberty" – were thoroughly creditable, but perhaps too visionary for this materialistic world, which resulted in the dissolution of the party shortly after the war. Unfortunately a few of its representatives, at least in the Liguria area with which this story is mainly concerned, were not worthy representatives of the Action Party. Deterioration in communications as the resistance movement spread throughout Northern Italy, and the subsequent loss of control by the Party chiefs, left increasing power in the hands of amateur politicians who, alas, thought more about increasing their own local status and political prestige, than about the future welfare of their country as a whole.

A representative of the Action Party suddenly arrived in Torpiana, and announced that the partisan formations to be formed would belong to his party, and to none other, and he promised the immediate delivery of arms, money, and clothing to those who would follow him. I watched this development with considerable misgiving, for it was plain that the politician in question was interested only in the possibility of elections in the near future. I made it clear that no-one under my command was to become involved in local politics, which in any case was not the intention of the Committee in Genoa. Attempts were then made to persuade the Poles to desert their English comrades. They hotly refused, causing a breach between the International Battalion and the Action Party which unfortunately widened as time went on. The population of the Rossano Valley were quick to realise the implications, suspicious as they were of all "foreigners" who lived outside their own domains. A century before they had fought a battle against the representatives of the Republic of Genoa on what was then the frontier, and the battlefield on the slopes of Monte Picchiara is pointed out with pride to this day. They were quick to offer us their protection, and I moved my headquarters back to the original cascina above the Valley where we had spent the first months of our freedom.

These complications produced disastrous results. Edoardo, strongly opposed to a policy that he considered was contrary to the interests of real patriotism, was hounded out of Torpiana, and obliged to flee with his family to a hide-out further north, where they remained till the end of the war. Other political parties, fearing the undisputed ascendancy of one, proceeded to form units of their own, thus creating a cross feud of personal jealousy between individuals that threatened to wreck the entire resistance movement. The partisans themselves became confused, and had more need than ever of capable leaders. A few commanders saw the red light, and endeavoured to create small non-political formations to fight independently.

One of these was Franco. With quiet determination he set to work to train a group of thirty patriots, and established his command on the northern slopes of Monte Picchiara whence, when the time came, he could harass the enemy garrison in the town of Sesta Godano.

The "International Battalion" had now grown out of all proportion to the arms that were available. Colonel Balbi continued to provide financial help, and fifteen of the youngsters from the Valley had joined us. They lived in their own villages, provided us with food and carried out liaison duties with formations outside our area. Otherwise there was nothing we could do but wait for the equipment that we knew the Allies would send us as soon as they could.

*   *   *

One day a letter reached me from Colonel Balbi. It contained good news. The Committee of Liberation in Genoa had received instructions from the Allied Command; among these instructions was an assurance that arms and supplies would be dropped by night on Monte Picchiara. There was to be one plane load at first. The date of its arrival would be signalled by the B.B.C. in a series of special messages transmitted immediately before the evening news bulletins in Italian.

At last our confidence in Allied support was to be justified. I passed on some of the information to the local Action Party leader who now controlled the strongest formation of partisans in the area. In doing so I had to break it to him tactfully that the Allies had ruled that I should be in charge of the dropping ground. Within ten days the warning message was received from London.

The dropping zone had been marked out on a wide grassy slope enclosed by two abutments of the mountain. Piles of brushwood were distributed in the shape of the letter "L" and were to be lighted when we heard the plane. On the edge of the field was a small stone cascina that served as a shelter in which to wait; a fire smouldered in one corner, emitting clouds of acrid smoke but little warmth. There was snow on the summit of the mountain and the sentries posted beside the signal fires shivered with the cold.

That night we waited in vain. The hours dragged on, and it was not until after three o'clock in the morning that I persuaded the assembled company that the plane would not come. The political leader was in a hostile frame of mind throughout and it was clear that he did not relish the conditions imposed upon him. I had done my best to improve our relations by arranging that when the plane arrived he should flash the appropriate Morse signal to the pilot indicating that we were ready to receive the drop.

Next night we stood by again in vain. This time the positive message had been given on the radio at four o'clock in the afternoon. The weather changed for the worse and heavy rain clouds swept in from the sea and obscured the summit of the mountain before midnight. And so it continued for a week.

Then came the night of March 14th.

We were in position as before – the International Battalion consisting of English, Poles, and a group of supporters from the Valley including Tarquinio and the miller; Franco the Sardinian and his force of thirty stalwarts, and many others of the Action Party.

It was just after eleven o'clock when we heard the sound of a plane in the distance moving towards us from the coast. There was a spontaneous rush to the door of the shelter. The sentries lit the fires; the dry brushwood flared up and burned brightly, throwing grotesque shadows against the slopes at the edge of the dropping ground. The plane came nearer. It was now possible to hear the throbbing of the twin engines. Watching closely, I saw the pilot flash his recognition signal.

"What about the torch?" I yelled to the politician standing beside me. "He's waiting for an answer."

He made no reply and seemed to be completely paralysed. Slowly the plane circled low over the field, and again the pilot signalled.

"For God's sake. Give him an answer!"

The politician came to life. He ran towards the nearest group of partisans and began asking feverishly if anybody had a torch. It was a futile question; such articles were as rare as gold in the mountains. Agents had been sent into the City of Pontremoli and elsewhere to buy them but they were not to be had. The only two available had been procured from Genoa. One of these had broken, the other had been handed over to the Action Party leader. It now appeared that he had lost it.

I sat down on the ground, and swore helplessly, cursing myself for having been so foolish as to rely on him.

In the dear sky above, the plane was completing a third run in over the dropping ground. Then the pilot turned out to sea and the throbbing of the engines grew fainter as he flew back to his base.

Mick and Paolo the Pole emerged from the darkness.

"Sir, the men want to know whether we can go back now. It's obvious the plane won't return."

"O.K., Mick, tell them to join me here."

"Perhaps it will come again to-morrow," said Paolo.

"Perhaps. If it doesn't we are going to be in a sorry state for a long time to come."

On our way back across the mountain the men were silent. After all our waiting and preparation, the event had been an awful anticlimax. Feeling was very tense when we left. The partisans began to talk about deserting the area in order to join other organisations in the north. None of them, even among the youngest peasant lads, attempted to blame the Allies for their disappointment. Only Franco was unmoved by the event. He gave orders to his force to march off and attack the garrison in Sesta Godano, and by that means collect some equipment. They had sufficient arms and ammunition for one short operation, provided that it went according to plan.

"Put not your faith in aeroplanes, my lads," he concluded. "Andiamo" – and they set forth into the dark forest.

Another day had passed, and we seemed to be no further with our plans. That dreamlike existence of "once upon a time", with its modern houses, beautiful women who spoke our own language, hot baths, and above all, security, seemed further away and more unattainable than ever before. Could it possibly be true that in the distant past one had travelled about in cars, and eaten sumptuous meals seated at tables where candlelight sparkled on silver plate, crystal, and polished mahogany? Yet all that had happened once, long ago, and had been called "normal life".

* * *

It was not only the partisans who had heard the plane during that memorable night; the enemy garrisons in Pontremoli and Sesta Godano had heard it too, and were spurred into action accordingly. For several days past their spies had brought news of an expected drop of supplies from the air, but the Fascists had refused to believe such a thing possible. And then they heard the plane.

They acted swiftly. As dawn broke on the 15th of March a large formation of armed troops, including for the first time a proportion of Germans, set out from the two garrison towns and made their way towards Monte Picchiara, where they were to combine forces and capture all the material that had been dropped. Warning reached us well in advance, and we dispersed as usual. Pickets were hidden on the surrounding hilltops to watch events.

The enemy duly appeared. It was obvious they had no doubt about the location of the dropping ground. The weather was hot that day, and they were arrayed in full battle order. It was a steep climb up the mountain, and when you imagine that behind any of the thousands of bushes that surround you on all sides there may be a rebel waiting to shoot, your feelings are inclined to become ruffled. The enemy, in the shape of some two hundred

Germans and Republicans, reached the hut by the field just after midday, and sat themselves down to rest.

By that time they realised clearly enough that they had come on a wild goose chase, for there was not a rebel to be seen. To justify their existence, the Commander of the force carried out a demonstration march. He gave his men the satisfaction of firing off their ammunition as they felt inclined, in order to impress the population. An old woman was killed by a stray shot while working in a field with her small grandson, and a girl standing on a balcony in Torpiana was seriously injured and died later.

By nightfall the disappointed enemy had withdrawn. The partisan scouts came down from their hide-outs, and commanders collected their scattered men. The International Battalion, joined by an embarrassing number of children from the Valley whose fathers had sent them to the English for "protection", had moved bodily to Monte Dragnone.

We returned late that night; hardly had we reached the cascina when we heard the sound of aeroplane engines again. There were two machines this time, making straight for the field where the pilot had seen the fires the night before.

We looked up into the sky. Slowly the roar of the engines drew nearer and passed overhead. For half an hour the pilots circled round the area, while their desperate countrymen below watched helplessly. To light the necessary fires, wood had to be collected beforehand, and the problem of the signal was still unsolved. To light the fires in the wrong place would bring down upon us bullets instead of parachutes. And so we stood in silence until the planes flew heavily away again. It was as well that we did not then know how many months were to pass before those aeroplanes would return.

March 1944 drew on towards its close. The supply of equipment from the cities was meagre, and recruits to the partisan formations increased out of all proportion to what was available. They were eagerly received into the ranks of the political leaders who at least had the money to provide them with food. Rumours began to reach the Valley of the existence of a new political party, the Communists. They had crossed the mountain range commanded by Monte Gottero, from the plains of Emilia to the north-east. It was common knowledge among the local population that Actionists and Communists did not enjoy each other's company; consequently we could expect further intrigues to arise once the new party had made its presence felt. The life of the Italian patriot, through no fault of his own, was becoming more complicated every day.

Allied bombardment of the communications in the north increased and reacted upon us by disrupting our contact with the city of Genoa, for the couriers made more than half of their journey by train. This enforced isolation of the operational areas from their directing base in the city threw the rank and file of the partisans completely into the hands of their respective leaders. It was a misfortune for which many were later to pay dearly with their lives, and it was at this stage that the lack of properly trained military commanders made itself most felt. Had such commanders been available at the end of March, the future history of the resistance movement, at any rate in Liguria, might have been very different.

With the coming of spring, life in the Valley became increasingly difficult for us all. Ravages made upon reserves of food by enemy patrols had reduced the Rossanesi to a state in which they found it difficult enough to provide for themselves, but they insisted on sending all that they could to the mountain, to feed "their" partisans. The older generation took pride in guiding their mules at night, laden with bread, cheese, and the inevitable chestnut flour, and there was always the fiasco of wine. One of these sturdy retainers was over seventy years old, and he carried his own rifle. Another couple were the brothers Grigoletti.

The elder brother was that mysterious stranger who had given us some anxious moments at Chiesa on Christmas night. My faith in Tarquinio's judgment was considerably strengthened when we got to know the Grigoletti brothers. It was due to indignation at one of them having been mistaken for a spy that the real culprit was discovered – a man who, as always in cases of betrayal, was not a native of the area, but was taking refuge there while making up his mind which side to back. It was he who had led the patrol to the cascina at dawn on January the 27th. When the operation failed he fled to the south, but not before Grigoletti had denounced him to the people of the Valley. The younger brother eventually became one of our most valuable couriers.

Then there was the problem of security. Enemy spies had increased owing to the bribes offered for their services. Although the Valley remained unaffected, the areas outside it became increasingly dangerous, served as they were by good roads and telephones. Our small force was obliged to keep continually on the move in the forests enclosing the Valley. The Militia patrols paid regular visits to the area, more for the purpose of looting than to search for the menfolk. There were few Carabinieri now, for many of them had taken to the hills and joined the resistance movement.

The first green leaves appeared on the trees at the end of April. Trivial as it might seem, the coming of the leaves was an important event for the partisan and one that was awaited with increasing impatience as the winter drew to an end. It meant that before long we could move at our ease across the mountains by day without fear of being observed by hostile eyes on the look-out for us, and we could begin to attack enemy vehicles on the roads. With leaves on the trees, the odds against survival were reduced a little.

One day Franco was sitting on a grassy slope beside the path leading into the village of Chiesa. Beside him lounged one of his men, a youth named Aristide who had joined his ranks only a few days before, having escaped from the village of Campiglia near La Spezia.

It was a bright, warm morning, and the little stream below them sparkled in the sunshine as it bounced its way over the pebbles. There was a fountain nearby, and a track led from it past the place where they were sitting. Tarquinio's mother had just filled a bucket at the fountain, and was returning along the path with the vessel balanced precariously on her head, after the fashion of the mountain people. As she reached the two partisans she paused for a moment.

"Buon Giorno," she said.

They returned her greeting. "What's the latest news, Mamma?" asked Franco.

"Niente di nuovo. The Carabinieri and some Militia are still at Coloretta, in the Zeri Valley. Is your friend a partisan?"

"Yes – he has never been here before."

The old lady went on her way.

It was pleasant sitting in the warm sunshine, with only the blue sky above them. Directly opposite, not more than fifty yards distant, the path climbed up again on the other side of the stream and lost itself among a cluster of chestnut trees on its way to the next village of Chioso. Franco looked at the sky above the wood, and fixed his gaze upon a hawk that hovered almost motionless in the limpid air. Fascinated, he continued to watch it.

"Look, Aristide, it's going to dive. I wonder what it has found?"

His companion, lying on his back with his eyes closed, grunted that he was far too comfortable to sit up. Franco continued to watch the bird; only occasionally could he detect the flutter of wings, so still did it hang. He watched it begin to dive – then suddenly it broke off its downward fall, and flew away. Obviously something must have frightened it. He dropped his gaze to the wood, to the little path leading into it.

Franco gave a cry of warning, and sprang to his feet. Aristide sat up with a start. As he did so, he saw three armed men coming towards them from the trees opposite. One was a Militia corporal wearing his distinguishing black shirt, the other two were elderly Carabinieri. At that moment the Republican saw them.

"Hi! You!" he shouted. "Come here!" and he raised his automatic rifle.

"Run for it!" yelled Franco, and dived down the slope into the bed of the stream. His companion began to run along the path to the village. The first house was only fifteen yards from him – if he could reach that he would be safe.

There was a burst of rifle fire. Aristide staggered forward two paces, and fell with his right leg shattered at the hip. Franco, thinking he was close behind, ran on and disappeared from sight.

The sound of the firing brought the women running to their windows, and then out into the street. The partisan was still conscious, and lay groaning where he had fallen. The patrol reached him, the corporal leading the way at the double. He stooped, panting, and looked down at his victim. Suddenly he kicked him viciously. The boy groaned and opened his eyes.

The Republican reloaded his rifle.

"Don't shoot again," said Aristide. "I can't run away. I surrender."

The Fascist bent down and forced the muzzle of the automatic into his mouth. He pulled the trigger.

"That's what we do to rebels," he said.

Suddenly he felt himself pushed roughly aside by Mamma. The old lady shook her fist at him, and shouted at the top of her voice,

"Murderer! You will pay for this!"

She fell on her knees, and, taking the bleeding remains of the boy's head on to her lap, she leant over him and burst into tears. The lad was still alive. He opened his eyes and looked at her. Then he died.

Meanwhile a crowd was fast gathering.

The Republican corporal, feeling that he could deal with the old women later, had begun to harangue them when he realised that his Carabinieri companions had disappeared. He looked about him anxiously and caught sight of them in the wood opposite, obviously beating a hasty but dignified retreat the way they had come.

Suddenly a voice spoke from the crowd.

"You'd better clear out," it said, "if you don't want the partisans to find you here."

The corporal did not feel nearly so brave.

"The body is to remain here until further orders," he said. "This rebel has been justly killed, and you are forbidden to bury him. If you disobey, you will be severely punished."

"The partisans are coming!" said the voice again.

The Fascist waited for no more. He scuttled along the path to rejoin his companions; as he disappeared in the woods he heard the angry murmur of the crowd.

Meanwhile, Franco was looking for his men, with the idea of ambushing the patrol on its return to Coloretta. They had left camp that day without firearms, except for a few revolvers. It had become an unwritten law in the Valley that by day no man would carry firearms that could not be concealed about his person, in order to avoid reprisals being taken against the villagers.

An hour passed before the Sardinian had collected together an armed force, and they set out. On the way they learnt what had happened and went on to Chiesa, where there were already some of the International Battalion.

The population carried the body into a little stone chapel that stands above the village, near the road leading from Pontremoli. They laid it on a table near the altar steps, and lit the candles. Two partisans mounted guard outside, while the people of the Valley came in an endless stream bringing tributes of wild flowers. The church bell was tolling, and the priest had arranged for the digging of the grave in the grey-walled cemetery. There was to be a special Mass the following morning.

From that day onwards the hatred of the Rossanesi towards the Fascist Republic became a deep-rooted, personal affair, that was shared by every man, woman, and child of the nine villages. The time was now to come when that hatred would prove to be a most effective weapon with which to fight the enemy.

Chapter Seven

Contact with Corsica

One night in the month of May, Carlino, the guide, knocked softly on the door of a cascina in the woods near the village of Bosco. It was dark, but not too dark for anybody who might be watching the scene to make out the figures of the guide and his companion as they waited in the shadow of a chestnut tree.

Inside the hut, Tarquinio, our new host, Zaffarino, and I sat on a wooden bench drawn up beside the smoking stove. It was Zaffarino who had arranged the meeting; he was an elderly farmer who owned two houses and an unknown quantity of chestnut flour, and had been chosen as the partisan leader of the village.

Young Carlino knocked again. This time Zaffarino seemed satisfied, for he went to the door and opened it a little way.

"Come in, Reverendo," he said, as the second figure appeared in the doorway. "Signor Maggiore, this is Don Davide from the village of Montereggio."

When we were seated again and the door shut, the priest began to speak. He was a short, slight figure of about thirty, and wore glasses. He had dressed in civilian clothes for his nocturnal visit and it would have been hard to guess his calling. The village of Montereggio lay in the next valley to the South West, in the direction of La Spezia. It too was connected with Pontremoli by means of a motor road, and it was close to another village famed for its pro-Fascist sympathies.

The population, said the priest, could not openly support the resistance movement at the moment, owing to their precarious position, but they could help with information and with a service of couriers. The village possessed a telephone that communicated direct with Pontremoli, and Don Davide was able to keep a watch on visitors to the suspected village of Parana.

At the moment he was more interested in a little matter concerning mules. Certain Fascists had stolen a number of mules from the local farmers before the Armistice. They really belonged to the Government of Badoglio –

therefore it was only right that the partisans should have them. Could we do something about it?

At the suggestion of removing Fascist property, Tarquinio became enthusiastic, and he, Carlino, and the elderly Zaffarino arranged the details between them. The discussion lasted late into the night. Don Davide and his guide departed at last, as it was essential that both should be back in Montereggio before dawn.

A few days later the animals arrived in the Valley, having been spirited away from their illegitimate owners under cover of darkness. Their departure was lamented, and threats of terrible reprisals were made but no action was taken, for at that time the Fascist authorities had their hands full elsewhere.

My own force of partisans had begun to expand, and we launched forth into small ambush operations against isolated Republican Army vehicles on the country roads near Pontremoli. These operations could only be of a hit-and-run nature, and we seemed to do more running than hitting, but at least they caused the enemy some anxiety. Our activities were still limited by lack of weapons, and particularly of ammunition, but the International Battalion began to earn a reputation for creating disturbances. The raids could only be carried out with small groups of three or four men, and the innocent population in the nearest village to the point of attack generally bore the consequences. I regretted this, but we were supposed to be fighting a war; the best I could do was to select ambush areas as far removed as possible from any village.

By the end of May we numbered thirty combatants, which meant thirty men armed with a variety of weapons that looked dangerous, although there was ammunition for only fifteen. We were now a truly "International" force; in addition to the British and Polish elements, we had been joined by two Yugoslavs, a Peruvian, and a somewhat bewildered Somali who had escaped from a ship in the port of La Spezia. Behind us we had the population of the Valley, ready to collaborate in whatever way they could.

The political situation became increasingly ominous, while the Allied Armies stagnated in front of Cassino. A strong formation of Communists had established themselves in the valley of Coloretta, in Zeri Commune, to the consternation of the Actionists. The population accepted them at first in a spirit of co-operation, but it was not long before they realised that the methods adopted by the new arrivals left much to be desired; they had begun to intimidate the country folk in their efforts to increase the party membership, and to "requisition" any food and livestock to which they took a liking. This resulted in a general exodus of youngsters from the villages in Zeri, who, liking neither Actionists or Communists, came unarmed and untrained to offer their services to the Maggiore Inglese. The success of "Operation Mule", and reports of our less light-hearted activities in the country lanes, had already resulted in an embarrassing flow of would-be recruits from the Montereggio region.

Most of these applicants had to be turned away, for we were not in a position to feed or clothe them, but I obtained three valuable recruits who later gave exemplary service to the International Battalion. The first was an Italian Air Force Lieutenant, Aldo Berti, whose home was in Pontremoli. The second was a swarthy Croat, of stocky build, with strong, hairy hands. He had been captured in Croatia, and interned in an Italian camp, and from time to time the expression in his eyes showed clearly that the experience had been far from pleasant. The third was a good-looking young Italian Army Corporal who had served two years on the French frontier, and who was gifted with a delightful sense of humour. He had learnt a good deal about his fellow men, in spite of his youth, and quickly proved himself a natural leader. His name was Nello Sani, and he came from the Spezia suburb of Valeriano. Nello's feelings were indicated by the fact that he chose as his nomme de guerre the name "Badoglio".

Aldo was appointed as Adjutant to the International Battalion, with the onerous task of instilling some form of training into our undisciplined mob, while Branco the Croat assumed the functions of Intelligence Officer, and was responsible for our security. His methods of obtaining information did not follow the Queensberry Rules; he had experienced the Axis methods of doing the job, and the hunted could not afford to be squeamish.

The accommodation difficulty was overcome by splitting the force into small groups of five, and each group occupied one of the many cascinas scattered throughout the forests. The owner of the building made himself responsible for providing food, contributed by the neighbours in his village, and the villagers would also look after the sick. There were few cases of illness.

Towards the end of May, there occurred an incident that brought the International Battalion another step nearer its goal.

After the expulsion of Edoardo from Torpiana, Colonel Henry Lowry Corry had joined me. Although he had had more than his fill of hardship in two world wars, he shared our trials and tribulations with a spirit of fortitude that was an everlasting encouragement to us of a younger generation, and I was indeed fortunate in having his wisdom and friendship to draw upon in moments of doubt.

One afternoon we were sitting outside our cascina basking in the sun, and digesting our one meal of the day. It had consisted of boiled potatoes, sent to us by Zaffarino of Bosco, and Henry Corry had just finished washing out the communal feeding bowl, having appointed himself chief cook and bottle washer for the day. I was in an irritable mood, due partly to an endless argument that had been going on at shouting pitch for over an hour between Nello and our latest recruit.

The newcomer was one Romeo, and the subject of discussion was who should be next for shooting. We knew practically nothing about Romeo, who had appeared out of the darkness two nights previously, thrown himself down on the chestnut leaves obviously exhausted, and gone to sleep, his carbine clutched to his side. All that we could ascertain next day was that Nello knew where he had come from – a village on the slopes above Alla in the Magra valley – and that he had the reputation of being a deadly marksman with any weapon that he might lay hands on. The local wine had loosened his tongue a little. As far as we could make out from Nello, who understood the patois of our uninvited guest, he gave himself the rank of Major (Nello explained that it was really Sergeant Major, but in partisan circles the "Sergeant" was conveniently ignored), he had a price on his head from the Fascist Government, and he had disposed of eleven "enemies" on as many different occasions between the time he left his village and found us – a journey of not more than four hours. He had been told of my whereabouts in Montereggio, and fervently declared that he had come to place himself at the disposal of the Allies.

Corry and I soon realised that there was something odd about Romeo. His mental process was extremely slow, he only understood the local dialect of the Spezia region, and his eyes were those of a fanatic. The difficulty was to discover what he was fanatical about.

He was of short sturdy build, and wore an incongruous assortment of garments that included riding breeches and black jackboots. His age could not have been more than forty-five.

Mick had gone down to Chiesa to find Dina that day. We were surprised to see him climbing up through the trees, followed in single file by three strangers, one of them carrying a suitcase. It was that unexpected article which caused the noisy argument to come to an abrupt end. Romeo turned coldly practical, and, releasing the safety catch on his rifle, brought it to the ready position.

"Nello!" I shouted, "What the hell is that madman doing now? Tell him to leave his rifle alone – I'll tell him when to start shooting!" This started another argument, which fortunately lasted until Mick reached the cascina.

I could see that he was excited.

"Sir, I found these chaps looking for you in Chiesa. They say they've come from Corsica."

Corsica had been occupied by Allied forces soon after the armistice of September. The remark made me look as I would expect to look if I saw fairies dancing on the lawn at the bottom of my garden. Apparently Corry's expression was similar, for Mick continued hurriedly:

"I know it sounds impossible. They might be spies, but they know your name, know you were with the East Surreys in India, and apparently had a long talk about you with Colonel Gore before they left."

The B.B.C. had sent a special message some months before telling us that Jerry Gore, our comrade in Chieti and Veano camps, had reached the island of Corsica in a sailing boat from Genoa. He carried a detailed report from Colonel Balbi.

The others had arrived by now, and stood uncertainly in the background, eyed with growing suspicion by Romeo. Eager to establish their bona fides, the leader of the three stepped forward. He was a tall, fair haired youngster, and looked very English.

"Perhaps I had better explain, Maggiore," he said in English. "My name is Giovanni, and the three of us represent a Mission sent by "A" Force, which has been set up in Corsica under a certain Captain Wheeler. Our instructions were to find you at all costs." He produced some documents, and the others did the same. These gave their names, and general details.

Corry and I began to cross-examine them. Giovanni was able to name several officers who had been in prison camps with us, whom we believed to have escaped. He confirmed what Mick had already said. He explained that the Mission had been brought close in to the Italian coast by submarine, and then landed in a rubber dinghy in the "Cinque Terre", the stretch of coast between Monterosso and Vernazza. They had some difficulty in climbing off the rocks, and had been seen by a worker on the railway, one "Baccicia" Sazzarini. He had come to their rescue, and had hidden them near Vernazza until he found a guide to take them to Montereggio. From there they had followed the trail to Chiesa, where they had met Mick.

The story seemed plausible enough, but we had suspicious minds in the mountains.

"What were you to do when you had found me?"

" 'A' Force is an ex-prisoner of war organisation. Our job is to collect as many escaped prisoners as possible and evacuate them by boat from the coast near where we landed. The boat is to call in a month's time. We were told that you would be able to help us, and that we could pass messages back about your requirements for the partisans."

"I see. And how will you let Headquarters know that you have found me?"

"By radio, Maggiore. We have brought a transmitting set with us."

They put the suitcase on the ground and opened it. There was no doubt about it containing a wireless set.

Nello showed interest at this point, as he had learnt something about wireless telegraphy during his Army training. While he was examining the suitcase I told the visitors to sit down and wait. There was no need to tell Romeo to guard them – he had not taken his eyes off them since their arrival.

Corry and I retired a short distance to consider the situation.

"What do you think?" I asked him.

"Probably the same as you. Their story could be genuine, but we only have their word for it. If they are spies they are doing a valuable job – it would be an excellent way of recapturing escapees. Once we had arrived on the coast they could complete the operation by taking us off in an enemy boat, and then send the "Mission" in for more."

"Then it seems to me," I replied, "that we will have to go by instinct. Do we instinctively feel that these chaps are telling the truth? It's a pretty dangerous way of deciding the issue, but it's about the only one we've got."

"I think they are genuine," said Corry, "but I shouldn't like to make a definite decision. If they were Englishmen, I'd be prepared to back my instincts and leave it at that. But they are Italians."

Nello joined us, his inspection completed. He was satisfied about the contents of the suitcase, but not about the bona fides of the men. We decided that there was one way, and one way only, whereby we could check the truth of their story. Nello said that he could get to Vernazza and back in four days. At Vernazza he would find the railway worker who had presumably rescued the party. During his absence the "Mission" would have to remain with us under observation.

"We'd better let them send a message, though," I said. "If they are genuine, headquarters in Corsica will be wondering what has happened."

We returned to the others, and I told Giovanni to transmit something. He explained that they could not be received until six o'clock in the evening, but he could send out a preliminary signal. He knelt beside the suitcase, while we watched. It was not long before it became obvious that the set was "dead". He looked at us in despair.

"It's broken," he said. "The case was swamped when we landed on the beach, and the sea water has got into the batteries."

In his agitation, Giovanni spoke in Italian, and Romeo for once understood what he said. There followed a noisy scene in which all three would have been shot, but for the restraining influence of Nello. I think the unfortunate members of the Mission believed their last moment had come. After a great deal of effort, Romeo was calmed down and I had the sudden inspiration of sending him off to Vernazza with Nello. They left that night.

By the end of the second day, Corry and I began to have more confidence in our instincts. We tried with some success to get our visitors drunk, and even then their story did not alter. In vino veritas was a well tried formula, but nevertheless we handed them over to Tarquinio and Branco for a while. Tarquinio applied wine in vast quantities, Branco applied what he was pleased to call "persuasion" and charm of manner, and still the story was the same.

On the third day, Fate intervened in a way that made us feel they needed our protection. The political leader put in an appearance at the cascina, followed by his inevitable armed escort of three, and informed us that our visitors were spies and that he had come to shoot them. For the first time I regretted the absence of Romeo.

There was a heated debate, during which I pointed out that I was responsible for any Allied Mission that might arrive in the Valley, that we believed their story, and that it was not the business of any amateur politician to interfere. The discussion became heated, and we reached the point where both sides began to finger the triggers of their rifles. One hasty move, and we would be the cause of a minor civil war that would grow into an internal political struggle, and wreck the resistance movement completely.

In a desperate effort to save the situation I resorted to bluff and stated that the Mission had brought two wireless sets with them, one of which had been damaged. The other we had already used on the night of their arrival, and had sent a long message giving full details as to our whereabouts and the strength of the partisan formations in the area, together with the names of their commanders. This message, I said, had been acknowledged, and we had been instructed to transmit similar messages at periodic intervals.

It was a wild throw, but I won.

Although I was sure the politician did not believe all this, there was an element of doubt about the explanation too dangerous to ignore – assuming a message had been sent through, giving his name. The deputation retreated with bad grace, and relations between us never recovered.

Nello and Romeo returned late on the night of the fourth day. They brought a note from Sazzarini confirming what Giovanni had said about the landing on the coast. In addition he included a brief description of each of the men.

We were greatly relieved, and only then did Corry and I begin to consider what the arrival of the "A" Force Mission meant to our future prospects. We had proof that our own people knew where we were, and were trying to help us. Even if we could not make contact with them by wireless, it would only be a question of time before they sent in another Mission.

A few days later Giovanni decided to take the damaged set to Genoa, where he could have it repaired. He possessed all the necessary money and forged documents, and, as his home was in the Genoese suburb of Sori, felt confident that he could complete the journey successfully. He left us early one sunny morning, to catch the bus at Sesta Godano, and that was the last we saw of him. He was murdered in the Torpiana valley, and his wireless set stolen. I was told later that the culprits believed that the set was in working order, and killed him to obtain possession of it. Thus Giovanni, fighting unselfishly for his country's freedom, fell a victim to political intrigue.

After his death the Mission did the best they could. The remaining members, Elio and Marco, travelled far and wide to dig escaped prisoners out of their hiding places, for the embarkation had been fixed for a set date in case communications broke down. Monte Picchiara was to be the rallying point; when the night came to set out for the coast, the two "A" Force men had collected twenty-eight escapees. I had decided to go with them as far as the sea, with the object of sending a written report and having a word with whoever was in the boat. Before we left the mountain, convoys of mules arrived from the Rossano Valley, laden with fruit, cheese, and the local "Yorkshire Pudding" made of chestnut flour. We filled our stomachs and our pockets, and began the march as night was falling.

Nello was our guide, and we reached Vernazza well on schedule the second evening, where Sazzarini took us all to a house on the outskirts of the town. Duly refreshed, we proceeded to the embarkation point on the beach half way between Vernazza and Monterosso. The boat failed to arrive.

Sazzarini, faced with the unenviable task of sheltering more than thirty "rebels" for a whole day, met the situation with praiseworthy initiative, and took us to his vineyard where we spent the daylight hours lying among the grapevines. Our host could do nothing about food, however, for he was not a wealthy man, so we existed on a diet of raw beans.

On the second night we arrived on the beach again in the middle of a thunderstorm, to see the boat coming in, clearly visible in the lightning flashes. The enemy coastal garrison at Monterosso saw it too, and fired everything they had at it. The alarm was sounded, and patrols were sent to comb the area. Sazzarini took us back to the heights above Vernazza, where he left us, and Nello became guide once again. We returned disconsolately to Monte Picchiara, and the ex-prisoners dispersed to their previous safety areas.

Chapter Eight

The Battle of Calice

At the end of May the Valley began to take on a more prosperous appearance, for the fields were sprouting grain shoots and cherry blossom flowered on the trees in the villages. This gave promise of a plentiful harvest and sufficient food for everybody by the end of the year. The Rossanesi now regarded themselves as under the protection of the International Battalion, though how we could be expected to protect them against a determined enemy was anybody's guess. Other partisan leaders began to impress themselves upon the public, the politicians, and the enemy in areas outside the Valley. Beyond Montereggio an Army Lieutenant, Danielli Bucchioni, had raised a force of his own. He was an energetic young fellow of athletic build, with thick, wavy black hair and dark brown eyes beneath bushy eyebrows. Like all those who adopted the partisan cause, he had grown a beard which he kept carefully trimmed. His father owned estates in the Calice area, and the son, realising that civilisation had slipped back six hundred years or so, decided to play the part of a warrior Baron. His dependents rallied to his call with enthusiasm.

Dani and I had first met in the early days when we joined forces to attack the castle of Calice, occupied after the 15th of March by a small garrison of pompous Militia from La Spezia. The Blackshirts made a nuisance of themselves strutting about the town looting the food supplies and requisitioning livestock. We came to the conclusion that it was time to give them a fright, for we learned that they believed the surrounding villages to be occupied by armed partisans and dared not venture far from the castle.

At the time we possessed only a dozen rifles between us, and not more than three rounds of ammunition for each of them. In addition we had a few Italian hand grenades. We decided that the morale of our men would benefit from an operation in which only Italians took part, as many as possible drawn from the Rossano Valley and from the Calice area. Bluff would be our main weapon, with the object of giving the garrison the impression that the "rebel" forces were much stronger than they had imagined.

In my innocence, I chose Sunday night for the attack, as being the most likely time to catch the Fascists off their guard. Alas, even war could not interfere with the traditional Sunday Festa, with the result that when my detachment of Rossanesi, led by Tarquinio, joined me at the rendezvous in a wood overlooking the castle, it was painfully obvious that they had spent the day imbibing deeply. Two fiascos of wine adorned the saddle of each of the two mules that accompanied them, for we hoped to acquire much enemy property. The attack could not be called off, as Dani's men were waiting for us on the outskirts of Calice. There were angry protests as I poured the wine into the surrounding bushes, and we went on our way.

Dani's contingent was in slightly better form. We decided to carry on, though we realised that the operation could not have a conspicuously successful ending.

I would prefer to draw a veil over what happened then, but one might as well be honest. At nightfall we approached the castle and reached a point where we could take up a firing position behind a bank less than a hundred yards from the northern face of the building. It looked, to my anxious eyes, incredibly large, and incredibly hostile, for silence reigned within and there were no lights showing. The windows glittered in the moonlight, and we told the men who possessed rifles to aim at those on the top floor, and fire together when the order was given.

The approach march had taken place silently enough, and I began to hope that it might have dispelled the alcoholic stupor of my "soldiers". My optimism was premature, for, without warning, Tarquinio took it upon himself to burst into song – a very rude version of the Fascist hymn "Giovanezza" – and the others joined in. Secrecy took wings and flew away.

"That's torn it," said Aldo, who was taking part in his first operation as Adjutant of the International Battalion.

Dani shouted, "Fuoco!" and a ragged volley echoed round the mountains, followed by the sound of tinkling glass. Regardless of preliminary instructions on the art of controlled fire all the ammunition was quickly expended in a furious feu de joi. Then fell an oppressive silence. We waited. The castle remained dark and foreboding.

Dani resorted to bluff.

"Is the mine laid under the door?" he shouted.

"Si!" came a happy chorus loud enough to be heard in Pontremoli.

"Right. Set it off," and he threw a hand grenade that burst with a roar near the door of the castle wall.

Silence fell again, to be broken by a sudden volley of rifle fire from the upper windows. In less time than it takes to read, Dani, Aldo and I found ourselves alone in the country lane, bathed in bright moonlight. Behind us we could hear scurrying footsteps and the snorting of mules as they were dragged along rocky paths into the woods. The incident is well remembered in Calice to this day, for in the resulting confusion I left my walking stick behind. It was discovered in the morning and kept by the townsfolk as an embarrassing souvenir.

It was not a very creditable performance, but such are the fortunes of war that it produced results greatly out of proportion to its military value, and thereby taught me a useful lesson.

The Blackshirts screamed for reinforcements. They arrived in lorry loads next day and combed the Calice valley for "rebels", watched by us with some amusement from various vantage points on the perimeter. Aldo narrowly avoided capture. Then they proceeded to bombard the empty mountain tops with mortar fire, for reasons best known to themselves. The enemy version of the affair must have been alarming indeed, for the Militia commander came to the conclusion that the area was too difficult to hold, and withdrew his garrison from the castle. Calice was left in peace for a while.

Then there were Guglielmo Cacchioli and his brother Gino, who had adopted the alias of "Beretta", and reigned supreme near Borgo Taro beyond the great mass of Monte Gottero. The Beretta brothers were the first to receive supplies from the air, and they contributed some sten guns and tinned rations to the needy "Internationals", a gesture that was warmly appreciated. They, with Dani, were trying hard to keep aloof from the political intrigues developing around them, to the chagrin of both Actionists and Communists.

It was during my visits to the Beretta brothers that I came to know the people in the village of Buzzo. They were led by old John Cura, who was born and bred in London and had served in the first world war in the British Army, a fact of which he was inordinately proud. John's chance came when the Allied captives escaped from their Italian prisons. He sent his son Dick to look for them and in spite of the danger that he ran, kept one permanently hidden in his house until the end. It was a lucky day for us when we first met him. He introduced his nephews Fred Brattisani and Gino, both of whom were British subjects and spoke broad Cockney better than they spoke Italian. Consequently they were of increasing help to us as interpreters and guides, as the International Battalion grew in size.

It is a long and tiring journey from the village of Buzzo over the pass of the Due Santi to Zeri, beyond which lies the Valley. The rocky path climbs upwards through the endless chestnut forests, past wooden huts where the charcoal burners toil day in and day out producing the charcoal that travels down to the city of Borgo Taro by means of an overhead cable; at last one comes in sight of the little chapel on the crest, known as the "Due Santi".

There is an impressive view of the mountain ranges beyond, reaching as far as the bay of La Spezia, and of the high green ridge sweeping in a semi-circle up to the crest of Monte Picchiara. Leaving the chapel, the path winds its way down through humble villages and over another low range of hills into the Valley. On looking back, one sees the sulking mass of Monte Gottero dominating the panorama. It is small wonder that these mountains are rich in legends, and that the poet Dante gained inspiration from them for his Inferno.

Towards the end of May we suddenly became aware of increased Allied air activity in the north. One morning a thundering roar of sound approached slowly from the direction of the Magra valley and a formation of four-engined planes crept into the sky, glistening high up in the sunlight. Then came another formation and another until the sky was full of them and no other sound could be heard above the roar of the engines. The peasants in their fields began to count. They reached three hundred, and still more machines appeared. Four hundred, five hundred, six hundred. They recovered from their stupefaction and began to shout and wave in the hope that the pilots would see them. Seven hundred, eight hundred, and they gave up counting. To us it was an unforgettable spectacle.

Then came rumours of preparations for an attack on the Cassino front. Aldo brought news from Pontremoli of unwieldy convoys struggling along the roads to the south and of growing consternation on the part of the enemy. The Republican forces began to desert in large numbers, impressed by reports of the bombardment of roads and transit camps and by stories of the guerilla warfare that was breaking out around them. Both Actionists and Communists doubled their numbers and the areas surrounding the Valley became overpopulated with new squads under new leaders.

Franco carried out a successful attack on the enemy barracks in Sesta Godano and captured all the arms and supplies deposited there. Most of the enemy took to their heels in the night, but a few prisoners were taken and carried into the hills. Then he turned his attention to the barracks at Coloretta in Zeri, the stronghold from which the Militia had so long irritated the Valley.

At the same time we took command of the largest building in Chiesa, the ancient "Palazzo degli Schiavi", which the Militia had occupied as a base for their punitive expeditions after the rastrallamento of January the 27th.

Coloretta fell without difficulty. The troops in occupation at the time surrendered willingly; they were disarmed and sent to their homes. The rations and livestock that had been removed from the population for the State depositories were redistributed by Franco, and a form of Martial Law established. Franco became the military commander of Coloretta, while I took over the Rossano Valley. Both operations were without bloodshed.

The moral effect of all this on the populations concerned was considerable. No longer was it necessary for partisans carrying arms to slink through the villages by night. We were now transformed into the acknowledged representatives of law and order. Chiesa became the military and administrative capital of the Valley. Sentries were posted at the door of the "Barracks", while armed patrols toured the mountain paths and the road leading to Pontremoli so that no stranger could cross our frontiers without being detected well in advance. My sphere of influence expanded as a result.

I was now able to begin planning operations on a larger scale. Among newcomers from the Borgo Taro area was Lieutenant Geoff Lockwood, who was my very able assistant for several months that followed. He acted as assistant Adjutant and quartermaster, and later carried out liaison duties with the "A" Force Mission and our colleagues in the Borgo Taro region. The "International" element increased with the addition of six Poles, four Russians, a Dutchman, a Belgian, and two Frenchmen. Our common language was Italian, while the Poles acted as interpreters for the Russians on whom, incidentally, they frequently vented their feelings when neither of the British officers was at hand to prevent them. The Russians had escaped from the German "Todt" forced labour organisations in the north; the others had deserted from merchant ships anchored in Genoa harbour, encouraged by Dina, Tarquinio's sister. Since the destruction of communications she had been acting as a special courier to that city, in liaison with the Polish representative of the underground movement, for our contact with Colonel Balbi had now broken down altogether. Branco enlarged his security organisation, and Aldo slowly began to make headway with the training of our cosmopolitan army.

By this time it had become the fashion among the partisans to wear bright coloured handkerchiefs round their necks, indicating the formation to which they belonged. This was particularly encouraged by the political parties, with the result that most of the handkerchiefs were a lurid red. Reluctantly I decided that we had better obey the dictates of fashion, for it became increasingly necessary that our men should not be confused in the minds of the population with their lesser brethren whose behaviour was beginning to cause a serious lack of confidence in the partisan movement. I decreed, therefore, that we should wear green scarves, and was careful to explain that the colour was not in homage to any political party, but to the first partisan of England, Robin Hood. Thus it was that the International Battalion became known as the "Fazzoletti Verdi", until the practice was abandoned.

In the month of June came news of the fall of Rome. The Rossanesi were not particularly enthusiastic about the liberation of the Italian capital – to them the liberation of Coloretta had been far more exciting, for they had little in common with their countrymen in the south. The event however was grist to the mill of the mountain politicians. Again the belief revived that liberation was at hand, and they redoubled their efforts. Underneath the noise and exuberance of those days of Allied victory in Italy and the landing in France, there were whispers of yet another German defence system north of Florence – the Gothic Line – but few heeded the rumours that began to circulate. The war was near its end, and then would come the elections. Meanwhile the influence of Actionists and Communists had grown, and so had their antagonism one for the other.

Between them, and coveted by both, lay the Valley.

Chapter Nine

The Power House

The acquisition of the Palazzo degli Schiavi provided ideal opportunities for training and supervision, compared with conditions that prevailed when we had lived in isolated detachments distributed throughout the countryside, and I began to cherish hopes of raising a force that really would harass the enemy and earn prompt support from the Allied Command. We still lacked uniforms and adequate supplies and had no modern weapons with which to fight, but at least the influence of the Polish contingent was such that recruits looked upon the International Battalion as a warlike formation, and not a refuge where they could find food and a means of escape from the hardships imposed upon them by the Fascists. I had learnt from the "A" Force Mission that the War Office with good reason were anxious that British ex-prisoners should not become involved in the Italian partisan war; therefore, with the exception of Geoff Lockwood and Mick, the others were billeted on families in the Valley and in the Borgo Taro area, until the time came for them to be taken through the Gothic Line.

By the end of May the aggressive spirit of the partisans had died down. In our own case, small ambush operations petered out for the very good reason that the enemy had appreciated them at their true value and took precautions accordingly, and we lacked the necessary equipment to make our efforts more effective. We would have sold our souls to the Devil for just one British machine gun and some gelignite. We waited hopefully, but nothing came.

The results of the efforts made by Colonel Balbi, Colonel Jerry Gore, and the head of the "A" Force Mission were sufficient to ensure that the right kind of help would arrive some time; it was my responsibility to see that we were still alive and kicking when it reached us. Those who were trying to help could not know of the many advantages we had on our side.

It became increasingly desirable that the International Battalion should carry out a special operation with the dual object of gaining experience, and of discouraging aggressive action against us by our political rivals. Nello had long shown signs of leadership, though he generally preferred to work alone or with one companion; his choice on such occasions was an intelligent young lad from Montereggio, who had chosen the battle name of "Cortez". He knew the surrounding country well, having lived there all his life, and this influenced me in selecting our target. Nello was promoted to the rank of Sergeant, and told to choose fifteen men to make up his command.

Some three hours from Chiesa, outside the boundaries of the Valley, there exists an important power house, fed by the Dam that collects the water from the southern slopes of Monte Picchiara. About two miles below the Dam stands the building that houses the machinery for distributing electric power along one of the main grid systems, and feeds the electric railway in the Magra valley connecting La Spezia with Parma.

To guard this important locality a garrison had been installed, believed not to number more than thirty men. It should be possible to dispose of them without much difficulty, provided we could collect sufficient information beforehand. Cortez had served with them before the armistice of September and was familiar with their daily routine. He and Nello went off to pay a friendly visit. They had no difficulty in finding out all they wanted and in visiting the barracks where the men slept. They returned to the barracks and made their report.

At the Dam itself were three Militia sentries, and four civilian engineers, two of them personal friends of Cortez. The Dam was connected by telephone with the power house, near which the main garrison lived in a wooden hut surrounded by barbed wire, alongside a metal road that connected the nearby village of Teglia with Pontremoli. The Militia were armed with rifles and grenades, and two Breda light machine guns. Their morale was very low indeed.

"They complain about being hungry, Maggiore," said Nello with a grin, "and they are frightened the partisans will attack them one day. They also say that the Germans won't give them boots. They are frightened of the Germans too. In fact they seem to be frightened of everything and only want to go home to their mothers."

Under the circumstances it seemed only right that we should help them to fulfil their desire. "Zero hour" was arranged for six o'clock on the evening of June the 15th, the day following that on which Nello and Cortez had made their inspection.

Dusk was falling as we set out from our base; we had to move at night in order that the curious could not guess what our objective was to be. In addition to the fifteen "combatants" armed with rifles, there were ten others from the Valley led by Tarquinio, bringing mules which we hoped would return heavily laden. The advance guard consisted of Cortez, Branco the Croat, and two others. I led the main party, which included three of our

Poles and the Dutchman, with the transport in the rear under the command of Aldo. Nello marched beside me, as I was anxious that he should try his hand at commanding when the time came.

A bright half moon climbed into the cloudless sky from behind the rugged outline of the mountains. In spite of this the track through the chestnut woods was difficult to follow, and we had to move silently in order to achieve surprise. After three hours we saw a dim light shining through the open door of the control room several hundred feet below us at the Dam. The advanced guard approached it while the transport animals were dispersed under the trees. The rest of us then moved on behind Branco and Cortez.

Cortez was to act as decoy duck, and make contact with his friends the engineers. Acting on what they had to tell him, he would call Branco and his companions to overpower the guard, or warn the rest of us to put in an attack. The signal for the general advance was to be given from an iron bridge that traversed the flood gates and connected the control room with the shore.

As we waited we could hear the hum of machinery and the lapping of water against the stone buttresses of the Dam. I hoped that it would not be necessary to open fire at this stage, for then we could not take the main garrison by surprise as they lay sleeping in their barracks. To reach them it was necessary to pass through the Dam. We had to put the telephone out of action, and retain control of the place for as long as we needed to complete the operation.

A light flashed from the bridge and its reflection shone for a moment in the dark waters beneath. We doubled across, to find Cortez waiting at the entrance to the building. There was an engineer with him.

"Welcome, Signor Maggiore, we are glad to see you. I have already disconnected the telephone." He pointed to where the instrument lay on the floor. The wires had been cut and hung untidily from the wall.

We lost no time. Lookouts were posted while the rest of us removed the military equipment and rations from the guardroom. Cortez took me to the kitchen and solemnly introduced the rest of the engineers. The guard were also with us, represented by three trembling figures clad only in their underpants. The first half of the plan had succeeded.

We left Branco on guard with three others. Led by Nello, the rest of us climbed on to an electric trolley that ran down through the foundations until we reached the big iron gates that protected the entrance, and gave on to the motor road leading to Teglia. Cortez unlocked them, the key having been obligingly provided by one of his friends, and we set off for our main target.

We now numbered eleven in all. Nello and I led the column in single file along the grass verge at the side of the road, while Aldo brought up the rear.

The next obstacle to be encountered was a sentry box about two hundred yards from the hut in which the Militia were billeted. We reached it after an hour.

The sentry box was conveniently situated round a bend in the road, and screened by a thick hedge. We halted, while Nello advanced with two of the Poles, their rifles at the ready. The sentry had to be disposed of in complete silence, for the vast black mass of the power house loomed close on our right, behind a high fence of iron railings, and there was a possibility that it too might contain an armed guard that we knew nothing about. The silence was broken by the hoot of an owl. Five minutes passed and then Nello crept back to us.

"All's well, Maggiore." His voice trembled with excitement. "There is no sentry – he must have gone to bed."

Presently I could make out the long dark shape of the barrack hut on the left of the road, and the moonlight showed a gap in the wire and a narrow path leading up to the only door. Opposite the hut there was a grass-covered mound at a range of less than a hundred yards from the windows.

Nello put the men in position on each side of Aldo and me, and then reported that they were ready.

"Give the challenge, Nello," I said, "It's your party from now on."

The men raised their rifles.

"Wake up, Fascisti, you are surrounded by partisans!" he shouted. The silence remained unbroken.

"Avanti, Fascisti! If you don't want to die, turn on the lights and surrender your arms!"

This time a confused murmur could be heard from behind the wooden walls across the road.

Nello called out for the third time.

"Turn on the lights, Fascisti, or we fire!"

The men aligned their sights. Suddenly the lights went on.

At that the squad jumped to their feet, and we rushed the door, grenades in hand in case of trouble. Again there was no difficulty; it swung open at the first push and we burst into the room, to be confronted with the sight of twenty men blinking at us from their beds. One was weeping bitterly, and several raised their hands above their heads in sign of surrender.

Once they had been assured that we did not intend to massacre them where they lay, the garrison became flatteringly co-operative and eagerly surrendered their arms and ammunition, while my partisans made short work of collecting everything else of value to us. During the process two of our captives approached Nello and asked permission to kill their Sergeant, for, they said, he had long been selling their rations on the black market.

They were firmly discouraged, when it suddenly dawned on me that the Sergeant in question was not present. Aldo and Cortez went off to look for him.

Even had the garrison been more hostile, we could not have shot them. Apart from the fact that they were young lads who had only recently been conscripted, such an action would have resulted in fiendish reprisals against the innocent inhabitants of the nearby village, and there had been too much of that kind of thing already in areas outside the Valley. Anxiety on their part as to their fate served our purpose well enough.

While the material was being stacked outside, Cortez reappeared and said that they had found the Sergeant in a hut nearby. I did not know of the other building, and immediately thought of a telephone. Cortez explained that there was no telephone, and the Sergeant was under guard, but there had been an unexpected development and would I please come at once and deal with it? As we crossed the patch of grass separating the two buildings, I thought it odd that the Fascist commander of the garrison had not made his presence felt earlier, especially as he must have heard Nello's first challenge. The mystery was soon explained.

The "unexpected development" was one that I hadn't thought of in planning the operation. On bursting into the billet with understandable lack of ceremony the partisans had found the commander in bed, but not alone. The lady was now in tears; with her arms locked tightly round her lover's neck, she was imploring the unwelcome visitors not to kill him. It took some perseverance to make her understand that we were not after her Don Juan's life, but were interested in a new pair of boots that had been discovered under the bed, and that she was endeavouring to hide by persistently standing in front of them. Tears and screams began anew when they were eventually removed by Aldo and the unfortunate siren transferred her attentions to Cortez, whose embarrassment was already great enough.

I managed to break up the party and we withdrew in good order having warned the Sergeant – who, like the others, was left without firearms, clothing, and the much disputed boots – that he had better make himself scarce the following day. Accompanied by Cortez and Aldo, I then crossed the road to examine the power house, where again we found two civilian engineers eager to co-operate. The ground floor was taken up by the dynamos, and we went up to the next floor to look at the instruments for controlling the power. I realised that only trained saboteurs could have done the necessary damage – for us it was like trying to destroy Battersea Power Station with a box of matches. In any case, the R.A.F. had already done part of the job for us. The engineers showed me a chart recording the expenditure of electric current for that day. The paper was covered with an erratic series of lines resembling the temperature chart of a hospital patient addicted to frequent bouts of fever. They said this was due to a heavy bombardment of the electric railway system that morning, and the line was now out of action for many months to come. In fact it remained so until the end of the war.

After a friendly leave-taking we rejoined the rest of the squad. The woebegone Republicans had been locked in their hut, duly impressed by their good fortune in not having been shot. Promises were extracted that they would return to their homes next day and never more play at being soldiers of Mussolini. We had no doubt about the promises being fulfilled if they wanted to remain alive, for under the Fascist Law the penalty was death for a soldier who lost his weapons. We returned to the Dam heavily laden with our loot.

All was quiet when we arrived, tired and very hot. The rearguard had made themselves useful in the kitchen and prepared hot soup for us and a cup of synthetic coffee made from the rations of the ex-sentries. Tarquinio brought the mules down to the iron bridge. When they were loaded, each of us carrying his quota as well, we set off for the valley.

Dawn was breaking when we came in sight of Chiesa. The men, though weary, were contented; the operation had succeeded beyond our wildest dreams, and I wondered whether Tarquinio and Aldo were comparing it with the "Battle of Calice". Our supply of arms had been more than doubled, and we had acquired valuable stores of equipment and clothing, especially boots – the latter, in those days, were worth their weight in gold.

As the column neared the Palazzo degli Schiavi the men began to sing. It was not long before the population knew what had happened, and great was their delight when they saw Tarquinio and the heavily laden mules struggling up the path behind us. The Rossanesi were proud of us that morning.

The enemy reacted by sending a fresh garrison, double the size of the original, to the power house. Their forerunners had kept their promise, for they found the barrack hut deserted, and they pulled it down to remove all evidence of the inglorious episode. The new guard, composed of Austrians and Poles under a German commander, were shut behind the gates of the main building. A platoon was sent to take control of the Dam itself. For the moment they did not dare advance nearer the Valley than that.

The incident had an unexpected sequel. A few days later two of my partisans came into our improvised Orderly Room bringing with them a prisoner. He was an extremely nervous lad dressed in the uniform of the Republican Army from which he had wisely removed the "Fasces", the badge of the new supporters of the Duce, and he had brought a rifle which his guard had requisitioned. On interrogation he explained that he was a

Corporal in the deposed garrison at Teglia, and was on leave at the time of our visit. On his return, finding that his unit was no more, and having heard the full story with embellishments from the villagers, he decided that he would join the "rebels" and made his way up to the Valley. I placed him under special supervision, during which he performed the more sordid duties in the cook-house. He proved his worth and was duly enrolled in our ranks under the battle name of "Spartaco".

It was shortly after the "Battle of Teglia" that the second "A" Force Mission arrived at Chiesa, and a great moment that was for us. They too had landed at Monterosso, in ideal weather conditions, and they reached the Valley without difficulty. I kept their arrival a secret, and by the time the politicians heard of it communication with the south had been securely established by wireless. What meant most to me was a message that Geoff Lockwood and I and our band of cut-throats had been finally recognised by Special Force, and were to be known in future as "Blundell Mission". A wireless team was on its way to me on foot, bringing with it two transmitting sets for our exclusive use.

Meanwhile, the duties of the Ruler of Rossano became more pressing, and I began to feel that I had taken on more than I could cope with. All kinds of administrative problems arose, for the trustful people of the Valley regarded the Palazzo as their legitimate Town Hall, with the result that I was expected to deal with the public health, communal law, registration of births and deaths, the settlement of private feuds, petty theft, and disputes concerning the ownership of isolated chestnut trees. Aldo and Branco did what they could to help, and Geoff took over the duties of Home Secretary, but nevertheless we were all getting rapidly out of our depth when help arrived in the form of two valuable recruits.

The first was a Doctor. Umberto Capiferri was of small physique, not more than five feet tall, and aged about thirty. He had an open, honest face, with keen grey eyes, and hair brushed back from his forehead. His hands were small, with long, tapering fingers. He had been in charge of a hospital at Villafranca, not far from Pontremoli, until he was obliged to take refuge in the hills, so he found his way to the Valley. He had brought some medical instruments with him, and a supply of medicines and bandages. He set up a hospital in the barracks, and became known to us as "the little Doctor". The quiet and efficient manner in which he carried out his duties as Minister of Health soon endeared him to the partisans of the International Battalion.

The second was a distinguished lawyer, whom we knew as Mario. He began his duties as Lord Chief Justice the day after his arrival.

We were in the Orderly Room, discussing the ominous political situation on our frontiers, when Tarquinio came in, and said that one of the peasants wanted to see me urgently. The man was shown in.

He was a friendly old fellow whom I knew well, and he brought with him a small bundle that contained the usual Rossano tribute of cheese, two eggs, and a piece of chestnut bread. This often denoted that a favour was to be requested. I asked him what it was.

He had brought with him a battered hat that he held in his hands, and kept twisting nervously as he sat on the edge of a chair. He was wearing his best suit, a shirt without a collar, and locally made boots covered with pork fat to preserve them from the damp.

"Maggiore," he said, when he had made up his mind to speak, "I want a divorce from my wife."

I began to wonder how to deal with this one, when I thought of Mario who at the moment was gazing out of the window at the fields of ripening corn.

"Well, now, let me see," I replied. "We may be able to do something for you. The Signor Avvocato here will deal with it."

Mario turned round and came over to the desk. He was an impressive figure at all times, but particularly so when dealing with the Law. Six foot tall, broad shouldered, and wearing a thick black beard, he had artistic hands and wore a ring on which a single diamond flashed as he gesticulated. His voice was deep and resonant, and he had the poise of one accustomed to addressing obstinate juries.

"Dunque," he boomed – he was famous for always beginning a legal affray with the word "Dunque" – "What is your problem, my good man?" and stroking his beard he looked down upon the plaintiff.

"Signor Avvocato, I want to get rid of my wife."

"But that is against the law – you should know that you cannot get a divorce in Italy," and the lawyer gave a deep laugh. "If we could, a lot of people I know would get rid of their wives."

The countryman considered this for a moment.

"But that was under the Fascists. Now we are an independent State, and the Maggiore makes the laws here."

I looked at Mario, with difficulty keeping a straight face, for the speaker was deadly serious. Mario produced a handkerchief and blew his nose.

"Dunque," he said at last, "How long have you been married?"

"Three years."

"Any children?"

"No."

"Why do you want to leave your wife?"

"She is older than I am," said the peasant, giving his long suffering hat another twist, "and she never stops talking, even when we are hoeing the fields."

"Did you like her when you married her?"

"Not really, but she owns a good cow. Now it would be very nice for me to get rid of her and keep the cow."

Mario let out a guffaw and slapped the surprised plaintiff on the back. "That's a good idea," he chuckled, "so you really married the cow?"

The man looked puzzled. "No," he protested. "The woman."

"Ah well, we won't go into that."

Mario paced up to the window and back again, while I wondered what would come next.

"Dunque – have you mentioned this to the priest?"

"No, what's it got to do with him? The Maggiore rules this valley."

We had reached an impasse. I looked at Mario and raised an eyebrow.

Mario stroked his beard, and stood contemplating the floor. "That's true," he said at last. "That's very true. But this is a matter that concerns the Pope, and the Maggiore has not yet had time to send an Ambassador to the Vatican State. You know, of course, that the Pope is head of the Vatican State in Rome, and is not ruled by the Italian Government?"

"But the Pope lives in Rome, so he must be a Fascist."

Mario looked horrified, and for a moment was quite speechless. Then he launched forth into a long explanation covering the relations between His Holiness and Mussolini during the past twenty years. It was all far above the head of my loyal subject of Rossano, but the lawyer warmed to his subject, and continued to the bitter end. At last he gave his judgement.

"The only thing to do is to send your wife back to her family until the war is over, and then we can bring the matter up again."

"Can I keep the cow?"

"That is for you to arrange. Legally, of course, a wife's possessions become the property of her husband on marriage."

The man's face lit up with pleasure.

"Grazie molto, Signor Avvocato – I will send you some fresh milk tomorrow, and you will see that it is the best in Rossano."

"But," continued Mario, unmoved by this gesture, "You will also be responsible for maintaining your wife until you are legally separated."

"That's all right," said the peasant, and scuttled out of the room in case the Avvocato should change his mind.

After that Mario, much to his surprise, found that he was as busy in Chiesa as if he had been in his office in La Spezia.

We felt we already owed a great deal to the goodwill of the Rossanesi. They had done what they could to protect and feed Allied refugees for nine months, in spite of bribes, threats, and reprisals by the Fascists – our presence in the Valley added to their hardships, and yet they gave us their support until the end. The population of the nine villages numbered more than three thousand souls, and never once was there an act of betrayal by any of them. Nor were their actions governed by thoughts of reward when the war was over, for they were far too occupied in the mere struggle for existence to give any thought to the future. Only Geoff and I could appreciate the full extent of the dangers that might come to them as the result of our having been raised to the status of a Military Mission, and I felt it my duty to do what we could to help them with their everyday problems, as long as we had the chance of doing so.

Except in those areas controlled by Dani, Franco, and the Beretta brothers, the population had been obliged to surrender their food and much of their live-stock to the troublesome partisan formations by whom they had been invaded. Actionists and Communists used intimidation to gain their ends, and threatened those who did not co-operate with imprisonment and death, with the result that a belief arose that partisans were political opportunists whose ambition was to disrupt the machinery of legal government. Unfortunately this belief has remained in Italy to the present day.

Chapter Ten

A Conference is Adjourned

The month of July brought an important change in the partisan world. The Actionists had managed to make contact with the American Special Services organisation. The Americans, with their usual generosity, and oblivious of the political implications, began to send supplies to them by air, which were dropped with carefree abandon on Actionists and Communists, and a few other formations that happened to be nearby. We were not included, as henceforth we were the responsibility of Special Force, but the Beretta brothers passed on to us what they could spare. Ugly incidents began to occur on the dropping zones between rival claimants, and I was glad that at least I did not have to contend with that additional problem.

The Communists had two large formations in the Zeri valley, one of which was stronger in numbers and armament than the other. The leader of the weaker unit became an embarrassment to the other, and a bitter rivalry sprang up between them. The stronger party decided that it was necessary to present a united front and a superiority in numbers to the Actionists, in order to discourage any bellicose intentions that the latter might entertain.

The leader of the weaker group was a young student and intellectual called Faccio, who had earned the respect of his men because he had the makings of a soldier and shared cheerfully with them the hardships of life in the mountains. He constituted an obstacle to the main plan and one morning his force found themselves surrounded. They were disarmed, and a summary trial was held, the commander of the stronger Communist force presiding. Faccio was accused of having stolen material from a drop that had taken place a few nights previously, and he was taken into the woods and shot.

As might have been expected, the murder of a partisan leader at the hands of another of the same political party had a profound effect upon the population, and upon the Actionists. The fiancee of the victim, feeling herself to be in danger, fled to the Valley and asked for asylum, and we took her in.

By this action the Communists gained the desired superiority in numbers over their political opponents; the latter, duly impressed, shut themselves up on the summit of Monte Picchiara and in the Torpiana valley to consider plans for readjusting the local balance of power.

It also gave us food for serious thought. Relations between the International Battalion and the Communists were far from happy. They had been further strained a week earlier, when a gentleman calling himself a "Political Commissar" arrived uninvited in my orderly room, and stated that he had come to instruct my men in the lessons taught by Marx and Engels. I told him I was not interested in politics, neither were the men under my command, nor the Allies whom we represented, and had him escorted over our northern frontier by the Poles, who made it clear that if he returned to the Valley it would be at his own risk. It was natural, therefore, to suppose that his colleagues would now adopt the offensive. I doubled the guards, warned the population, and we waited, while the "A" Force Mission sent a report of the development by wireless.

A day or two later, a young partisan officer came to the barracks and asked to see me. He was brought into the Orderly Room, and we were left alone.

The newcomer was a pleasant looking fellow, with fair hair and honest grey eyes. Although he could not have been more than twenty six, his face bore traces of a life of hardship. He was wearing round his neck the customary red scarf of the Communists.

"What can I do for you?" I asked.

He did not reply at once, and it was obvious that he felt extremely uncomfortable.

"Maggiore," he said eventually, "I should first of all explain that I am a Lieutenant of the Air Force, and I have come here alone. The truth is" – he paused a moment for words – "The truth is that I have left the partisan formation in which I was enrolled, and want to join you."

"Why, Lieutenant?"

"One reason is that the leader of the formation to which I belonged was my closest friend. The other day he was shot by another Communist leader."

"I know all about that."

"Another reason, Maggiore – and I hope you won't think any the worse of me for telling you – is that yesterday the newly appointed leader ordered me to bring a squad here to disarm the International Battalion."

So our suspicions were justified.

"Thank you, Lieutenant, I am grateful for that information – it was not altogether unexpected."

"Then you believe what I say about wanting to join your Command?"

"Yes, I believe you, but first I would like to know your own feelings about the International Battalion, and why it is not popular with your comrades."

"To answer the second question first, the more irresponsible believe that the war will end very soon, and they want to be in a strong position when the time comes and voting begins for the new Government. They are also afraid of your power."

"Power?"

"Yes. They think that you have direct means of communication with the Allies, but they are not sure. They are afraid that if you are not "liquidated" you will send adverse reports about them, that might make things awkward after the liberation."

"I'm glad they have some idea of what I represent. And now for your own opinions?"

"I know, Maggiore, that Italy can only be freed with the help of the Allied armies who are fighting alongside our own Army on the battle front. Povera Italia, she has suffered so much from a dictatorship that most of the people did not want. How can we possibly save our honour and our King, if we don't collaborate with those who are trying to help us?"

"As far as I am concerned," I said, "I am prepared to trust you, but you are doing a very dangerous thing. If you throw in your lot with the International Battalion, you will run the risk of being murdered. I personally cannot guarantee your safety."

"I realise that. I also realise that if I stay as I am, I shan't be able to do anything to help my country." Suddenly realising that he was wearing the badge of the Communists, he self-consciously removed the handkerchief and put it in his pocket.

"Maggiore, you cannot know how difficult it is for us! I have been a prisoner of the Germans. I escaped from France to Switzerland, and was interned in a concentration camp. I then escaped from Switzerland into Italy, and after many hardships, reached the Zeri valley, where I joined the first partisan formation that I met. My home is in Pontremoli, and naturally I want to help my family as much as I can. But I know that it is useless to expect that our leaders can solve the problem on their own."

"Very well," I said, "I shall be glad to have you in our ranks."

Thus it was that Lieutenant Avio joined the International Battalion.

This event proved clearly enough that our position in the Valley was becoming precarious, and that we had to consider the two political groups as potential enemies, as well as the Axis troops. We would be in a stronger position once the Special Force wireless sets arrived, but, in the meantime, the more we could do to increase the fighting reputation of the International Battalion, the better it would be for us. In their latest contribution of equipment received from the air, the Beretta brothers had included a dozen suits of British battle dress, and I decided to put these into use at once.

Branco the Croat had left us, and gone south in an attempt to cross the lines, and, as he came from Pontremoli, I appointed Avio as Intelligence Officer with the duty of keeping us well informed of enemy movements in the Magra valley. His first report brought news that the garrison at the Teglia power house had now been replaced by Germans, and that a lorry travelled from Pontremoli to Teglia every day, with rations and leave details. It was not long before we discovered that, with usual German thoroughness, the lorry driver followed a set routine, and left punctually at 8 o'clock each morning, except on Sundays.

I decided that we would carry out an ambush with twelve men clothed in battle dress. I would lead the operation, and give the fire orders in English. The result should be that the enemy would spread word that English parachutists had landed in the area, and would be duly alarmed thereby. Such a rumour would impress those city dwellers who were still uncertain as to which side to back, and might lead to large scale desertions among the enemy troops.

The party included three Poles, to whom we had given Italian names, Paolo, Alfredo, and Edmundo, one Russian, a Yugoslav, Riboncia the courier from La Spezia, Nello, three other Italians chosen partly because they had fair hair and might have been mistaken for Englishmen, and myself. The day before the attack, we went down into a glade near Chiesa and practised firing with the sten guns that had been given us, and throwing British-made hand grenades. That night we set forth carrying only our arms and ammunition, and, after a long march down into the Magra valley, arrived at a point on the country road half way between Pontremoli and Teglia just after 7 o'clock.

The ambush point was chosen with some care, for I had to do what I reasonably could to ensure that our escapade would not react unpleasantly on the civilian population. It was at a point where the road passed over a ridge to dip down and round a sharp bend, before it crossed a bridge over a gulley. On each side was a thick hedge of quickthorn backed by shrubs and trees, in which we could lie hidden until the right moment. I dispersed the men at points along the hedge on both sides of the road, and we waited. I toyed with the idea of setting up a barricade to stop the lorry altogether, but abandoned it, as there was some civilian traffic as well. If we stopped all cars and kept them under guard until the operation was over, the occupants would probably be shot as accomplices; if we let them go, after due warning, they might give us away. So we lay hidden, and watched two cars go by.

Suddenly we heard the vehicle approaching from Pontremoli. The Poles got so excited at the prospect of shooting a German that I had to warn them to wait for the order to fire. The sound came nearer and we heard the driver rev. up his engine to mount the rise.

A fifteen hundredweight lorry came into sight. There was the driver and a German corporal in the cabin, but what pleased us more were six German soldiers sitting at the back, unprotected by any superstructure. There was a stir along the hedgerows.

"Wait for it," I said in Italian. "Not yet."

I raised my gun, and aligned the sights. The lorry began to gain speed again as it came down the slope towards us. When the bonnet of the engine was level with the near end of our firing line, I stood up and gave the order at the top of my voice.

"Fire! Give them all you've got!"

A fusillade broke out from both sides of the road. As I fired and reloaded, I was conscious of the Germans struggling to their feet, frantically loading their rifles. One, quicker than the rest, began to return the fire with his revolver. The lorry swayed, but kept on, and as it passed we emptied our magazines into it. Shots were flying in all directions, and we had the satisfaction of seeing one of the Germans throw up his hands and pitch out to lie in a crumpled heap on the road. The lorry swayed round the bend, and we heard a crash and the sound of tinkling glass as it toppled over the bridge into the stream below. Then silence reigned again, mainly due to the fact that our magazines were empty.

The Poles and the Russian leapt on the dead German and proceeded to remove his uniform and boots, for nothing could restrain them now. Taking Nello with me, I made my way to the bridge, and looked at the wreck. It lay upside down in the mud, and blood and glass were scattered round it, while seven bodies lay sprawled in various positions on the banks. It seemed to me unlikely that they were all dead, but at least they would not be in circulation for some time to come.

I collected the men, and we started on our way back to the Valley. We had been on the march for about an hour, when we heard other vehicles moving rapidly along the road from Pontremoli on the way to investigate; one of the wounded must have given the alarm by telephone from the power house.

The reaction to this incident was more or less what I had hoped it would be, except for the fact that the infuriated German command collected a number of hostages from the village nearest to the point of attack, and issued an order that they were to be shot, in return for the death of three of our victims. It was only due to the strenuous intervention of the Bishop of Pontremoli, and, to give him his due, to the Fascist Prefect of the city not supporting the decision, that the sentence was changed to one of imprisonment. The argument used in defence of the hostages was that the attack had been carried out by the English, and therefore the civilian population could not be blamed for it. A rumour flourished for a short time that there were dreaded British parachutists about, and there were a number of desertions from the Fascist garrisons stationed in the area. The Germans added another black mark against the Valley, and decided to bide their time. For a while the political groups turned their attentions to other areas.

A clandestine Committee of Liberation had been set up in La Spezia, and towards the middle of July they sent a representative into the hills to form a central command of all the partisan formations in the name of the liberated Government of Italy. He was a Colonel of the Italian regular army who had seen service in Greece and elsewhere. Following the abortive armistice, he had retired to his home in Monterosso after exhorting those under his command to disband with their arms. Colonel Mario Fontana had been set an insuperable task; in so far as his appointment was intended to create a central authority that all partisans in the area would recognise, he had arrived three months too late.

He arrived without warning one day at the Palazzo in Chiesa to pay a courtesy visit, and I was glad that the sentry on duty at the main door was intelligent enough to present arms on seeing his badges of rank. The Colonel presented himself in the Orderly Room; we shook hands, and I settled him in an arm-chair.

He was of short stature, of wiry build, with a dark complexion and greying hair, and delicate hands, and he carried a monocle which he wore in his left eye. His movements showed a nervous energy that portrayed a mind constantly on the alert. From the first moment I saw him, I realised that there was something fundamentally honest about the man. I got to know him well as time went on, and came to love his sense of humour, and his philosophical bearing in all the adversities that we shared together.

He looked at me for a moment through his monocle.

"Well, Maggiore," he said at last, "I have heard a great deal about you and your International Battalion. The 'Battle of Calice', for example," and he gave a quick smile.

I felt myself blushing.

"That wasn't a very good example, Signore Colonello."

"It's all right," he said, "I was only pulling your leg. I know that the International Battalion has done useful work for Italy, and so I have come to ask you whether you would be prepared to place your unit at my disposal. I shall have need of good men at my Headquarters. "

He obviously did not want to say any more, and pulled out his cigarette case and offered me a cigarette. "English," he added. "Dropped by our friends from above."

I understood the implications of his remark, as he intended that I should. He had already been in the area for a week, and had realised that his task was not going to be easy. As a loyal Italian he was not prepared to discuss the failings of his compatriots with a foreigner, but the fact remained that, in the initial stages, he had urgent need of a body of men who would carry out his orders and who would encourage more reluctant elements to do likewise.

My silence apparently worried him, for he added, "Of course, the Battalion will remain under your command, but I would like to have them closer to hand."

"Where will you establish your headquarters, Colonello?"

"In the village of Adelana in the Zeri valley, for the moment."

"You know, of course, that we are not exactly on brotherly terms with the Communists?"

My lack of finesse temporarily embarrassed the Colonel. He flicked the ash off his cigarette, and then looked at me.

"I know what you mean," he said, "But at the moment I am not prepared to express an opinion either way. I prefer to believe that all Italians in the mountains to-day are true patriots, and they only need the proper guidance to concentrate their efforts against our common enemy. You can, if you will, help me to prove that I am right."

We relapsed into silence while I thought this out. Nobody knew better than I that the Colonel needed support in his mission. From my point of view, it would be an advantage to work in close collaboration with the legitimate representative of the Italian Government, especially once I was in wireless contact with Special Force, and the rank and file would have something to occupy them while I was busy with liaison duties. Knowing what I did of the partisan world, however, I had grave doubts as to how long the Italian Government Representative would remain in the area. I decided there was nothing to lose by complying with his wishes, at least to begin with.

"Very well, Signor Colonello," I said at last. "I shall be very pleased to place the International Battalion at your disposal. You would like us to move to Adelana?"

"Yes," he said. "Thank you, Maggiore. How many men have you, and what armament?"

"I have fifty combatants at the moment," I said, "mainly armed with Italian rifles and Sten guns. We have a quantity of ammunition and grenades, and three Breda machine guns. We have no explosives, stores, or clothing, as we have not yet received supplies from the air."

"Oh, how is that?"

"They are being dropped by the Americans, and we come under the British command."

"I see. But I understand that you are in contact with the British by wireless?"

"I am," I said. "But at present that only concerns the evacuation of ex-prisoners of war. Our supplies are to come later."

"You may rest assured that I shall give you all the help I can," said the Colonel. His visit ended with my arranging to move the combatant squad, and some selected couriers, to Adelana within the next few days.

The village of Adelana consisted of a church, a school, and a group of rugged houses, with the inevitable chestnut forest surrounding it. I moved the detachment from the International Battalion to a site half an hour's walking distance from the Colonel's Headquarters, and Geoff and Aldo took command. The day before they left the Valley, the team arrived from Special Force. It consisted of two wireless operators, Alfonso and Bianchi, with two transmitting sets, and all the necessary paraphernalia for sending and receiving messages. I took them with me at the end of July – with communications established, our prospects for the future looked brighter than they had ever done.

It was on the night of the Ist of August that I finally moved to Adelana, to the house of the Priest, Don Grigoletti. He had ruled supreme in his little kingdom for many years. He had seen his seventieth summer, and hoped to end his days in the old grey house opposite the church. There was something distinctly Dickensian about him, with his quaint clothes, ruddy complexion, twinkling brown eyes, and prominent nose of a startling hue that bore testimony to many years' appreciation of the local wine. He recognised the hand of Fate in the arrival of the partisan command, and contented himself by offering hospitality to all and sundry.

He showed me into the little kitchen, and we sat talking until late that night about the progress of the war. I was surprised to find that he had an accurate knowledge of the general situation on the battle front, for he listened regularly to the B.B.C. broadcasts in Italian, and could recite extracts from commentaries made by Colonel Stevens and "Candidus". He told me, too, about the Bishop of Pontremoli, and how successfully he was holding his own against the German commander in that city, basing his actions on the laws of the Vatican State. The Bishop's diocese extended over a large part of the mountains in which we were, and he took a keen, if clandestine, interest in what was going on.

The next morning the Colonel held his first "staff" conference at Command Headquarters. He explained that the area that he commanded was henceforth to be known as the 4th Partisan Zone, and included the valleys of Borgo Taro, Torpiana, Brugnato (below Monte Dragone) Calice, Rossano, and Zeri. There were rumbles from the far end of the table, where a cluster of red handkerchiefs blossomed, and doubtful looks from the representatives of the Actionists. He then went on to say that his intention was to establish control over all the formations, through their respective commanders – a control that would be essentially military in character.

It was at that point that the conference really warmed up and I realised that it would end in failure. The Communists had no intention of kissing the Actionists on both cheeks, and Actionists and Communists were united – for the first and last time in the history of the war in the 4th Zone – in their dislike of the International Battalion. The conference deteriorated into an exciting battle of words. The Colonel, handicapped by his regular army training, endeavoured more and more ineffectually to act as mediator, for he, poor fellow, had not yet had time to appreciate the fact that he was sitting on a dangerously active volcano. Actionists and Communists had decided that a lamb must be slaughtered to mark the occasion, and that lamb was to be the International Battalion, represented by Mario, old John's nephew Fred Brattisani, and myself. Franco, Dani, and the Beretta brothers would have supported us, but they had not reached Adelana in time. The crisis came when one of the Actionists declared that it was the intention of his formation to take over the Valley, but that the International Battalion might be allowed to remain in Chiesa on certain conditions.

Mario sprang to his feet, looking most impressive. He had acquired a suit of battle dress uniform, to which he had attached a revolver holster complete with revolver, and a thick lanyard plaited from white silk parachute cords. He wore the green scarf of the International Battalion round his neck, and the Battalion badge – the Union Jack and the Italian flag – sewn over the left pocket of his tunic.

"Dunque," he began, and went on for a quarter of an hour, voice booming, eyes flashing, hands gesticulating. At the end, he turned to the Colonel. "I see no reason why, in the interests of this battle for liberation in which we are all supposed to be collaborating, the Valley should not be regarded as a kind of San Marino – it is clear that the English Major and his men have a strong influence there – why shouldn't they remain?"

I didn't quite like his reference to San Marino, but I got the general idea.

He sat down amid a storm of protest. The colonel asked me whether I would agree to the International Battalion leaving the Valley altogether.

"No, Signore Colonello," I replied. "I have no intention whatever of abandoning the people of Rossano, and I would like that to be clearly understood once and for all."

At this one of the Communists jumped to his feet. Banging the table with his fist, he shouted to the assembled company: "The English Major can do nothing without our approval – I do not agree to his absurd proposal!"

"It was not a proposal," I replied with a smile. "It was a fact."

"Nevertheless," he shouted, "I refuse to accept it!"

There was a storm of applause, and violent clapping broke out. The Colonel and my two supporters remained silent. Fred was a big, quick tempered fellow, and the taunt raised his anger. When the clapping died down, he looked at the last speaker.

"In other words, you want to make a concentration camp for the English and Internationals," he said quietly. "The sooner the Allies hear about this the better," whereupon he got up and walked out of the room.

A surprised silence fell on the assembled company. I lit my pipe, and sat back to watch. The Colonel, obviously shocked by the remark, was the first to speak.

"I am sorry that this matter has caused so much irritation. I must confess I was under the impression that the Maggiore was prepared, to transfer the International Battalion to this command, and did not realise that he still wished to retain a garrison in the Valley. At the same time, it is not unnatural that he should wish to maintain contact with a population that has protected him and his men for nearly a year. I propose that we leave this for decision another time."

"No," shouted one of the Actionists. "We demand a decision now. The English Major must agree to leave Rossano at once. Let us prepare a written declaration to that effect. As my colleague has said, he can do nothing without us!"

There was another pregnant silence while the speaker began to write. I realised that the situation was beyond the control of Colonel Fontana – there was nothing he could do, dependent as he was on army discipline.

Just as the law-maker had finished writing, Nello entered the conference room. He was conspicuous in his green scarf, and the badges of his unit; quite unperturbed by the hostile looks, he made his way to where I was sitting and saluted. I was conscious of a murmur of anger from the audience, and an expression of pleased surprise on the face of the Colonel.

"A message for you, Signore Maggiore. It is very urgent."

I felt that I was the object of all eyes as I read the note, and hoped that my expression did not betray my sense of relief. The message, sent by Alfonso, had been received from Special Force that morning.

"Signor Colonello, I gather that our friend has something further to say," I remarked, indicating the last speaker.

The Colonel turned to him.

"Have you finished writing?"

"Yes, Colonello, I have written a report of what we have decided, and now we will get the Englishman to sign it. It is a statement to the effect that he renounces all claim to the Rossano Valley and in return we guarantee him our help and protection for himself and his ex-prisoners, and we will also give his men any food and supplies they may require."

The Colonel looked annoyed. He took the paper and slowly read it through.

"I do not feel that this is really necessary," he remarked.

I heard Nello whistle silently, and turned round.

"They can't get rid of us as easily as that, Maggiore," he whispered.

Meanwhile the other members of the conference were becoming restless At last one of them stood up.

"Of course it's necessary," he shouted. "Let us have it signed and get on with the other business!"

Applause broke out again. The Colonel, with an angry expression, passed me the document, and Mario leant across and read it. He said nothing, and began to stroke his beard – a sign that I now well knew meant he was about to adopt the offensive

"Well, Signor Colonello," I said slowly. "This document will be an interesting souvenir after the war. I am sorry to find that the International Battalion is the cause of so much friction – our colleagues do not seem to realise that we are all fighting for the same cause, just as much as the Italian and Allied armies on the front are doing."

An angry murmur broke out again. I looked at Alfonso's message.

"Naturally I would not dream of signing this peculiar ultimatum, and I have no need of assistance from other formations, even for arms and supplies." I felt Mario stiffen in his chair. "Our political friends don't seem to realise that I represent the Allied Command in this area, and that I have direct communication with them through two wireless sets. Anything that I may require for the International Battalion will be sent to me by air. This is a message to say that the first drop of supplies will be made here to-morrow night. Naturally, should I decide that my position is insecure, I shall inform my superiors accordingly, and transfer my unit to another area where I can be sure of co-operation."

I paused to watch the effect. It was pleasing to find that the announcement had come as a shock; the Colonel's expression was non-committal; Mario continued to stroke his beard; Nello was grinning broadly. So far, so good. Now came the tricky part, and I hoped that nobody would call my bluff.

"Naturally these supplies will be followed by further supplies of arms and equipment to the partisan formations in this area, provided that I have recommended them. You must understand that the Allies have no interest whatever in your political differences. In the meantime, should I disappear, or should the wireless sets at my disposal cease to operate, the Allies will suspect the worst, and will act accordingly, both now and after the liberation."

The bluff lay in the facts that, firstly, the message was for "A" Force, and stated that a plane would drop food and clothing only on the following night, for ex-prisoners of war, and secondly, I very much doubted whether the "Allied Command" would be in the least interested as to my fate amid the bigger issues involved when victory had been achieved.

I proceeded to rub salt into the wound.

"Signor Avvocato, would you please repeat what I have said? There may be some who have not understood my Italian. There can be no question of my abandoning Rossano, as I consider it an area essential to the Allies for future operations that I may be ordered to carry out."

Mario stopped stroking his beard, and rose to his feet. He thoroughly enjoyed himself for ten minutes, at the end of which nobody was left in any doubt whatever. The Colonel was the first to make a remark when he had finished. "Ho capito."

After that there was little more to say. One of the Communists tried to protest, but his efforts lacked conviction. The Colonel proposed that the conference should be adjourned. As a last shot the Communist leant across the table,

"We shall still prove to you, Maggiore, that you can do nothing without our approval!"

"We shall see," I replied.

The meeting broke up.

*　　*　　*

That night there was a further lengthy discussion in the village hostelry. A political commissar arrived just before the evening meal, deeply incensed because he had been prevented from making a speech to the Rossanesi. After he left the conference, Fred had returned to the Valley, and arrived just before the would-be orator, to find a small crowd collected outside the Palazzo degli Schiavi waiting for the speaker to appear on the balcony. Fred made no bones about it. An armed guard met the Commissar and persuaded him to abandon the attempt, and the population returned to their houses with relief.

The Commissar had brought a few supporters to uphold him in his protest. The dining table became a political arena, for several of our friends had turned up – including Guglielmo Beretta – some of whom had been whipped in by Nello, who had decided that our team was not strong enough. The fun grew fast and furious, and in vain the Colonel, as commander of the whole Zone, endeavoured to explain that the political question must take a secondary place until after the end of the war. Mario – for the first and only time during the long period that we worked together – lost his temper, and let fly in terms that, for once, were not strictly legal.

At two o'clock in the morning I left them at it. Nello was waiting outside the door and we walked down to Don Grigoletti's house.

"Maggiore," he said as we reached it. "Is it true that an aeroplane will come to-morrow night?"

"Yes, Nello, it will come, provided the weather keeps as fine as it is now."

"And we won't desert the Rossanesi, will we?"

"No fear of that," I said.

"Bene. Good-night, Maggiore."

It was the night of the 2nd of August, 1944.

Chapter Eleven

Fire in the Hills

It was Mario who woke me in the morning, shortly after dawn; Nello was with him.

"The Colonel wants you to come up to the command as quickly as possible. There is the sound of machine gun fire from the direction of Pontremoli, but we don't know what it means." Before I left the house, I could hear the firing quite distinctly.

At Headquarters I found the Colonel had given orders to pack up, ready to move. An orderly brought news that a Fascist and German force, armed with mortars as well as machine guns, had begun to advance into the mountains. One of the partisan formations had opened fire against them, and then retreated over-hastily, in spite of orders to stay where they were. We were therefore obliged to evacuate Adelana in favour of a position higher up the slopes of Monte Gottero.

The detachment of the International Battalion had been encamped near the village for a week, under the command of Geoff and Aldo. I set off to find them, after despatching Nello with orders to the "A" Force and Blundell Mission wireless operators to withdraw at once to the Monte Gottero Pass, with Nello as their guide. There could be no question of the partisans, still untrained and badly led as they were, defeating the enemy, but there was hope that they might inflict heavy losses, and then withdraw to the heights in true guerilla fashion.

I took with me one of our special couriers, Falco, who, like Nello, came from the La Spezia village of Valeriano. He was a courageous youngster, with an independent spirit that had caused him to rebel against the evils of Fascism at a very early age. He had suffered accordingly, and his sufferings had bitten into his soul so that at nineteen he possessed a deep rooted suspicion of all persons wielding authority, in whatever form. Poor Falco was never to recover his faith in human nature. Together we made our way along a path through the woods, and over a crest dividing us from the valley of Zeri, with its small villages grouped round the termination of the motor road that led to the Magra valley. It was a sunny day, and there were no clouds in the pale blue sky. The sound of firing died down, and then flared up again with an intensity which indicated that the enemy had picked up an important target. A column of thick black smoke began to rise sluggishly from amid a group of houses near the road. A mortar shell exploded at the foot of the slope in front of us. Presently another column of smoke rose into the air, and this time we could see the bright orange flames of an angry fire.

"They are burning the villages," said Falco.

We stopped in our tracks, and I watched the fire for a moment shielding my eyes against the glare of the morning sun. The situation was already hopeless, for it was the population who were going to suffer the brunt of enemy ferocity, and we were incapable of protecting them. I looked towards the tree-covered ridge that divided us from the Valley and my heart sank. What would happen there? We could not see any smoke on the horizon. Perhaps the invaders had not reached it, perhaps they would not penetrate so far into the mountains. The small garrison left behind in the Palazzo degli Schiavi was armed mainly with out-of-date Italian rifles – what hope had they against machine guns and mortars? They would be given ample warning by the population, in time for Doctor Capiferri to evacuate his hospital patients.

Two mortar shells burst in quick succession on the forward slopes of Monte Picchiara just about where the International Battalion should be.

"Come on, Falco, we must find the others."

We walked on through the chestnut woods. Shells began to drop with increasing regularity on each side of us, and we could hear the distinctive "tack-pum" of German rifles fired by isolated snipers. We listened for the sound of opposition from the partisans who should have been in the area of the burning villages; it was only too obvious that there was none.

As we reached the woods above the now deserted village of Castello, a group of partisans crossed the path that we were following. The men were moving silently in single file. I called to the leader, Elio Fantoni from Pontremoli, whom I recognised as one of Franco's men.

"Where are you going?"

"We're escaping, Maggiore," he said, without halting. "They are too many for us. What can we do against mortars? I am going to the summit of Monte Picchiara; from there we may be able to get out of the area." He spoke in a hushed whisper, and in his eyes was that dazed look that I had seen in the eyes of my comrades in the prison camp at Tobruk.

Elio disappeared among the trees. Falco asked another for news of our own men, but the lad either did not know, or was too bewildered by the succession of events to answer him.

For an hour we searched in vain – there was no sign of the International Battalion nor did we encounter any other unit. By the time we returned to Adelana, the enemy had reached the centre of Zeri. A thick pall of smoke hung over the scene. The mortars had been moved forward, for we could see the flash of the guns, and the shells were falling in a creeping barrage nearer and nearer to the summit of Monte Picchiara. A clock in the deserted village chimed ten.

Two Allied 'planes droned across the sky, making for La Spezia. I noticed that the firing ceased and wondered whether the pilots could see the smoke below them, and what they would think. Surely they would realise what it meant, for the Hun was doing this kind of thing all over occupied Europe. If only they would send help!

On reaching Adelana, we found the Command deserted except for Guglielmo Beretta and one of his junior officers. The Colonel had left a message for me, asking for the International Battalion to be brought to his new position on a spur some way below the Monte Gottero Pass. From there it was possible to watch developments on Monte Picchiara, divided from us by a deep and impassable ravine, and the exits from Adelana.

It was painfully obvious by this time that communications had completely broken down, and the Colonel had lost control of the situation. The only course of action that remained open to us was to gather as many men together as we could, and withdraw by night to the other side of the Gottero range. I hoped that the enemy were not awaiting us over there as well.

We took one last look at the scene of devastation, and then set off to find the Colonel. Each of us carried as much food, in the form of potatoes, as he could find. Adelana was now deserted, for the terrified population had fled into the woods leaving their houses and possessions to the mercy of the enemy. Only the old priest Don Grigoletti had remained in his church, gathering round him those of his parishioners too aged and infirm to seek refuge.

The enemy began to close on the summit of Monte Picchiara, the stronghold of the Actionists. The partisans gave a good account of themselves until they were nearly surrounded. Then they dispersed, leaving behind them large quantities of arms and stores that they had been steadily accumulating over the past month. Demoralised groups wandered helplessly about the open slopes in full view of the German snipers until, in desperation, they were forced into the deep ravine that offered the only protection.

We watched all this from the new Command Headquarters. Everything possible was done in an attempt to regain contact with the besieged party on the mountain opposite, but it was in vain. We could only look on helplessly as the grim drama drew to its inevitable conclusion. A hot sun beat down on us and the peaceful scene presented by the green woods, and a multitude of flowers that carpeted the grassy slopes, added a macabre touch. The Colonel, tired and harassed, was sitting on a bench outside a house normally used as a summer lodging by a farmer and his family. The men were dispersed around it, some sitting on the grass, some snatching a few moments' sleep in the shade of a gnarled fir tree, some standing silently watching the battle. Despite the sunshine, the air seemed heavy with a premonition of approaching disaster.

The enemy duly reached Adelana, and soon the familiar columns of smoke began to rise from the village. As we watched, we tried to make out which houses were burning. Firing had ceased, and we turned our attention on the path leading towards us from the village. If only the enemy would emerge on to it, we would be able to pick them off like flies.

The arms we had with us were disposed in defensive positions to cover the approaches, and we had a well-covered line of retreat behind us, but the afternoon dragged on and the path remained empty. All sounds of combat died down on Monte Picchiara after four o'clock. In vain we waited for news, but it was not until an hour later that two bedraggled messengers arrived from the other side of the ravine. They had little to say. When the position on the mountain became untenable, the commander had given the order to scatter. A squad of the International Battalion, with Geoff and Aldo, had been in action near the summit, but they could not tell us what had happened to them later. One of them, Dante Armanetti, had been killed by a sniper while firing his Bren gun at the enemy troops in Coloretta, the first of many who were to die in battle before the end came.

Towards dusk two figures appeared on the green slope of the mountain opposite. Even at that distance we could recognise their uniform. They were studying us through field glasses. I thought of the mortars – we would make an excellent target massed as we were near the prominent stone building. The range could not be more than 1,500 yards, it was only a question of whether the enemy could bring their mortars into position before dark.

The Colonel seemed to read my thoughts.

"As soon as it is dark," he said, "we will withdraw to the summit of Monte Gottero, and wait there until dawn."

"What news is there, Signor Colonello, of developments on the other side of the mountain?"

Guglielmo intervened, "A company of my men, under command of Richetto, an ex-Carabiniere, is in action there, near the Cento Croce Pass. His opponents seem to be all Militia and things are going well for us at the moment."

"Let us hope that Richetto will hold out," I said. "If the enemy manage to surround this mountain as well, then it won't be very funny."

At length Colonel Fontana gave the order to withdraw. The men, tired and discouraged, were slow to respond. One of them looked sullenly at him and remarked that he would not move on until he had had something to eat, whereupon he sat down on the grass and began to munch a piece of dry bread. The Colonel said nothing. I knew the way across the Gottero Pass by night only too well, as did all the ex-prisoners. I set off with a group of seven men – all who had been found of the International Battalion. Gradually other groups fell in behind us, and followed silently. We made our way through a thick wood of fir trees climbing upwards, and when after an hour we reached an open clearing, it was quite dark. As we left the shelter of the trees, the men gasped, and halted in their tracks amazed at what they saw.

Below us spreading as far as the horizon of dark mountains that marked the coastline, was a myriad of lights – lights that wavered, and changed colour intermittently from bright orange to dull red. Hundreds and hundreds of fires were burning, each of them representing the house of some unfortunate peasant. The activities of the enemy that day were clearly registered.

"God, what an example of German culture," I murmured, unconscious that I was speaking in Italian.

The Colonel had come out of the wood behind me, and overheard the remark.

"It is a pity," he said, "That the whole world cannot see this. Nobody in England or America would believe that such a thing could happen in the present century."

There was bitterness in his voice.

Turning our backs on the scene we continued to climb, oblivious of the boulders and tree-stumps that lay in our way, thinking of the tragic shambles below, and wondering what we would find in the morning. What had happened in the Valley? Where were the rest of the International Battalion? A number of wounded had remained in the Palazzo degli Schiavi in the care of the gallant little Doctor Capiferri. There was no news of Avio who had been sent on a special mission two days before to collect information from the villages on the outskirts of Pontremoli. This very night the first British 'plane was due to arrive with supplies for the ex-prisoners of war who were collecting for their journey to freedom.

It was nearly ten o'clock when the column reached the small chapel with its stone statue of the Madonna that marks the head of the Pass over Monte Gottero to the valley of the river Taro. To the left of it was a thick wood of beech trees. The men dispersed in small groups and lay down to wait for dawn. Sentries were posted on the track leading through the wood.

We now numbered forty-five in all, and one prisoner, a Fascist Colonel of Artillery, who had been kidnapped by Franco while indulging in an afternoon stroll with his family on the outskirts of the coastal town of Sestri Levante. As I lay on my back looking at the stars shining through the branches of the trees, I made a mental list of those who were present. They included men of the Actionist and Communist parties; in face of common adversity their political differences had faded into the background. If only we survived, good might come of the disaster, and a patriotic force would be created having as its single common interest the liberation of Italy.

Towards midnight, the sound of an aeroplane engine broke the silence. Gradually it grew louder, and it was clear that the 'plane was flying at a low altitude. The Colonel sat up, and several of the men sprang to their feet, to stare hopefully into the dark sky. We heard the 'plane pass over Adelana and then turn towards the mountain. It came closer, skimming the tops of the trees under which we sheltered, then circled slowly and returned towards the fires that continued to blaze in the village where we had been that morning. The pilot was obviously confused by what he saw, and awaited a signal of recognition from the ground. He passed over the village a third time. Suddenly there was a burst of sound from the shadows below – the enemy, growing over anxious as to the intentions of their unwelcome visitor, had opened fire. The pilot was quick to respond and we saw a string of tracer bullets leave the 'plane and hurtle into the darkness. The aviator circled again and repeated his attack, sweeping the hills below him with what resembled a shower of glowing white cinders. Then the 'plane flew away into the night.

"That's good-bye to our supplies," I said.

Ardito, one of my couriers, was standing beside me, and swore loudly. This tall, sturdy seafaring lad had joined the International Battalion a month before. His home was in the little fishing village of Fezzano on the bay of La Spezia, where his family remained under close observation of the Fascist police following the disappearance of their eldest son. Ardito was shaping well as a recruit, and his standard of loyalty was very high.

The alarm was sounded shortly before dawn by one of the sentries, who heard movement on the path leading from Adelana. The men stood up silently and cocked their rifles. We could all hear the unmistakable sound of footsteps approaching over the stony surface of the mule track. A sentry challenged.

"Chi va la?"

"Amici!" came the prompt reply.

A Rossano family at work.

Amelia.

Memorial to the people of the Rossano Valley.

The church at Chiesa, Rossano.

'Lofty' Rose, with two of our friends in Valley.

The Deluchi family, Chiesa, 1954. (L. to R.) Richetto, Babbo, Mamma, Tarquinio and Amelia, with their children.

A section of the International Battalion, March, 1944.

The Valley of Rossano, Monte Picchiara on left, Monte Gottero on skyline. The white buildings are in Chiesa village.

Amelia's family, Sperinde, in Valle, 1954. (L. to R.) The father, brother Silvio with wife, daughter and neighbour, Amelia's mother, and Romeo.

'Palazzo degli Schiavi,' barracks of the International Battalion, after the enemy attack of August, 1944.

Supplies descend on Rossano, January, 1945.

Lieutenant Dani of Calice.   Nello Sani ('Badoglio').   Nino Ferrari, Franco's
Quartermaster.

Don Battista Ravini of
Torpiana.   Nino Siligato.   Ardito.

The city of Pontremoli, showing the Cathedral dome, and castle in the background.

Monsignor Giovanni Sismondo,
Prince of the Vatican State,
Bishop and Count of Pontremoli.

The Valley of the River Magra, looking North towards Villafranca and Pontremoli.

The 'Fortezza della Brunella' at Aulla.

"Che amici? What group do you belong to?"

"International Battalion."

"Approach one at a time."

The partisans formed a circle ready to open fire. A figure emerged from the obscurity. A sentry peered into his face.

"Is the English Major here?"

I recognised the voice and stepped forward. It was Mick. I told the sentry to let the others pass.

"Who have you got with you, Mick?"

"Only four, sir – Arthur the sailor, two of the Poles, Paolo and Alfredo, and Riboncia the courier you left with us at the Barracks."

I led them into the wood at the side of the path, where the Colonel joined us.

"What have you got to tell us, Mick?"

"Not much. I was in the Valley when they came this morning. They arrived at dawn, and we only had half an hour's warning. They opened fire with mortars on the Palazzo degli Schiavi and it caught fire; Arthur was the last to clear out, and we made our way to Monte Picchiara. Fred Brattisani was with us as far as that. When we got there, everything was in confusion and nobody seemed to be in command, but I found out from one of the Actionists that you were still with the Colonel, so we made our way to Adelana. The Huns got to the village before us, so we had to make a wide diversion, but here we are."

"What was the last news of Chiesa?"

"The last we saw of it was from a wood near the cascina where we lived last winter. There were a great many fires, especially in Chiesa, but there was too much smoke to see which houses were burning."

"And the patients in the hospital?"

"Doctor Capiferri managed to get the serious cases out of the building and hid them under the leaves in a ravine. The others were told to scatter and look after themselves."

Arthur spoke for the first time.

"There's not much hope for the wounded. We only just managed to get away in time. The population had already cleared out, and we found some of them hiding in the woods."

"Have you any news of Adelana?" asked the Colonel.

"They say that somebody has been shot there, but I don't know for certain. The enemy suffered a few casualties in the beginning and were all out to make reprisals."

Mick and the others lay down under the trees and fell asleep. There were only a few hours before daylight, and then we would be on the move again.

I passed the time trying to think up some plan of action. The safest place in which to re-assemble my scattered forces seemed to be near the house of old John at Buzzo, but that would depend on how well things had gone for Richetto in the Taro valley; we would also have to find the wireless sets, and hope that the operators had not considered the situation to be so serious that they had destroyed them together with the code books – at least, in Nello they had the best guide in the partisan forces.

In the grey light of dawn, the Colonel rallied his men and gave them their orders. Guglielmo Beretta had left during the night, to find out the situation in his area, and until we heard from him we dispersed among the undergrowth. Beneath the bushes grew masses of wild strawberries, which we ate ravenously.

At last a courier arrived from Beretta, who told us that Richetto's men had not only driven off the Militia, but had inflicted heavy casualties on them, with the result that they had been obliged to withdraw to Borgo Taro. With that we descended from the Monte Gottero Pass, and dispersed to the pre-arranged villages.

In due course we assembled at Buzzo, and turned John Cura's house into our new battle headquarters, ably assisted by his wife. Rosa Cura could poach eggs better than anyone I have ever known, and she looked after us all like a mother. During the following weeks, stragglers came in from all directions, picked up by the Beretta brothers and Richetto. The latter began to form his own unit as part of what became the Beretta Division. The titles of partisan formations were imposing; a brigade, for example, generally did not number more than a hundred men, by no means all of them armed, but the names of the formations reached enemy ears and encouraged the illusion that our forces were very numerous.

Richetto and I became firm friends. He was an ex-Carabiniere of some thirty-five years of age, tall, thickset and sporting a luxurious black beard of which he was inordinately proud. Following the traditions of the fine Corps to which he belonged, he was fighting the war for the good of his country and his King, and despised the political party wrangling as much as I did. A happy spirit of cooperation was created between our two commands, equal to that of Dani and the Beretta brothers, and this was to be of inestimable value in the future.

A week after we had installed ourselves in Buzzo, Geoff and Fred turned up. They had had a hard time, during which they had existed for two days in a cave without food, surrounded by the enemy. After emerging from that, they had returned to the Valley, to find that it was still occupied by a Militia patrol, so they were obliged to return on their tracks. They had seen Tarquinio, and the news he gave them confirmed our worst fears. The whole of the village of Chiesa had been burnt to the ground, including his own house. Some of the wounded from the hospital had been found and shot on the road outside the village. All the villages had been looted, and the reserves of grain burnt. Doctor Capiferri returned after a few days and discovered that typhoid germs had been planted in the wine at one of the village inns, and he was awaiting an epidemic.

In Adelana, too, there had been disaster. Half of the village was destroyed, and some of the houses had been blown up with dynamite. Two German patrols passed by. Then came a third, composed of Militia. They entered the church where Don Grigoletti had remained with the aged and infirm of his parish and dragged the old man outside to watch them while they ransacked his house and set fire to the room in which I had slept the night previously.

The patrol leader turned to the priest.

"Do you want to say your prayers before you die?" he asked brusquely.

Don Grigoletti knelt in the dust in the shadow of his house and prayed. There was a volley of rifle fire. They dragged his body to the door and threw it down the cellar steps. Don Grigoletti, Priest of Adelana, was seventy five years old.

It was on that same morning that Don Quiligotti who, on our arrival eleven months before, had guided us to the Valley of Rossano, was caught and murdered in the village of Coloretta.

For the rest of that month we set to work to reorganise the International Battalion. Numbers were reduced, for many of our original members had not returned, but I did not want to take on new recruits for a while, except for more promising candidates from the village of Buzzo itself. Alfonso and Bianchi were established at Albareto, in Richetto's area, and the wireless sets were henceforth under his protection. So effective was his security that until the end the politicians, try as they did, could not discover where the wireless team was housed. "A" Force began to send small parties of ex prisoners through the lines, while those who were waiting were found safe billets in the Borgo Taro area. One of these was Colonel Corry, who for a long time remained the appreciative guest of old John. Colonel Fontana eventually returned to Torpiana and set to work once again to build up a unified command, and it looked at first as if he would succeed, for the old political jealousies had died down, and many of the sleeping partners in the Resistance Movement – notably the "Political Commissars" – had fled far afield when the enemy attacked; one of them broke all records and arrived on the Swiss frontier. Communications were re-established with Special Force by radio and there were promises that we would soon receive our own supplies by plane.

We returned to the Valley during the first week in September.

Part III

The Coming of the Allies

Chapter Twelve

Return to Rossano

There were only a few of us on the return journey to the people who had shared our misfortunes for so long, and I was anxious as to our reception following the disaster of which we had been partly the cause.

Tarquinio met us as we began the descent from Monte Pichiara. He was genuinely glad to see us and was emphatic in his assurance that the population bore us no grudge. I felt dubious; it was impossible that some should not be angry with the partisans.

We passed below the village of Montedelama. No houses had been burnt there, and the peasants at work in the fields waved as we passed. We crossed the two streams and entered the village of Valle. Amelia came out of her house and greeted Tarquinio. She looked serious, but there was no sign of hostility in her manner. No houses had been burnt, but there had been extensive looting.

Peretola was the third village. The inhabitants greeted us with the same friendliness. On the edge of the village two houses had been burnt. We continued along the path and turned a corner.

And then we saw what remained of Chiesa.

Geoff was leading the way. He stopped suddenly and I heard him gasp.

Staring in gaunt obscenity emphasised by the bright sunlight was a blackened heap of ruins. The Palazzo degli Schiavi that had been our barracks consisted now of four high walls, with gaping windows, and broken tiles and rubble littered the grass at its base. The priest's house had been the first to receive the attention of the barbarians and was just another blackened shell. Only the church remained intact.

We walked on through the ruins until we came to the house that had been Tarquinio's. He pointed to it, and said nothing. I was suddenly conscious of a lump in my throat, and a feeling of helpless rage. Apart from the blackened walls nothing remained except a heap of rubble and twisted ironwork. An oil lamp with its glass broken still hung on a nail in what had been one of the bedrooms. There lingered over the scene that queer, unforgettable pungent smell of burnt steel and masonry that the people of London knew so well. It was the same with the house of old Gattino the painter who at Christmas 1943 we had strongly suspected of being a spy, and with the Inn belonging to Tarquinio's aunt. The whole village had been reduced to a powdery skeleton, its outlines marked by scorched stone walls. We passed on, and reached the metal road.

"Where are you living now?" I asked Tarquinio, when I had found my voice again.

"We are living in a shed in the fields until I have built a hut," he said. "My aunt and uncle are sharing a stable in another village. You mustn't mind if they are angry, Maggiore. They have lost everything now and they are dazed. They are not country people like us – they have lived most of their lives in Genoa, where Uncle was one of the chauffeurs to the Royal Family."

You mustn't mind if they are angry! I said nothing, for there seemed no way of answering that remark. Geoff had also heard it

"They would have every reason to chase us out of the area, let alone 'seem angry'," he said.

We reached a bend in the road and saw a figure running to meet us. It was old Mamma, Tarquinio's mother. She came to me, Giuseppe following, and the tears were streaming down their cheeks. The old lady threw her arms round my neck.

"Welcome back, Luigi," she sobbed. "I was afraid that you would not return." She rested her head on my shoulder. Old Babbo was embracing Geoff. They led us back to the cascina that had taken the place of their house.

After a while they began of their own accord to talk of the day of the fire. It was much as we had already heard. The dead had been buried in the fields nearby, most of them unidentified, for the documents that they carried had been removed by the enemy. Only after careful questioning did I realise how much this family had suffered. They had managed to save very little from the ruins. Their neighbours, in their immediate reaction after the fire, had blamed them for the disaster because they had encouraged us to stay in Chiesa. "They are stupid people," said the old lady, "for it would have happened anyway. There were no English in the next valley, but they burnt the villages just the same."

"We are glad you have come back to us," said Babbo. "There is a place for you in another village. Amelia's father wants you to live with them."

* * *

With the passing of time, a new spirit was born in the Valley. The ferocity of the enemy, instead of reducing the people to a stage of abject fear, created a greater sense of unity and a hostility that proved far more dangerous than the semi-benevolent attitude shown to the fugitives in the mountains before the rastrellamento. The typhoid epidemic was checked, so that menace was not added to the hardships of the partisans. I had sent a message to Special Force headquarters, now in Florence, and a doctor was sent through the lines to investigate. He eventually reported that there was no danger of infection. The Rossanesi now felt that they were all partisans by force of circumstances. Even the children learnt not to chatter in front of strangers lest they should be spies.

The month of September drew to a close. In the first week of October the enemy staged a rastrellamento in the region of Montereggio. Another of the International Battalion was killed – a lad named Carlo who was one of the original recruits and whose brother Cortez had played such an important part in the attack at the Dam two months previously. When they found him in a ravine not far from his home his body had been mutilated by Fascist troops. More houses were burnt and more hostages shot.

Colonel Fontana established his headquarters near Torpiana, and endeavoured to generate a sense of discipline and responsibility into the forces under his command. The old inter-political rivalry sprang up anew. Groups of ex-prisoners of all nationalities arrived in the Valley in increasing numbers, and were passed on by us to Dani who provided guides to cross the river Magra on the final stage of their journey towards the front line and freedom. Colonel Corry and Arthur the sailor went with them. British and American planes began bombing raids on targets indicated by the partisans.

The month of October brought increasing activity in all directions. The enemy began to suffer heavy casualties on the roads and in their isolated garrisons, and the people in the mountains witnessed with satisfaction the birth of that fear that eventually paralysed the troops of the "Little Republic" altogether. Arms, food, and clothing poured down upon the partisans from the sky, and printed news bulletins from which we learnt that the outside world was watching our activities with hope and admiration. Orders were received by radio and messages and money sent by special couriers who came through the Gothic Line on foot or were dropped into neighbouring areas by parachute. For a time the partisans of all formations collaborated with a will.

Franco, and Lieutenant Ermano – a worthy representative of the more patriotic elements in the Action Party who had moved into the Valley – carried out frequent attacks on the coast road leading to Genoa; the gallant little force under the command of Dani tirelessly molested enemy columns on the road that led from La Spezia to Parma, and wrought such havoc that the Fascists put a price on his head, but were too frightened to venture into the mountains to look for him. Richetto's brigade held the Cento Croce Pass and continued the splendid record that they had begun in August. The forces of Guglielmo Beretta and his brother Gino kept the enemy confined to the lowlands of Borgo Taro. Heroes were not hard to find in the different sectors surrounding the Valley and the Allied news broadcasts paid frequent tribute to the work of the partisans.

The International Battalion was now fully occupied with its work of liaison between the partisan formations and the Allied Command in the South. A selected squad of youngsters from Rossano, the sons of those families who had helped us for so long, acted as guides and muleteers for the transport column when attacks were carried out on the roads. The leader of these was the indefatigable Nello and he had with him four others from La Spezia – Ardito from the suburb of Fezzano, Riboncia, only son of the de Santo family in the same suburb, Falco from Valeriano, and a newcomer, Roberto, from the other side of the river Magra. The rest of the battalion, under the command of Aldo, operated as an independent unit and sallied forth from time to time to harass the enemy on the outskirts of Pontremoli.

Lieutenant Ermano had established his headquarters in the village of Montedelama. Before the war he had been a station-master and he had relations in America. He was tall, young, and like most of us wore the beard of the partisan. Following the August rastrellamento he had been made responsible with Franco for the policing of the Valley, for that region had now become of some strategical importance in the battle of Liberation.

By slow degrees, the influence of Colonel Fontana began to take effect as he strove to create unity among the different formations. It was a frustrating task, and the fact that he made any headway at all was proof of his strength of character and determination. By the end of October, the most rebellious spirits had begun reluctantly to look upon him as their leader.

For a while, then, Fortune favoured the partisans.

One chilly day in early November when snow had already appeared on the summit of Monte Gottero, the International Battalion made its first direct contact with our forces in the South. I was working in my office at the Colonel's command when a stranger was shown in by one of the partisan guards. He was loaded with a heavy pack of British Army pattern, and produced a document signed in ink with the name of a Special Force officer beyond the Gothic Line. I looked at the signature dubiously.

"What is your name?"

"Lieutenant Gambarotta."

"What further proof have you got that you come from the South?" I asked.

He winked at me, and, slinging the pack from his shoulders, he opened the flap.

"I thought you'd need further proof. Major Mackintosh in Florence said this would satisfy you."

He placed on the table an object wrapped in brown paper. The wrapping removed, it revealed a bottle of Scotch Whisky. For a moment I gazed at it in silent wonder. The label seemed authentic. I called the Colonel and we opened it with reverence. There was no doubt that it was the real thing. Gambarotta could not have been provided with a better passport.

"I was also told to give you this package," he said, and laid down an envelope containing one hundred thousand Lire in notes.

We called for glasses from the local hostelry and drank a suitable toast. That was a day never to be forgotten, for it marked another step forward in our plans.

I prepared a report giving details of the partisan situation, and a list of our immediate requirements. Gambarotta left us next day to visit another British officer who was in command of a Mission in the province of Parma.

Air activity increased further during the month of November. A plane was shot down near Borgo Taro, and the American pilot escaped unhurt. A special guide brought him to Torpiana. We had received a message that we were to expect a drop of arms and rations that night. The weather was stormy but one plane arrived over the field and dropped its load in more or less the appointed place.

I arrived on the dropping ground at dawn accompanied by the American pilot. Franco was on duty with some of his stalwarts and had collected the containers together ready for loading on to mules. Several of the containers had burst open.

As he saw us approaching, Franco gave an order and six of his men stepped forward into line holding extraordinary objects with which they proceded, by various slow and complicated manoeuvres, to present arms. Each was wearing on his head a cardboard contraption intended to represent a military shako. Nino Ferrari, Franco's bearded quartermaster, knelt on the ground arranging behind each man a pile of cotton waste and a box of matches.

Franco stepped forward, a twinkle in his eyes.

"Ho, honoured Commander – I present ye antique Guard with ye antique blunderbusses."

He handed me one of the rifles and the American laughed outright. The thing I held was nearly five feet long, had a ramrod attached to the barrel, and a beautiful embossed butt inscribed with the date 1890.

"As they have forgotten the flints," added Franco, "each soldier is to be provided with tinder and a box of matches. We have sufficient nails for ammunition."

The American couldn't believe his eyes, no more could I. "Where did you get these?"

"Ye flying bird dropped them last night. Here is the container."

Those rifles quite cheered us on that chilly morning. We wondered whether their antiquity was a subtle hint on the part of Special Force Headquarters as to what they thought of our methods of warfare. In the other containers we found bags of dried potatoes which met with little enthusiasm, as potatoes were one of the few foodstuffs of which there was an abundance. The American pilot was to continue his journey that night, and I impressed on him the need for making it clear at Base that we needed more modern weapons. If the next drop should contain dried chestnuts, I could not be responsible for the consequences. The quality of our supplies improved considerably after that, so our messenger must have made the point clear.

Ex-prisoners of all nationalities congregated in the Valley; they arrived in tens and twenties – Dutch, French and Belgians who had escaped from ships commandeered by the Axis, and anchored in Genoa harbour – Russians and Yugoslavs who had deserted from the infamous Todt organisations, and Poles helped in their flight by Dina and their courageous countrywoman who, married to a German, lived at Sori near Genoa. The Rossanesi accepted them all, and did their utmost to provide them with lodging and food for their arduous journey to the South.

One squad of nine Yugoslavs arrived, commanded by a woman clad in British battle dress uniform. She carried a rifle and on its butt had carved a niche for every German that she had killed, and she had accounted for more than any of the men under her command. She had suffered the horrors of a concentration camp for a year, had a son in Rome of whom she had not heard for many months, and parents in Yugoslavia of whom she had not had news since the outbreak of war.

It was only to be expected that the enemy should grow increasingly anxious about the resistance movement which their punitive expeditions failed to obliterate and which offered so serious a threat to the lines of communication. They knew that Allied planes were dropping arms by night. Deserters from their forces began to find their way into the hills from the battalions stationed in Pontremoli and in the area of the Cisa Pass, and they told tales of ever increasing death and destruction on the roads leading to the front line. There were not very many German deserters. The enemy were doing their best to bolster up the flagging morale of their troops by pumping into them propaganda about the secret weapons that Hitler was nearly ready to launch; this propaganda began to lose effect after the Allied landing in France.

The treatment of deserters provided a problem for the partisan Command that was not easy to handle. There was no means of constructing adequate concentration camps and the difficulty of providing food for the partisan forces alone would have been insoluble had it not been for the supplies of tinned rations dropped from the air. The partisans were reluctant to share these supplies with their prisoners. After the first rush, therefore, deserters were discouraged. In due course this problem solved itself.

By the end of the month of November the genuine partisan began to feel that it was already too late for his Fascist kinsmen to escape his just deserts in a last minute endeavour to become "patriots", in spite of the desire of the politicians to swell their ranks at any price. This attitude hardened when reports reached us of the torture carried out on prisoners in La Spezia who had been captured in local rastrellamenti. The "Brigata Nera" became experts in refined cruelty as taught by a certain notorious Maggiore Carita. This creature had committed such gruesome acts in the early stages of his career in Florence that when he was obliged to retreat to La Spezia the population knew what to expect. He was denounced by the B.B.C. as a war criminal. After that there began an exciting game between him and me. Carita's thugs were sent out to find me, tempted by a bribe of 50,000 Lire if they brought me back alive; I offered double the amount for the head of Carita and made it clear that I would prefer him dead.

A messenger arrived at the Command one morning with a message from the Spezia Liberation Committee. It was marked "urgent", and contained a warning that a certain sergeant of the Fascist garrison with two of his men had been sent into the hills with special instructions to kill as many of the partisan leaders as they could find by whatever means they chose. Security patrols were increased and sentries doubled, but in spite of these precautions victims could not be avoided. One morning a patrol moving along a mule track in the woods came upon a mound of newly turned earth. Under a bush nearby lay the head of a partisan, its eyes gouged out and lying on the grass beside it. On the forehead had been carved the letters "M.M." representing the Fascist "Mad Morti" unit. After that, the "quality of mercy" died for a while in the hearts of the partisans.

During the month of November political intrigue began again to exert its damaging influence upon the liberation movement, encouraged by agents who drifted into the 4th Zone from other regions to the north and east. This influence was impossible to eradicate, for most of the funds necessary for the maintenance of the forces were still distributed by the committees of liberation in the cities. These committees represented all the political parties of the recognised Government of free Italy. Among them were her finest Statesmen, but they could not control the activities of their less scrupulous colleagues. Thus it was that the Colonel had no power to dismiss a partisan commander without first obtaining the permission of the Liberation Committee, the majority of whose members had a tendency to judge the partisan leaders by their political value rather than by their military prowess. It became painfully obvious that if the tragedy of August was not to be repeated, the Allied Command in the south would have to take a more active part in the directing of operations.

The situation deteriorated rapidly as the month drew to its close. Once again certain formations began to dissolve into small independent bands. Franco, finding himself unpopular with the Action Party to which he nominally belonged, reduced his command to forty men and based himself on the Valley, in the village of Chioso. Richetto, sensing the peril ahead, raised another brigade in the area of the Cento Croce Pass and struggled to keep it non political. An order went forth that a "Political Commissar" was to be attached to all formations; Colonel Fontana could do nothing to oppose this, and Franco and I were the only ones that did, with the result that we became still more unpopular than before. The International Battalion was reduced for a time to a nucleus of trained men in order to discourage reprisals, and the rest of its personnel were dispersed among the commands of Richetto, Dani, and the Beretta brothers. Aldo Berti was sent through the lines with a detailed report and the blessings of the Colonel. He joined Special Force, was trained as a parachutist, and was later dropped behind the enemy lines further to the north. Ermano remained with us in the Valley, while Dani withdrew to his own estates at Calice to continue his special task of evacuating refugees. The political storm was rising, and we knew that it could not be long before it burst upon us with full force.

By December, Rossano was again surrounded by elements that eyed it with jealousy. This time, however, the constant stream of escaped prisoners across the River Magra provided an additional method of communication with the Allied Command in Florence that effectively discouraged any hasty action on the part of the agitators.

Then, to complicate matters still further, Alfonso's wireless contact broke down altogether. A week before Christmas the operators sent a message to say that they could no longer make contact with Base. Richetto and his men of the Cento Croce Brigade had been given several special drops of arms and supplies with which to protect them, so that his force became the most strongly equipped of all.

In view of the circumstances this breakdown was the most serious thing that could have happened. Back at the Base, Headquarters would not realise that it was due to a technical defect but would attribute it to enemy action and would discontinue the dropping of supplies. My two last remaining Poles, Paolo and Alfredo, volunteered to go through the lines, and I sent them off with an explanation. They left after I had moved back to the Valley from Torpiana.

Snow began to fall, and soon the great mass of Monte Gottero was white. My Headquarters was now in Valle, in the house of Amelia's brother, Domenico. I had been given a bedroom that possessed a large iron bedstead, a washstand, and a table. The floor was covered with loose tiles and the small iron-barred window overlooked the narrow path that ran through the village. It might have been said that this improvement in the standard of living was a measure of how the importance of the International Battalion had grown.

One evening four days before Christmas I returned from the summit of Monte Picchiara where I had been waiting fruitlessly all day with a small squad of couriers for the arrival of a long expected aeroplane. Amelia's mother was waiting for me.

"You are to sleep upstairs to-night, Luigi," she said, and continued to stir the large cauldron of minestrone that simmered on the fire in the smoky kitchen.

I took off my pack and dropped it on the floor.

"Why is that, Mother?"

"It's safer upstairs," she said, without looking at me. "There are too many strangers who are angry with you and they might throw a bomb through the window when you are asleep."

"I think they would be too frightened of the Rossanesi to do a thing like that."

"You never know," replied the old lady. "You can't trust them. They come from places near the sea."

With that she lifted the heavy cooking pot and took it into the next room. "Come and have your supper before it gets cold," she said.

I wondered what was worrying her, as she was a brave old soul who did not allow herself to be alarmed by the idle chatter of the other womenfolk.

After supper Tarquinio, Romeo, Silvio (the brother of Amelia), Antonio the Carabiniere, and old Rossi who kept the village hostelry, collected round the fire and held a council of war. They spoke in the dialect of the Valley, but I could understand enough of it to realise that they were worried about the turn that events were taking. I did not interrupt them, for I had learnt by this time that their deep rooted sense of caution was a valuable asset – in fact, the attitude of suspicion which the whole population adopted towards newcomers was one of our greatest safeguards.

They had been talking together for some time when we heard the sound of running footsteps outside. The door was pushed open, to admit a breathless Dina.

"Tarquinio, there are some people coming along the road to Chiesa. Come quickly. They are asking for the Maggiore. They speak with a strange accent and I think they are Germans." She had not noticed me sitting in my dark corner smoking a rank toscana cigar given me by my hostess.

Tarquinio spoke.

"It's better for you to remain here, Luigi. I will go and see who they are, with Antonio. It is easy for us to pretend that we are on our way to the next village and if there is any danger we can run back and warn you. It's too dark for them to see far, and they can't shoot well enough to do any harm." With that the two men left the room.

Chapter Thirteen

Descent from the Skies

It was a black night, and a strong wind blew down from the heights with the promise of more snow. The little group by the fire had stopped talking. Antonio's wife joined us and took her place on the end of the wooden bench on which her two small children lay curled up asleep. The old lady sat motionless staring into the red embers of the fire, and it was plain to see that they were listening for some sound in the night that would tell them whether the enemy was near. The situation in the areas around us had been growing uglier for the past week; there was an unnatural lack of news from the cities and the B.B.C. had already given a general warning that the enemy were preparing fresh expeditions against the partisans in Northern Italy. There was an unpleasant similarity between the present atmosphere and that of the last week in July – the same political wrangling, the same feeling of isolation from the outside world, and that same sense of anxiety hanging over the Valley like a vast and invisible cloud. This time we should be better prepared for trouble, but there was not that unity of command among the forces that could prevent the burning of houses and the persecution of the population. Further proof of the approaching crisis had reached us a few days previously with the news of a strong rastrellamento in the provinces of Piacenza and Parma, and fugitives from the formations that had been overrun had already begun to reach the Valley. I looked at the old lady.

"If the Germans come again, you must escape with us, Mother," I said.

She continued to gaze into the fire.

"I shall stay here," she replied. "All our valuables are hidden and they can only burn the house. It is a very old house, dirty and dark, and I shall not be sorry to see it burn."

"The English will build us a new one," said Silvio with an air of certainty, "and then we shall be better off than we are now."

I hope to God they will, I thought.

Silence returned, and we continued to listen to the wind. Presently there were footsteps outside again, and Tarquinio came in. He had been running.

"Luigi," he said "I have spoken to the leader. He has several men with him and they are all armed. He says he has a letter for you. I wouldn't trust them. They are coming along the road with Antonio who is leading them down to the burnt houses and I came back to ask what we should do."

"Could you see what kind of arms they were carrying?"

"Not very well, but they seem to be automatic rifles like the ones dropped by the aeroplanes."

"See if you can bring the leader here alone," I said. "But warn everybody in the village to be ready to escape if there is trouble."

"They are all ready waiting by the road, with hand grenades to throw at them," he said as he departed.

A few minutes later Tarquinio returned, and we heard another with him. The stranger stooped as he came through the door, and then stood still, accustoming his eyes to the gloom and smoke. Then:

"Is Major Lett here?" he said.

I was relieved at the friendly American accent, and stood up.

"What can I do for you?"

The stranger smiled.

"You've got darned good security," he said. "I and my men have been wandering round this God-darned Valley for hours, and nobody would tell us where you were." He dropped on to the bench. "My name is Wheeler. We've come from the 6th Zone. Here's a letter I was given for you."

I tore open the crumpled envelope. It was a short message written by the Special Force colonel who was head of the British Mission in the Genoa area, and it explained that the bearer required assistance to travel through the lines.

"You're American?"

"Yeh. Mission Wala Wala. I've got seventeen guys with me."

I explained to the other occupants of the room that all was well, and Tarquinio went to collect the rest of the party. Captain Wheeler was given a glass of wine, and while he drank it he told his story.

There had been a general attack in the 6th partisan zone which comprised the whole of the area to the north-west as far as Genoa. The partisans had resisted for three days, and had then been forced to disperse. The American Mission, seeing that the position was hopeless, had reported by wireless and received orders to return to Base by way of the Rossano Valley. The 6th Zone had been well armed, but as usual there was poor leadership for the most part and the same political dissension existed there that made the creation of an effective central command impossible. The last news that they had had, three days before, confirmed that the enemy were in force to the north-east as well. We also knew that they had begun a rastrellamento to the south, beyond the Magra. There remained only the 4th Zone, of which the centre was the Valley, and it looked very much as if that would receive the concentrated attention of the enemy from all directions before long. The Germans were preparing for a big attack along the Gothic Line and were intent on making secure their lines of communication before it began.

"Do you think we can get through all right?" asked Wheeler.

"I think so, but we've had no news for a week. Our radio has broken down."

"I've brought mine with me. If you like, the operator can try to get through for you in the morning."

"That's the best news I've heard for a long time," I said, and meant it.

The other members of the Mission entered one by one. Another American, Lieutenant Smith, was with them. The rest were all Italian Americans recruited in the United States. They were well armed, and equipped with American uniforms, and this gave a sense of security to the onlookers that they had not experienced for many days past. The newcomers quickly fraternised with their hosts, and other members of the village crowded into the room to talk and watch them eating. That night they slept on the floor, while the villagers kept guard outside.

It took some time to make contact by radio next morning. Meanwhile I collected a small party of guides to take the Mission Wala Wala on their way, and wrote a note for Dani, explaining who they were. It was nearly eleven o'clock when the wireless operator brought me a report.

"There is a special message for you, Major. They say it is very urgent and they want an answer immediately."

I read the message through once, and looked at the operator. I read it again, and still could not believe what it said. I read it a third time. The long months spent in the mountains must have played havoc with my emotions, for I felt a sudden desire to cry like a child. Then I realised that I was repeating over and over again "At last – at long last!" The American watching me tactfully looked away, and went back to his set. For some minutes I stood staring at the ring of mountains that made up the horizon. Then I sat down on the wall of the ruined village chapel, and wrote a reply. I took it to the operator.

"Here is the answer. Will you please send it in code?"

The soldier looked at it and read:

"No repeat no stop ready to receive twenty seventh repeat twenty seventh stop signal letter H for Harry repeat H for Harry and British and Italian flags on field already indicated stop regards."

"O.K. Major," he said.

It was the morning of the 22nd December 1944.

* * *

On Christmas Eve, accompanied by Nello and the couriers Ardito, Falco, Riboncia, and Chella, I set off through the snow to cross the mountain ridge that separated us from Dani's kingdom of Calice. The men were armed with automatic rifles given them by the American Mission before they left to continue their journey, as it was rightly felt that these weapons would be too conspicuous. At least, that was the explanation given by Nello. Knowing my partisans, I had an uneasy feeling that the arms might have been "acquired" rather than given, and could only hope that Captain Wheeler was not cursing us as he approached the danger zone. There was a cloudless sky that morning, and the glare of the sunlight was almost painful in its intensity.

Dani had invited us some time before – the "Diplomatic Mission" as he jokingly called the International Battalion – to spend Christmas with him. There had always been a strong alliance between our two formations, and Dani regarded his force as a kind of auxiliary to my own and was ready to move into the Valley and support us if the need should arise. Dani and his men had done more than anybody else to assist the ex-prisoners on their journey to freedom. The "A" Force command in liberated Italy had sent him a special message of thanks for his services, and a personal drop of supplies from the air, with the result that the politicians were not pleased. Little did he care about that.

As we made our way through the bare chestnut forest I thought of the last Christmas spent in these mountains. The faithful Mick was no longer with me, as I had reluctantly sent him through the lines to rejoin his regiment, the Rifle Brigade. He was later awarded the Military Medal for his work with the partisans, and certainly deserved it. Colonel Corry, Bob the Australian who had escaped with me from Veano, and Arthur the sailor had all arrived safely in Florence. Their places had been taken by the group of special couriers led by Nello. None of them was involved in the rastrellamento of December the 27th 1943. On the anniversary of that event, I hoped that the unpleasant memories in the minds of the population would be obliterated by others more encouraging.

It had been arranged that the families of the couriers would meet us in Calice. Two had walked from Valeriano near La Spezia, but those from Fezzano near the naval arsenal were under enemy observation and could not leave their homes, so Ardito and Riboncia had no relations with whom to share the Christmas feast.

On Christmas day I took Ardito with me to a conference in the house of Dani's father. After lunch, we sat on a bench in the warm living-room, and for a while discussed the general situation. Eventually I came to the main object of my visit.

"As from to-morrow, Dani, I want you to help me with a special task, but, while asking you to do this, I can't give you all the information that you would probably like to have."

"That's all right – I'll do my best," he replied. "What is the job?"

"The whole of the Valley is to be shut off from the rest of the zone." I took a map from my pocket and spread it out on the bench between us. "I have decided that all our frontiers must be guarded and nobody, no matter to what formation he may belong, is to be allowed to enter the Rossano area for forty-eight hours, unless he has a special pass signed by me. I want you to make yourself responsible for the frontier between us and Montereggio. On the twenty-seventh, your men posted in that area will see some strange sights. Will you impress on them that they are not to talk about what they will see?"

Dani studied the map for a moment in silence.

"This sounds interesting," he said at length. "I can guarantee a squad of reliable lads to guard the frontier. Can I send you any reinforcements into the Valley?"

"Yes, I'd be grateful if you would. A dozen men, well armed, to help with police duties. After the first forty-eight hours we shall be able to look after ourselves."

"Right, Maggiore, I'll send my brother with the best men I've got."

"Thanks," I said. "Sorry I can't tell you more, but it is better not, in case something goes wrong. We've had so many great expectations during the past three months, but not much has come of them so far. I've told the Colonel, by the way, that we are closing our frontiers."

" Va bene," said Dani. "Let us hope we'll have fine weather on the 27th There seems to be a big party going on, south of the River Magra. Roberto came back yesterday after taking the American Mission across. Apparently everything is in confusion and all the partisan formations have been disbanded. We seem to be safe enough here for another week – after that, who knows?"

"Anything might happen," I said with a smile.

Dani grinned. "It all depends on the Diplomatic Mission."

We returned to the Valley next evening, as the tree trunks began to cast shadows creeping like long black fingers across the snow-covered fields. Bruno Cura and a squad of the lads from Buzzo were awaiting us as a result of a warning order sent out two days before. There was also a report from Avio, from his station in the plains, to say that there was no unusual movement of enemy forces in the city of Pontremoli; most of the garrison appeared to be fully occupied with their punitive expeditions to the South, and there was no immediate danger to the Valley. Ermano had reorganised his men into small patrols to watch our frontiers by day and night. The stage was set, and we prayed for fine weather on the morrow for the rise of the curtain. There was little sleep for me that night. The transmitting set was still out of touch with base, but I knew that the Poles had crossed the lines. I kept thinking of the year before, and wished that Colonel Balbi, and Edoardo and Maria Rita could have been with me now. I had had no news of Edoardo after he had been forced to leave Torpiana by the Action Party leader.

The morning of the 27th dawned cloudy, with a slight wind. Throughout the morning we busied ourselves with the necessary preparations and our glances at the leaden sky became more and more anxious as the morning changed to afternoon. We had a British and Italian flag made from pieces of coloured parachute sewn together by the women, and these were spread on the ground at one end of a field above the burnt village of Chiesa. In the centre of this field other pieces had been spread out to form the letter "H". Passers-by stopped to watch.

The cascina in which Tarquinio's family had been living since the fire was near the field, and old Mamma had been given certain careful instructions that puzzled her somewhat, but she set to work vigorously with the help of Dina and old Babbo. The afternoon dragged on. The suspense grew, as the weather continued cloudy and the wind increased in strength. Three o'clock chimed from the church tower in the village. The partisans raised the flags on their wooden poles and continued to wait. Half past three. I strained my ears to catch that distant sound that would mean so much to us, and began to imagine what would happen if my countrymen failed me this time. The troublemakers would be convinced that I had no direct contact, and would fall upon the Valley like hungry wolves.

Then we heard the distant drone of aeroplane engines from the direction of the Magra valley. Slowly it drew nearer, and the machine came into sight, and followed the frontiers of the Valley. Over Monte Picchiara the pilot seemed uncertain as to his whereabouts and he circled twice. Then the plane turned back towards us. A few seconds later the pilot spotted our signals, and the plane circled lower. It passed over the field, and suddenly we saw six packages flung out. Six coloured parachutes unfolded in the air above us and floated slowly to rest on the field. The plane circled again, and then swooped low enough for us to see the pilot in the cockpit. He waved to us, and then flew away.

It was the first daylight drop that we had had in the Valley. The parachutes were collected and brought into the middle of the field. People began to run towards us from all directions to watch the proceedings.

There was a small bundle attached to one of the containers. I opened it, and found mail from home – letters from the girl who was still waiting patiently for me in bomb-blitzed London. We hoped to be married one day, but the war was taking an awful long time to finish! There was also a message from Special Force Headquarters. I read it and called Nello.

"Collect the others here," I said.

When they had all gathered round, I read the message.

"Partisan Nello Sani has been awarded the Italian bronze medal for distinguished service with your Mission. Congratulations from us all."

We shook Nello by the hand, and somebody procured a flask of wine with which we drank his health. It was a grand gesture on the part of H.Q. and the medal had been well earned. It was the first award to be made to any partisan in the field.

We set to work to remove the stores to a prearranged stronghold. Tarquinio had produced two mules which were duly loaded and taken away. Again the men settled down to wait, a little mystified that they had been told to remain at their posts. The clouds had thickened, and there was promise of snow to come during the night. The spectators gradually dispersed to their villages, convinced that the party was over. The partisans stood in huddled groups about the field, their rifles slung across their shoulders. Presently Dani's brother asked if they could light a fire to warm themselves. They heaped some brushwood together and set alight to it.

And then, as the church clock began to chime the hour of five, again we heard the distant drone of aeroplane engines, and this time it was clear that there was more than one machine.

I had been squatting beside the fire with the others. I jumped to my feet.

"A posto ragazzi!" I shouted. "Stand by the flags, and keep them waving!"

The planes came into sight – six heavy grey shapes that, like their forerunner, crawled along the skyline above the Montereggio frontier of the Valley, and slowly circled, one after the other, towards the summit of Monte Picchiara.

On the field, the partisans waited expectantly, staring in silence at the planes, their faces showing a mixed expression of bewilderment and hope.

* * *

A shaft of sunlight broke through the clouds for a moment, making the aircraft glitter like silver fish as they passed slowly over the summit of Monte Picchiara. Twice they circled over the mountain. The partisans held their breath, as they waited expectantly near the burnt village, and wondered if the machines would drop their cargo in the wrong place. After an anxious five minutes the aircraft turned back towards the Valley.

Meanwhile, the population had seen them, and had begun to collect once more on the edge of the field. The flags were ready; for the hundredth time, I looked anxiously at the shape of the letter "H", which stood out against the mottled background of snow and dark earth. The leading aeroplane came on, and passed overhead. We could see the open doors in the fuselage, and white packages ready to be thrown out. Slowly the plane circled to the right, followed by the others, and passed overhead a second time. The partisans began to wave frantically, and, forgetting they could not be heard, shouted encouragement to the pilots.

The leading aircraft approached a third time, gradually losing height as it did so. Then we saw a figure jump from the doorway; a silk parachute burst open above him, and a murmur of surprise arose from the watching crowds.

"Un uomo, un uomo!"

The people of the Valley stared open-mouthed as the parachutist floated to earth, landed neatly in the centre of the field, and then became enveloped in the cords of his parachute, which crumpled to the ground beside him. Tarquinio was nearest, and ran forward to assist. I reached the khaki–clad figure just as he had extricated himself from the last ropes. It was a fair haired young captain, and, as I was to discover within the next few minutes, one with a phlegmatic outlook and dry sense of humour which at once placed him in the category of "typically English".

"Are you Major Lett?" he asked.

"I am, and I'm very glad to see you."

"My name is Chris Leng, of Special Force," said the newcomer, holding out his hand. Then he laughed. "This is rather like the 'Doctor Livingstone, I presume' touch. I'll give the others the signal, as they are waiting to come down and join us."

He pulled a Very light pistol from his haversack, and fired a green signal, which rose into the air in a wide arc, leaving a trail of white smoke behind it, and then fell into the nearby trees. The planes were continuing to circle round the area. On seeing the signal, the leading pilot dived his plane again. Six bundles shot into the sky this time, and then another six from the following aircraft, until the whole sky seemed full of coloured parachutes, with the men attached to them, hanging ready to make contact with the ground.

"Now we're O.K." said Chris. "We were a bit puzzled at first as to where you were. Somebody has put out a lot of signals on the mountain up there, and we were going to come down on them, when we caught sight of your two flags."

"Some of the political gentry are responsible for that," I said, "They are getting rather troublesome just now."

The commander of the parachute squadron was the first to touch down – a perfect landing, practically in the middle of the letter "H". As he struggled to his feet, he grinned at me.

"You didn't expect to see me, I bet. The last time we met was in that foul prison camp No. 21, at Chieti." He undid the parachute harness as he spoke, and taking his binoculars from their case, began to watch the aircraft unloading. Captain Bob Walker Brown was certainly the last person I expected – I had last seen him a prisoner on the day that I left for Veano.

"Sorry about all this theatrical stuff, but yesterday morning a message came through to base saying that you had been murdered, and so we weren't quite sure what we would find in this part of the world."

I did not reply, absorbed as I was in watching the men descending. The wind had dropped, and the parachutes were floating down very slowly. Some had been launched beyond the field, and appeared to be drifting into the deep gorge where lay the river that led to the Dam. Others had been caught in the surrounding chestnut trees. It seemed unbelievable that I now had behind me a force of sturdy, well trained, well-led British troops. I glanced quickly at the crowd of local inhabitants, watching the scene with me. They were silent with wonder, as load after load of parachutes descended on their Valley. All the men had landed, and after collecting their personal kit, were closing in on the flags. Their helmets were removed, and replaced by the typical red beret of the Special Air Service.

For half an hour the planes continued to unload equipment, arms, and rations. More than three hundred parachutes lay scattered on the ground, and the partisans were collecting them, and bringing what they could carry to a central dump. At last the launching was complete. The planes circled for the last time, dipped in salute as they passed overhead, and then flew away to the South.

Meanwhile the troops had formed up on the field, and their officers called the roll. All were present, and the only casualty, in spite of the trees and rocks among which they had landed, was one man with a bruised thigh. Bob called them to attention, and asked me to address them. I walked forward, and stood in front of them feeling strangely out of place.

"There's not much that I can say. You can guess, without my explaining, how glad we are to see you lads, after more than a year on our own in these mountains. You may have heard something of the partisans here – whatever you have heard, you can take it from me that they are good chaps, and they are putting up a very fine show, against tremendous odds. The people of this Valley are all our friends, and you can trust them to look after you. The nearest enemy garrison is in the town of Pontremoli, about four hours' march from here, and there are partisan patrols watching the area all round us. I can promise you that there is no possibility of danger for at least forty-eight hours – after that, it will be as well to be prepared. Now, if you go over to that hut which you see among the trees" – I pointed to the cascina of Tarquinio's family – "you will find a very courageous old lady who has prepared some hot tea for you. There's no sugar in this part of the world, but otherwise it should be fairly drinkable!"

As the commander gave final orders to his men, I walked across to the watching spectators. It did not take long to find volunteers from all of the villages to provide lodging where the various detachments could eat and sleep – there was some competition between them for the duty of acting as host. Mules were called up, on which to load the kit. Tarquinio, with Amelia's brother Silvio, Ernesto of Valle, Antonio, Marcello, Giulio Rossi and the rest, then set to work to transfer the heavy loads of weapons and rations to the storehouse in Peretola. I climbed up the hill to the improvised teahouse.

In the cascina fraternisation was taking place in a big way. Old Mamma, wielding a large ladle, was serving out tea, whilst Tarquinio's brother Richetto contributed milk from a copper saucepan. Dina was offering the newcomers pieces of hot chestnut bread. They had never seen anything like it before, but they accepted it with the natural politeness of the British Tommy. They were a fine-looking squad of men, and it was easy to see that the population were very favourably impressed by them. The special partisan couriers of the International Battalion, Nello, Falco, Ardito, Riboncia, Mazzini and Chella were already beginning to make themselves friends. The lads from Buzzo were there as well, and I watched with interest the growth of comradeship between my Italian patriots and my fellow countrymen. Bob Walker-Brown and Chris Leng came in when all the material had been cleared from the field. They were followed by three other Lieutenants of the S.A.S. One, Riccamini, had jumped by parachute for the first time that day. He had not had time to carry out the usual preparatory course at the base, and, rather than miss the opportunity of taking part in an operation behind the enemy lines, he had decided to take a chance. His parachute had been caught in a tree, and he had been extricated from it by the somewhat startled inhabitants of the village of Peretola.

It was quite dark by the time that the various hosts came to collect their guests, and led them away to the houses that had been arranged as billets. The headquarters section of the formation, with the radio sets and operators, accompanied me to the village of Valle. We marched down the road from the cascina, to the point where it ended among the ruins of the burnt village. The gaping windows of the Palazzo degli Schiavi stood out gauntly against the starlit sky. A wooden shutter banged to and fro, for a gentle wind had sprung up after dusk, and the sound echoed eerily in the darkness.

"This village was burnt last August," I said. "It was my headquarters."

The party halted, and looked at the ruins.

"I thought the place looked a bit blitzed from the air," said Bob. "Rather tough on the population, wasn't it?"

"Very. Several people were shot, and they were all badly frightened. But it made them more determined than ever to help us. They are a grand people."

"We have certainly had a surprising reception," said Chris. "I never imagined it would be possible to land right behind the enemy lines like this, with people waiting to offer you cups of tea when you arrived! We expected to have to begin fighting within an hour of landing."

"There's no fear of that. The enemy cannot take us by surprise, however much they may want to. On the contrary, I think that, having seen the planes arrive – and they have obviously seen them from Pontremoli – they will send out spies to obtain more information. The spies will take back fantastic reports about thousands of parachutists having landed all over the mountains, complete with armoured cars, guns, and anything else you can think of, with the result that the little "Republicans" will be so alarmed that they will scream for help from Uncle Adolph. Uncle cannot help at present, however, as he has his work cut out harassing the unfortunate partisan formations in all the areas surrounding us. Therefore I don't anticipate any interference for some time. It would be just as well, though, to be ready to go into action the day after to-morrow."

We walked on in silence for a while, until we came to the stone bridge over the stream near Valle. Amelia's tall fair haired brother was awaiting us. He carried a carbide gas lamp, which showed us the rocky path leading up into his village. I heard the troops talking amongst themselves as they followed.

"Cor Blimey!" said one of them suddenly, "Just like Piccadilly Circus, ain't it?"

"They've forgotten Eros," answered his companion. "We'll bring it with us on our next trip."

At Amelia's house great preparations had been going on and we found the old lady her mother beside herself with delight. A party of her chosen friends had been collected together to welcome the strangers, and they all assisted at the evening meal. The troops consumed their first plates of minestra with a polite lack of comment. They were then treated to roast chicken, followed by cheese. Fiaschi of wine circulated freely. It was past midnight when they were taken to their respective billets, each host having been careful to bring a lamp with him to light the way, and leading his guest by the arm, in case he should stumble on the slippery cobblestones.

The officers were conducted to Antonio's house. Mattresses had been spread out on the floor, and a crackling wood fire in the iron stove gave warmth to the otherwise bare room. As we entered, Silvio called to me from the path below.

"Maggiore, there is a courier from the Partisan Command."

"Send him up here," I said. Bob, Chris, and the others began to unroll their sleeping bags. Silvio came in, bringing a partisan dressed in a battle-dress jacket, and trousers of Italian naval uniform. He had a Sten gun slung over his shoulder. He saluted, and handed me a note.

"Come va, Lelino?"

"Bene, Signor Maggiore," he grinned happily, and looked at the parachutists. "We saw the aeroplanes arrive to-day, and we think that now the war will be finished very quickly."

"I hope so."

I opened the letter and the messenger, Lelino, watched me as I read it. He was a seafaring lad, from the village of Fezzano, near La Spezia, and had come into the mountains with Ardito and Falco. He had been one of the first to join the International Battalion, and, when Aldo had been sent through the lines, Lelino had been transferred to the Colonel as his special courier.

The letter was from Colonel Fontana.

"Congratulations and good wishes to your compatriots," it read, "I was on the summit of Monte Picchiara to-day, and saw them arrive. I wanted to come down and see them, but thought that perhaps you would rather have them to yourself for this evening. Please let me meet them as soon as possible. Auguri."

"A note of welcome from the Colonel, Bob," I said. "He wants to meet you all as soon as possible. He's a very good fellow, and you'll find him most helpful." I turned to Lelino.

"Thank the Signor Colonnello very much, and tell him that we shall try and come up to see him the day after to-morrow."

"Si Signore," Lelino saluted, and left the room. We gathered round the fire, to smoke a last pipe before turning in for the night; it was a treat to smoke real tobacco after dried chestnut and tea leaves. I felt that I wanted to talk to them until dawn. Bob was a tough Scot, and a born soldier. As he sat puffing at a weather-beaten briar I could see that he was already turning over the details of the situation in his mind, and that fact alone filled me with gratitude towards whatever power was responsible for having sent the right man to the right place. We had both been taken prisoner in Tobruk in June, 1942, and had been unwelcome guests together in various prison camps in North Africa and Italy. We had plenty to talk about.

He was anxious to know about the people of the Valley, and I told him what they had done for us. We stopped talking at last, and went to bed.

Before I went to sleep, I thought of the message that the American operator had shown me.

"Reply if ready to receive bodies repeat bodies on twenty fourth stop force standing by stop urgent."

I could not receive them on that date, as preparations had to be made. Furthermore, I was anxious to make the anniversary of the first rastrellamento a date to remember. And it had all come about according to plan. A whole squadron of S.A.S. had arrived, and in the course of half an hour had completely changed the local balance of power. I thought with some satisfaction of the politicians gnashing their teeth on the summit of Monte Picchiara, and of how the men of Ermano, Franco, and Dani had cheered wildly that afternoon as they saw the first parachutes unfolding over the dropping ground. The enthusiasm of the population had been as great; they had shown no fear at this rain from the skies of armed men whose language they could not understand. They had accepted them as colleagues of the ex-prisoners whom they had known for so long – for whom they had been unconsciously waiting.

The population felt secure that night.

Chapter Fourteen

The Fortunes of War

Two days after their arrival, the S.A.S. moved out of the Valley to carry out their first attacks against the main enemy lines of communication. One squad, with Bruno Cura and Falco as guides, went to the village of Buzzo to molest enemy columns in the Borgo Taro area. Another, with the partisan Chella as guide, set off to cross the river Magra and attack columns using the road through the mountains from Modena. Chella knew the country well, for the route lay through Dani's territory and then to the South. They set out on the morning of December the 28th I went with Bob, Chris, and the rest of the force to a village above the coast road where Colonel Fontana had temporarily established his headquarters.

We left the Valley on the morning of the 29th. The weather was bad that day; hard snow covered the mountain paths and a cold wind from the North swept the slopes, piling up snow drifts across the mule tracks. The heavily-laden animals found the going difficult. The muleteers were all youngsters from the Valley who had volunteered for the task and they were led by Salvatore the innkeeper of Chioso. It was after hard going that we reached our destination the same afternoon. More than once the mules had had to be unloaded, the loads carried by the squad over slippery patches of ice, and then packed once more on to the animals. As we entered the small village, four American planes flew low overhead, directed towards the Valley. Chris looked at them and swore. He had been careful to send a message the evening before warning Base that no further supplies should be sent for the moment; in any case the force of the wind was now so great that all the parachutes would be carried away and lost in the river gorge. The message had not been received. The planes flew on, and were hidden behind the dark mass of Monte Dragone.

The Colonel gave us an enthusiastic welcome. Commanders of various formations, accompanied in some cases by curious and hostile "political Commissars", were with him. It was not long before they had overcome the language difficulty and were amicably discussing past adventures and planning fresh attacks. The Colonel was anxious to carry out a large scale operation using parachutists and partisans, but he could not make the necessary arrangements for some time, owing to the difficulty of communications. Bob decided to carry out a small operation that night. At dusk we prepared to move to Sero, a village nearer to the Via Aurelia, the vital coast road that led from Genoa to Rome.

The column had formed up and was about to move off when an orderly ran out of the partisan headquarters and told me that the Colonel had something to say. Chris came with me. Colonel Fontana murmured, "It is the fortunes of war," and handed me a note.

It was from one of Dani's men who had remained in the Valley to guard the parachutists' stores. It stated that when the planes had arrived that afternoon, one of the machines had got into an air pocket and crashed in the woods beyond the village of Chiesa. The machine had instantly caught fire and the entire crew of seven were killed.

I handed the note to Chris, who read it in silence. There was nothing to be done and so we returned to the waiting column and moved off to our new rendezvous.

Headquarters that night was in the house of one Pippo Siboldi, an Italian who had lived in the United States for some time before the war. Although he was no longer young, he had taken a vigorous part in the resistance movement from the first. His real name was Loius, as we all knew within a few minutes of meeting him, and it was not long before he was thoroughly at home with us all. He then began to show a marked interest in the leader of the mortar section, a tall young fellow from the Channel Islands named Gordon Rose who, following the age-old tradition of the British Army, was known to all and sundry as "Lofty". Pippo was imbued with an insatiable love of adventure, and prided himself upon being a marksman of no mean prowess. Lofty, drawing him on, proceeded to cast doubts upon his skill, and hinted darkly that the numerous hares and partridges that Pippo claimed to have bagged in the past year had really been caught in traps or purchased in the nearest market town unknown to his wife. The result of the argument was that Pippo insisted on taking part in the attack that night and a bet was made between them as to who would shoot the first German. Having thus prepared the ground Lofty referred the matter to Bob. Since he needed a guide to take them to the nearest ambush point, Bob raised no objection to the partisan going along with them.

As we finished supper another message was received from the Colonel. This time it was to say that a squad of refugees, all from the Spezia suburb of Fezzano, whom I had sent off ten days before, had gone astray somewhere behind the Gothic Line and walked on to a minefield. Of eight men in the party five had been killed, one had arrived wounded in the Allied lines, and two were missing. The leader was an Italian Air Force Lieutenant whom I had hoped would be able to guide planes to us in the future. It seemed to be an unlucky day.

The force set off some time after dark. Pippo's house had now been transformed into Battle Headquarters. The radio set was installed under the watchful eye of the S.A.S. Corporal Johnston, and the transport animals with their leaders and spare ammunition and equipment waited on the path outside. I accompanied the column part of the way, and then watched as they began the descent through the pine forest. Pippo had taken up his position behind Lofty and I heard him whisper, "Now then, Lofty, you son of a gun, I teach you how to kill 'em," and Lofty responded with a quiet chuckle at the quaint accent of the partisan.

I returned to the house and settled down with Chris to await their return, while Pippo's daughter Lina made us innumerable cups of tea. She was a village schoolteacher by profession, a short, strongly built young woman with chestnut-coloured hair parted in the middle, an honest, open face and ready smile. Lina was certainly a chip off the old block. Some months previously she had been imprisoned in La Spezia by the Brigata Nera, who had hoped to use her as a hostage and hand her over to the attentions of "Carita", whose private torture chamber had become notorious. Lina was quick witted, and had made a clever escape after only twenty-four hours. She rounded off the incident by sending a personal note to the Fascist Commander, describing in unladylike but accurate phrases exactly what she thought of him and his cut-throats. It was hardly surprising that her name, with that of her father, had been added to the Republican "Black List".

Three hours after the parachutists had left, there was another interruption. Chris had been given Pippo's bedroom and was snatching some hard-earned rest, while I kept watch in the entrance hall. Lina came in from the kitchen, where she was preparing a hot meal for the return of the saboteurs.

"There is a courier for you, Maggiore – he says he has an urgent message, but won't tell me anything about it. Shall I bring him in?"

"Yes, please, Lina."

She returned with the orderly, and then left us. "A message from Lieutenant Dani, Maggiore," he said, "I'm afraid it's bad news."

"I'm not surprised – there has been plenty of bad news to-day."

The message was in Dani's handwriting, and explained briefly that the squad of S.A.S. who had set out to cross the river had all been captured in a village called Montebello, not far from the River Magra. Further particulars of their capture were not yet available.

"How do you know of this?"

"We heard about it this afternoon. A friend of mine was in the village when it happened. There was a rastrellamento nearby, and a spy brought the Brigata Nera to Montebello during the night. They found the English in a shed, just before dawn."

"What happened to Chella, the courier who was guiding them?"

"They dragged him into the village street, Maggiore," the lad said slowly. "A Fascist lieutenant saw that he was wearing the British and Italian flags on his tunic, and recognised it as the badge of the International Battalion. He ordered his men to beat Chella with sticks, and then they shot him. They took his uniform away with them."

"What did they do with the parachutists?"

"They were put in a lorry and taken to La Spezia."

I walked out on to the terrace of the house, unconsciously crumpling the note in my hand. At least it was fortunate that the others had left before this news arrived, for it was a serious blow to their fortunes after only three days in the area. I thought of Chella. He had been killed doing his job, and fully conscious of the risks that it entailed – it was just like him to insist on wearing the badges of his formation, in spite of the consequences if he was caught. Had it not been for that, he might have been imprisoned with the others. For some time I stayed on the terrace, hidden by the darkness. There were no lights to be seen in the village, and the night was wrapped in so deep a silence that it seemed as if all the world were dead.

I was still there when the partisan sentry called out a challenge. There was a muffled reply, and the silence was broken by the sound of marching feet. The parachutists were returning. They were in high spirits, for the action had gone well. Pippo launched forth into a vivid description of the attack that had been made on an enemy transport column on the Via Aurelia. Two vehicles had been set on fire, and there were casualties among the German troops travelling in them. Pippo had borne himself well, and for the rest of their stay in the mountains, Pippo and the men of the S.A.S. became inseparable.

When they had drunk the hot coffee prepared for them by Lina, I took Bob outside and told him of the fate of the squad sent to cross the Magra. He swore, and drew silently at his pipe.

"What is likely to happen to the prisoners?"

"I don't think they will be shot," I replied, "but we can't be certain. A good deal depends on what prison they have been taken to in La Spezia. The partisan squads in the city responsible for underground activities may be able to find out for us in a few days, as news of the incident must have spread all through the province by now."

"What about torture?"

"It's better not to think of that. There is a good chance that the Fascists will be afraid of torturing them for the present. The partisan information services down there are pretty good, and the enemy know that we have wireless communication with the Allies, because several of the worst types in La Spezia have already been denounced on the B.B.C. as war criminals. Our chaps should be all right, provided they are not handed over to Carita and his pal Gallo – they are the torturers-in-chief."

Bob refilled his pipe and lit it before he spoke again.

"We'll send a message through to Base first thing in the morning," he said. "It would be useless before then, as we cannot make contact. I'm very sorry indeed about your courier – we certainly won't forget when we have a few of those swine in our hands."

The eastern horizon was suffused with a dull red glow as we settled down to snatch a few hours' sleep. It was as well that we did not know then that we would never again have news of our missing comrades.

Chapter Fifteen

A Race for Time

The victims of the plane crash were brought to the little cemetery at Chiesa and buried with full military honours on a sunny morning in January. All the partisan formations were represented, including Richetto's Cento Croce brigade and that of the Beretta brothers, who were located two days' march away. From the day of the funeral the weather changed for the worse.

On the high ground in the region of Buzzo and the Cisa Pass movement became well nigh impossible, and in consequence most of the operations were confined to the Via Aurelia and the road along the Magra Valley leading from La Spezia to Pontremoli.

As a result of the arrival of the S.A.S. squadron, attacks by the partisans increased. Following the success of his first action, Bob developed an interest in the Via Aurelia that quickly spread alarm among enemy garrisons stationed along it. The road provided the only means by which enemy convoys could move by land from Genoa to La Spezia, and it was essential that free passage should be maintained in order to ensure rapid support for the German forces preparing an attack along the Gothic Line. Bob and his S.A.S. carried out ambush after ambush. The enemy strengthened their garrisons and unwisely established a headquarters in Borghetto, the largest town on the road nearest to the 4th Partisan Zone.

Borghetto held a special significance for us; it was to the commander of the Militia stationed there that the ex-prisoners had been denounced during our residence in the Fortezza Maria Rita. Taking advantage of the panic he was causing, Bob carried out a daylight attack on it, and bombarded the Fascist barracks with mortar fire. Lofty had need of a mule to accompany him to the firing point. He called for volunteers from the Valley, and Salvatore the innkeeper leapt into the breach before anybody else had a chance. He was warned that the operation would be dangerous, but Salvatore insisted, though he was by no means a youngster. The attack took place at dawn one morning; as they reached their action stations Lofty was not a little worried to find that the mule, laden with precious mortar shells, was leading

Salvatore, who, filled to the brim with wine from his inn, was clinging to its tail, and nothing would persuade him to leave it. The action over, the mule pulled him up the hill again to Sero where Salvatore, still in an alcoholic daze, described to all and sundry the wonderful "festa" in which he had taken part. After that he accompanied us everywhere, his mule taking charge when he reached a state of happy abandon.

There was keen competition among the partisans to take part in operations side by side with the S.A.S., and they excelled themselves in individual actions. The most outstanding formation among the small independent groups was that of Franco which, as time went on, was adopted by the parachutists more or less as an auxiliary unit.

In the Valley, the population lost that sense of impending disaster that had been oppressing them when the American Mission passed through. Their aggressiveness was further encouraged by news from the B.B.C. implying that the final advance on the Gothic Line was imminent. The punitive expeditions in northern Liguria and south of the Magra had worn themselves out, with the loss of much time and some casualties. Desertion began again among the enemy troops, who brought reports of a rapid deterioration in the morale of the German and Fascist soldiery, particularly among those units that were being hustled along the main roads to the south at the mercy of partisans and aerial bombardment.

Avio continued to send from the plains intelligence reports which showed that the local commanders were exasperated by the growing strength of the resistance in the 4th Operative Zone commanded by Colonel Fontana. By the middle of January they came to the conclusion that the parachutists did not number more than sixty. We soon became aware that we were due for another large scale mopping-up operation, unless the Allies launched an attack. The situation developed into a race for time on both sides. Our orders were to prevent the enemy completing his preparations until the Allied Forces were ready.

The passes out of the Valley had become ice-covered and blocked with deep snow drifts. Fortunately for us, the protection of the Valley from marauders outside it during the past year meant that there was animal transport available. When the S.A.S. went into the attack, a column of mules and donkeys followed them to the assembly point, watched over by the Rossanesi, for it was a duty jealously guarded by them, which could not be given to "outsiders". They worked heroically, those men of the Valley, as they struggled up the snow-covered slopes of Monte Picchiara and slithered down the icecoated paths leading to the battle areas, often cold, often hungry, and with their feet and hands frost-bitten. Garibaldi would surely have smiled with approval and acknowledged them true descendants of his own gallant red-shirts.

As the moment of crisis drew nearer, the reports of enemy movements became more detailed, for Avio's collaborators redoubled their efforts. These collaborators were drawn from all walks of life. In Pontremoli there was a distinguished Professor, an ex-Italian Consul, and a lawyer, who had established a network of informers astride the river, extending as far as the towns of Villafranca, Bagnone, and the small village of Filetto, where the German Command had a detachment watched over by the village priest, Don Manoni, who lived in their midst not entirely unsuspected. The most active and hard tried of these collaborators was the Bishop of Pontremoli, Monsignor Giovanni Sismondo.

Following the 8th of September 1943, the Bishop had thrown himself heart and soul into the difficult task of guiding the clergy of his extensive diocese. At first he, like many others, had hoped that the Church would be able to exert its influence as a Christian and neutral force, taking its example from the Vatican State. It soon became apparent, however, that the enemy had no intention of regarding it as such. The persecution of the clergy began at once, and the priests in small country villages known to harbour partisans bore the full brunt of their wrath.

Following the murder of Don Grigoletti and Don Quiligotti in the Zeri valley during the rastrellamento of August 1944, the Bishop published an angry denunciation of the enemy, which he had had circulated throughout his diocese. This drew him under suspicion. Confident of the power that he had in the land, he remained at his post, and the Germans were wise enough to realise that, in view of the unpleasant reaction that had followed their treatment of high Church dignitaries in the North, they would have to treat him with caution. He was placed under permanent observation, but he continued to use his influence as a restraining force on the enemy and more irresponsible partisan formations alike. Towards the end' both were dependent on him for exchanges of prisoners.

The Bishop was supported in his difficult task by the affection of his people, nearly all of whom showed him an unswerving loyalty throughout. His clergy found themselves between the danger of enemy reprisals on the one hand, and the actions of a few undisciplined groups of partisans on the other; it was only natural that in a few rare cases, the weaker brethren among them gave way under the strain – their task was the most difficult of any section among the harassed population of Northern Italy.

It was no surprise to us when, at the end of the second week in January, reports reached us from these sources of enemy preparations for a combined attack on the 4th Zone, on a much larger scale than ever before. These reports were supported by others from La Spezia, from Richetto's headquarters at Varese Ligure, and through old John at Buzzo, on the other side of Monte Gottero. At the same time warning messages were sent us by wireless. We were better prepared this time, but our strength in men and equipment was offset by the bad weather conditions that successfully wrecked communications with formations outside the frontiers of the Valley. Owing to the dangers of the political background, it had been considered inadvisable to establish a wireless intercommunication system, but even that would not have overcome the physical difficulties presented by the snow. It was rumoured that the enemy intended to use Mongol ski troops. Colonel Fontana wisely decreed that attack was the best form of defence, and drew up a plan whereby the partisan formations were to strike a hard blow at the enemy at widely dispersed points, before the general offensive began.

A council of war was called with all the partisan leaders. The Colonel, Bob, and I reviewed the situation, and battle positions were allotted to the various formations. We were to strike on the night of the 19th of January at selected points. Dani was to descend into the valley of the Magra to create panic among the Fascist troops in the outskirts of the town of Aulla. The S.A.S. and what there was of the International Battalion were to attack enemy columns moving into Pontremoli from the direction of Villafranca, while Richetto and the Beretta brothers were to take up a defensive position on the Northern frontier, much as they had done in the August battle, to prevent infiltration into the Zone through Vares Ligure and the Due Santi Pass below Monte Gottero.

In the Valley, the strength of the parachutists had been reduced by sickness, and they were to be reinforced by picked men of Richetto's Cento Croce brigade, under the command of one of their best leaders, the sailor Nino Siligato.

Once these orders had been issued, we returned to our respective areas to carry them out.

* * *

On the afternoon of the 18th January, the S.A.S. and partisans of the International Battalion, with their transport animals fully loaded, moved to the outpost village of Arzelato. The village possesses a high church tower, from the summit of which one can see Pontremoli below and a considerable length of the River Magra threading its way like a silver ribbon through fields and villages to the next town of Villafranca. From the church the country falls away in steep wooded slopes to the outskirts of the city.

Taking advantage of a bright interval in the weather just before sunset, Bob, Chris, and I climbed the tower and studied the landscape through field glasses. A partisan guide from the village was with us, and pointed out the main buildings – the cathedral with its large green copper dome rising above the houses in the market square, the Bishop's Palace, and the Fascist barracks. At the northern end of the city we could see the old castle – once a stronghold of the Visconti family and later a fortress of the Emperor Charles V – standing proudly on a hill. It commanded the road built by Napoleon to the Cisa Pass, where many a German vehicle had already met its doom. Everything appeared normal, and there was no unusual movement on the roads. The bombed railway station stood out clearly, but it was little used. Owing to the damage done to the bridges in the Borgo Taro area by the Beretta brigades, no trains could reach Pontremoli from Parma, and we knew that the long tunnel was filled with railway wagons loaded with art treasures looted from Florence. A few coaches, drawn by a steam engine of ancient design, made spasmodic journeys from Villafranca to Pontremoli. The bridge at Villafranca had been destroyed some months before by Avio and our sabotage squad, and it had not been repaired, which meant that rail communication was cut off with La Spezia. We remained in the tower until darkness covered the landscape below.

When I went back to the local Inn, I found the detachment from the Cento Croce brigade arriving. They had been on the march for two days, and Nino the commander was anxious lest they should not arrive in time. He was suffering from an attack of mountain fever and had travelled on a pony that belonged to a collaborator in Varese Ligure. On seeing me, he vaulted from the saddle and shook hands.

Nino Siligato was a young sailor from southern Italy. His hair hung down to his shoulders, for he had made a vow that he would not cut it, or shave his beard, until his country had been liberated; this gave him an air of ferocity that belied his years. He was noted for his peculiarity of always speaking of himself in the third person.

"Here is Nino, Maggiore," he said. "The march took longer than we thought, owing to the snow. The men haven't brought any heavy weapons with them, as we were told that you had enough."

"Bravo, Nino! – I knew we could count on Richetto's boys. Let them rest now, and give them a drink. I'll tell you the plan later."

We were to stage an ambush on the main road leading to Pontremoli from Villafranca. Following the successful outcome of that, the force was to switch over to Codolo, at the entrance to the Zeri valley. They were then to fall back before dawn to Zeri itself and reassemble in the Valley to await enemy reactions. This meant that, to facilitate movement over the ice-covered tracks, the spare mortar and ammunition was to be sent to Codolo from Arzelato to await their arrival. In the event of any unexpected development on the part of the enemy, the force was to return to Arzelato, and back to the Valley by the same route that we had followed that morning. The wireless sets, spare transport and ammunition were to be left with me in the village until the next morning, when they too would be withdrawn to the Valley.

Owing to the intercommunication problem, once the manoeuvre had started there was no means of informing the assault troops as to any developments either in their rear, or at Codolo. At Arzelato, therefore, we would have to judge what was happening from the sounds of battle.

The latest information about the enemy was useful. There had been a massing of Fascist troops in Pontremoli during the past week, and the strength of the force was quoted as anything between 800 and 1,800 men. No convoys had reached Pontremoli during the day, but we knew that they moved by night, often with full headlights, protected by the stormy weather conditions. With ordinary luck, the ambush should be successful. There was a small garrison of German troops near Codolo, but rumour had it that they shut themselves into their billets at night, as they felt none too safe. By nightfall that day, there had been no news of enemy patrol activities. The plan had a reasonable chance of success – provided the enemy knew nothing about it.

At ten o'clock the expedition set out for its first target area. The S.A.S. contingent gathered on the road outside the Inn and moved off into the night. Behind them came the partisans from Varese Ligure. Nino approached me as they filed past.

"Good-bye, Maggiore," he said. "If Nino should not return, he wants you to have his horse. Buona fortuna," and he hurried after his men.

I waited until I could no longer hear their receding footsteps. I had known Nino for a long time, and a great friendship had grown between us. He had come to our rescue as fugitive ex-prisoners many times during the past year and his personal courage had won him a hero's reputation with his companions. It was for these reasons that Richetto had sent him to represent the Cento Croce brigade in this most critical of all operations.

Nello was waiting for me at my billet.

"Nello," I said, "You are to take the mortar and spare ammunition to the village of Codolo. Wait there for the parachutists who will arrive after they have carried out the ambush on the road. Be careful to move in silence. The enemy are preparing an attack at any moment, and may have spies watching for us. If you see anything suspicious on the way, send a message back to me here. You had better leave at once."

"Va bene, Maggiore." He went off to collect the mules.

I went outside again, and paced up and down the road, thinking of possible developments. We could not know for some time how the various operations had succeeded. Bob had arranged to send back a message as soon as the first operation was completed. Chris had gone with him so that he could send a first-hand report to Special Force in the morning. On receipt of the message, I would move back to the Valley with the wireless team. This was still in charge of Corporal Johnston. Several of the S.A.S. men, among them Lofty, were in hospital in the Valley under the care of our efficient little Doctor Capiferri. In the event of a counter-attack, they would have to be evacuated. I was thinking of all this when a figure approached. I recognised the village priest.

Don Pasquale, well in his sixties, had been involved in the partisan war from the beginning. He was one of the first of his cloth to be precipitated into the arms of the patriots by force of circumstances. Six months before, a gang of Mongols arrived in Arzelato on a looting expedition and, according to custom, made straight for the vicarage. It was raining hard at the time, and the poor man was obliged to have food prepared and watch them drink his wine and remove his few possessions. The news of their presence reached the Valley, and we set out in the hope of surprising the intruders at their drunken orgy. By the time we reached the house, the Mongols had returned to Pontremoli. We found the old priest alone in his village, greatly distressed by the event. In spite of that, he refused to go into hiding, and remained there until the end.

"Buona sera, Reverendo."

"Buona sera, Signor Maggiore. Please excuse me if I am disturbing you. I only want to say that I am glad to help you and your compatriots. But you must be careful, Maggiore. There may be spies in this village who are in contact with the enemy down below. One never knows these days who are good and who are bad."

"You are right, Reverendo, but I think we are prepared. I only hope that your parish will not be made to suffer if the enemy carry out an attack to-morrow."

"You needn't think of that." The old priest smiled. "The lads of this village are on guard to-night, with my nephew Ugo, and they have the firearms that you have given us; the population – or at least those of them who are good Italians – are ready to risk the consequences if things should go badly."

"We shall see," I replied. "It is likely that there will be an enemy attack soon, if not to-morrow."

Don Pasquale shrugged his shoulders. "As to that, it is in the hands of the Almighty. Buona notte, Maggiore," and he went on his way.

Meanwhile Nello, with three heavily laden mules and accompanied by Salvatore, Silvio, Marcello and several others from the Valley, was half-way to Codolo. They were obliged to move slowly along the track, for the night was silent as the grave. Often an iron shod hoof would click against a stone in spite of their precautions.

Suddenly they heard the sound of machine gun fire from the Pontremoli road. The attack had begun. The column stopped to listen. The firing died down as abruptly as it had started, and they were about to move on when Nello heard a suspicious sound in front of them. They drew the animals into the darker shadows of the trees while he crept forward to investigate. He came to a bend in the track, and fell flat on his face and lay still.

Not far from him two figures stood blocking the route. They were talking in low whispers, but the partisan was close enough to realise that they spoke in German. He retreated as silently as he had come.

The others collected round him. "We must go back," he whispered. "The Germans are waiting for us further on. We must tell the Maggiore. There is no other path, and we would make too much noise travelling through the woods."

Silently the little column made its way back to Arzelato, and Nello duly reported.

"You did the only thing possible," I said, when he had finished. "We can't risk the mortar being captured. Warn all the guards, and then we had better move to one of the houses on the edge of the village. We must wait till dawn, in case the parachutists discover that the route to Codolo is blocked, and return here."

Falco the dentist, the leader of the partisans of Arzelato, took us to his house, overlooking the way back to the Valley. It was now obvious that the enemy was on the alert, and he had posted his men as sentries to watch for the outcome. We did not have long to wait. Hardly had the darkness turned to grey when we heard rifle fire nearby.

I ran into the roadway, Nello beside me. The inhabitants of Arzelato were streaming away as fast as they could run towards the woods. Some of the womenfolk were frantically hiding their possessions in the snow near their doors. Nello called up the mules, already loaded. The wireless sets had been hidden by Johnston, in case of damage during the retreat, but we felt that the spare mortar and ammunition had to be taken with us at all costs. We began to withdraw towards the Valley, and left the village just as the sun was rising.

To gain the shelter of the trees, we had to cross an empty mountain slope covered with snow. As we began, a German machine gun opened fire from the base of the church tower. The black figures of men and animals made a perfect target, and the range was such that the gunner could pick us off at his ease. To make matters worse, one of the mules overbalanced. It belonged to Salvatore, and nothing would induce him to leave it. We unloaded the beast, after which it deigned to get to its feet again, and we moved on. The machine gun spat at us, but the bursts were aimed high, and scattered the snow on the slope a foot above our heads. There was still a long way to go, and the next burst would get us. Somehow we struggled on, and it was with some surprise that, bringing up the rear of the column, I eventually found myself under cover, and realised at the same time that the gun had not fired again. Our escape seemed nothing short of miraculous, and it was not until some two weeks later that we learnt the reason for it.

Two of the partisan sentries, on guard at the entrance to the village, heard a movement on the road below them shortly before sunrise. They waited until three figures came into view, when they challenged. The partisans realised that they were not the parachutists whom they were expecting, but a German patrol. They opened fire. The enemy responded with what arms they had, for their main column was still in the rear, but they could not see at what they were aiming. The partisans continued to fire until they heard the machine gun open up near the church behind them. They then knew that they were surrounded, and managed to slip quietly away into the river gorge below.

When it grew lighter, and just as the machine gunner had seen his victims struggling across the slope in front of him, the German officer commanding the patrol saw that one of his men was dead, spread-eagled across the road on the edge of the village. In accordance with their custom he called off the gun team and set the patrol to work putting the body in a sack, after which it was strapped on to a mule and sent back to their base. Thus the partisans of Arzelato had saved their comrades of the Valley.

It was at that same hour, in the nearby village of Codolo, that Nino and six of his comrades of the Cento Croce Brigade were massacred by another enemy patrol.

Chapter Sixteen

The Enemy Advances

The days that followed were among the most exciting that we had ever known.

When we reached the Valley that morning the enemy was already approaching it from all sides. We found out later that the patrol which killed Nino and his men had followed the S.A.S. squadron along the road to Zeri, where a brisk action took place in the village of Noce, whose gaunt ruins still bore witness to the last visit by the supporters of the "Little Republic". The parachutists, greatly outnumbered, had then withdrawn to Coloretta, and took to the surrounding heights; Bob, Chris, and Riccamini were with them. The enemy broke off the engagement in search of less hostile victims.

In the Valley there was only time to collect the sick men from the hospital. Fortunately, all of them were walking cases. Lofty insisted on carrying the mortar, assisted by Parachutist Gargan, who had endeared himself to the Rossanesi and on account of his youthful appearance, had earned from them the nickname of "The Boy Bandit". There were only thirty rounds of ammunition for the mortar, and it was doubtful whether it could be used, but Lofty felt about it as Salvatore had felt about his mule – it could not be left behind. Avio joined us, but the news that he brought was now outdated by events. Some of the parachutists from the Borgo Taro area were there as well. Nello and the courier Riboncia went off to collect certain vital possessions from the village of Castoglio, and I told them to follow us as quickly as possible to the summit of Monte Picchiara.

We set off on the two hour walk through snow drifts to the upper slopes of the mountain that was so closely connected with our destiny.

Early in the afternoon the weather changed again. Heavy clouds covered the leaden sky and cold blasts of wind swept the snow into swirling eddies of white powder. Eventually we reached the edge of the plateau where so many drops had been made from Allied planes during the past months, and Lofty posted the mortar in position overlooking the Valley. Through binoculars we could see enemy patrols marching along the road to the skeleton village of

Chiesa – at least there was nothing left for them to burn there. They offered a provoking target to our trained gunners. After a while, Lofty could not resist the temptation any longer, and asked me whether he could open fire.

It would have given us great satisfaction to have done so, but the enemy had not started to burn houses, and there was a chance that if we did not attack, the population might be treated with less harshness than on the previous occasion. In any case, we had not sufficient ammunition available to warrant a pitched battle, and, unless we could drive the enemy back and keep him out of the area, the action would achieve little of value. Furthermore, the partisans who had already reached the mountain were not in a position to launch an attack with us. Ermano was there with some of his men, but confusion had been created by the arrival of disorderly groups from other areas where things had gone badly since dawn. The situation had already deteriorated to such an extent that whatever action took place in the future would depend upon the fighting spirit of each individual partisan, or the decision of a commonly elected leader. The official "Commanders" and political Commissars, except in rare cases where they happened to be sufficiently military-minded, had lost control altogether and faded from the scene. The men, by force of circumstances, automatically adopted the tactics of true guerilla fighters. In the course of the six days that followed, there were more cases of individual heroism among the partisans than at any time in the history of the resistance movement.

So, to Lofty's obvious distress, the mortar was hidden beneath the snow, and he and Gargan carried out the burial service.

In the middle of the afternoon we received a valuable addition to our numbers in the person of Pippo Siboldi from Sero. He told us the enemy had already reached his village, but they had had to fight for its occupation. The whole of the area adjacent to the Via Aurelia had been overrun, and so he had come in search of his friend Lofty, and to act as our guide.

When dusk fell, it was clear that the partisan offensive had failed dismally, and that the enemy was fast establishing himself in all the main villages. I decided to withdraw to the last stronghold, the slopes of Monte Gottero, in the hope that the Cento Croce Brigade had managed to hold out. If that front had collapsed as well, we would be properly in the soup. Nello and Riboncia had not arrived by nightfall, and I left a message with several of the Rossanesi who had decided to return to the Valley, that they were to follow us to Monte Gottero.

Armed with two light machine guns, rifles, and as much ammunition as we could carry, we set off towards the north.

On Monte Gottero all was lost. The Cento Croce Brigade, like the other formations, had split into small groups, and Richetto with a few of his men crossed the mountain to the village of Monte Groppo, where they went to ground. There was no news of Bob and the other members of the S.A.S.

This was one of the trickiest situations that I ever had to deal with during my life as a partisan, and it was some consolation to know that I was not facing it alone. King's Regulations, the soldier's Bible, had not done much to prepare one for this kind of thing, nor had Regular Army training. But out of the past came memories of service with the Ist Battalion of the East Surreys in India. I had joined the Ist Battalion as a very junior subaltern, and at the time we had an adjutant who instilled the fear of God into us. He was a small man, with a particularly vitriolic tongue, and one of the finest soldiers that ever wore uniform. For some reason, while trying to make up my mind what to do next, I suddenly remembered one awful day when I was called into the orderly room to receive what was commonly known as the periodical raspberry. I have forgotten the cause, but the adjutant ended what was undoubtedly a painful interview with the remark:

"Remember, young fellow, that in this battalion, nobody is considered indispensable. If he thinks he is, he must prove it. Very few young officers manage to do so!"

It was odd that that remark should have come back to me over the years. Perhaps, for the first time in my life, I was indispensable in that I knew the terrain in which we were moving much better than did the enemy. And so I decided that we might stand a better chance of survival by retracing our steps and patrolling the mountains and villages that were so well known to all members of the International Battalion. With Pippo to guide us, we held a trump card in our hand. This decision was influenced to a great extent by the prospect of having with me a few well trained soldiers of the S.A.S., who could be relied upon to do the right thing in moments of crisis.

Those who did not like this plan were given the choice of going to earth, or chancing their luck outside the 4th Zone. Eight of the parachutists remained with me, including Lofty and Gargan. In addition there were Avio, the courier Mazzini, and two partisans who joined us on Monte Gottero – Spartaco, who had deserted to the International Battalion after the affair of the Teglia Dam, and Ivan, a Russian refugee who had been welcomed with enthusiasm in the ranks of one of the Communist units. With Pippo our group numbered fourteen, and we were well armed.

We started to move back to the northern slopes of Monte Picchiara the next afternoon, Pippo leading the way. We had not slept for forty eight hours, and the men were feeling the effects of scrambling along the slippery tracks, ankle deep in snow. Night came on – a clear, moonlit night, and bitterly cold. As the next day promised to be a lively one, it was essential that we should get some rest.

We reached a point where a main road had to be crossed, on the opposite side of which there was an isolated house. We crossed over in single file and while the others took cover in the shadows, Pippo and I went in search of the householder. It was important to know whether there were enemy patrols in the vicinity, and to find a cascina in which to rest. Pippo knocked at the door. A light showed, and it was opened a few inches. Judging by the whispered conversation that ensued it was clear that the light-carrier regarded our presence with acute discomfort, and was anxious to be rid of us. Reluctantly he supplied the information that there were Mongols in the next village and directed us to a cascina an hour's march up the mountain slope. Then he shut and barred the door, and the light was extinguished.

We climbed wearily through the forest, and at length arrived at our resting place, a delapidated hut built of chestnut wood, the floor barely covered with prickly leaves. The men crowded into it and settled down to sleep after sentry duty had been arranged at two hour intervals. It was by then nearing midnight, and a full moon was high above, throwing the landscape into a clear cut pattern of black and white.

Two hours later Ivan and I took over sentry duty. For the first time that night, the brilliant moonlight was our ally, for the cascina was built on the edge of a steep gully leading down to the road, and we had an uninterrupted view of the white slopes beneath the trees.

In that life of semi-barbarism, it was strange how quickly our instincts became adapted to circumstances. Like hunted animals, we had developed a kind of sixth sense that gave warning of approaching danger before it took visible form. Our watch was half over when suddenly we both knew that something was wrong. We had no common language, as Ivan only spoke half a dozen words of broken Italian, and yet when the moment came we found ourselves acting in unison.

I was endeavouring to explain to him, by whispers and signs, that if he saw anything suspicious he was not to fire, but warn me and then rouse the sleepers; the cascina was to be evacuated in complete silence, and we would move further up the mountain. In the middle of my dumb play, I suddenly stopped, and we froze in the shadow. There was dead silence around us. We stared into the moonlight at the opposite bank of the gully. Then something moved. Ivan instinctively gripped his rifle, and I put my hand on his arm to restrain him. We saw two figures dressed in white creeping towards us.

We waited. The figures climbed down into the gully and began to cross it. We let them come to within twenty yards of us, and then I challenged softly.

"Chi va la."

There was a scuffle, and they vanished as silently as they had come.

We jumped to the entrance of the cascina. Ivan shook the men awake, while I kept guard outside. Swiftly they picked themselves up, and I took them along the track that led to the more thickly wooded heights. We had covered about a quarter of a mile when a green Very light shot into the sky and burst above our recent resting place. I stopped and, while Pippo led the squad past, checked to see that they were all present. There were twelve of them – with myself thirteen. One was missing.

I called a halt and checked again to find that Lofty was not with us. I sent the squad on its way and waited. Perhaps he was straggling behind. I became aware that Ivan was with me. He insisted on taking the light machine gun that I was carrying, slung over my shoulder. He tried to explain that it was my duty to give orders and his to carry things. There was no time to argue the point so I let him have his way, but my heart warmed towards Ivan. His Communist colleagues had not been generous to this representative of their El Dorado, for his uniform was in rags, he had no overcoat, and his bare feet were encased in sandals held together with string. He must have been in agony from the cold.

Another Very light was fired. In the last resort we would have to return to the hut, if it was not surrounded. I called softly.

"Lofty, where are you?"

There was no answer, and I gave a low whistle. It was answered from below. It might be the enemy, so we waited where we were. Presently a tall figure staggered into view. By its height and the shape of the dark beret against the snow it could only be our missing parachutist. His relief was as great as ours, though mine expressed itself in a flow of abusive language.

He confessed that he had fallen asleep again, and then had woken by instinct to hear us scrambling up the slope outside. Our parachutists were beginning to react to circumstances as effectively as the partisans.

We caught up with the rest of the squad. As we did so, all Hell was let loose in the woods below. We could hear rapid machine gun fire and the intermittent explosion of grenades, and soon a dull red glow lit up the sky. The cascina had been transformed into a frying pan in which the enemy intended that we should fry. Tired as we were, this spurred us to greater effort, and we continued climbing for another two hours.

We reached a clearing in the forest, in the middle of which stood a house. Apart from fatigue, we were ravenously hungry, for it had not been possible to carry rations with us in any large quantity. There were no lights showing. A dog barked angrily, rattling its chain as it tried to escape from captivity. Pippo found the door, and we waited while he knocked. A woman spoke in a low mumble, and Pippo replied. The door remained closed.

"She's got the wind up," whispered Pippo. "She's frightened to let us in because of the Germans."

I then did a thing that I have ever since regretted, but our need was desperate; in view of what the new day would bring, we must have food. I went to the door, and banged loudly on it.

"We're Germans," I shouted. "Let us in at once, or it will be the worse for you."

The door swung open, to reveal a trembling elderly peasant woman.

"Come in," she said, "Come in. I meant no harm – I only wanted to be left in peace."

We filed into the kitchen, and clustered round the warm stove. Continuing to act my unsavoury part, I truculently demanded food. The woman opened a large wooden chest that stood in a corner and produced some cold slabs of chestnut bread and a flask of wine. "This is all I have."

"Liar! You have potatoes. I saw your fields on the way here "

She left the room, to return with a heavy sack. Pippo took it and emptied the potatoes on the floor.

Unknown to our reluctant hostess, one of our number had been posted as guard outside the house. We proceeded to bake the potatoes in the fire, while attacking the bread, and passing the wine flask from mouth to mouth.

Pippo, rather sadistically I thought, began to cross-examine our hostess.

"Why are you afraid, if you are a friend of the Germans?"

"I am always afraid," she said. "My husband is a prisoner in Russia, and my daughter-in-law is in bed expecting her third child. I have to look after the house and the two children."

"Where is your son?"

"I don't know," she replied, and diving once more into the chest she produced another flask of wine.

Pippo was not to be side-tracked.

"What do you mean, you don't know?"

"He disappeared last August. He went over to Chiesa."

"Where?" I interrupted.

"To Chiesa in the Rossano Valley. There was fighting, and he never came back."

I felt a desire to tell her who we really were, but Pippo continued before I could think what to say.

"That sounds as if he was a partisan rebel – what do you know of the partisans?"

This put the fear of God into the poor soul, and she began to tremble again.

"Nothing," she said. "O Dio come ho paura!"

"You must have heard something. We are looking for the English parachutists – tell us about them."

"I have never seen them," she said – as indeed she had not until that night – "But they say that there are a lot of them in Rossano."

"How many?"

"Three hundred – four hundred – I don't know."

"Well, you will be all right. The Germans are here to protect you – have you seen any before us?"

"Some passed this morning," she said slowly. "They were dressed in white clothes, and had long wooden things on their feet and moved quickly over the snow. They took away " She stopped, and her eyes filled with tears.

"What did they take away?"

"They took – I gave them – my pig."

We knew only too well that that pig represented half of her capital.

"Which way did they go?"

"Down to the next village. They were going to Monte Gottero, because one of them asked me the way."

"Good. We will soon catch the English and kill them, and then they will not do you any harm."

The woman surprised us with an angry retort.

"They have never done us any harm like – " she stopped and put her hand to her mouth. "O Dio, what have I said!"

This was getting too much for me. To cover her confusion I said in English that we had better start on the move again. We collected some money together and while Pippo diverted the attention of the peasant woman I dropped it into the wooden chest. I have often wondered if she ever found it, and how she thought it had got there.

Stuffing the rest of the potatoes into our pockets, we emerged into the night. The woman shut the door, glad to be rid of us.

"You rubbed it in a bit thick, Pippo," I said.

He grinned. "That's nothin' to what the Germans will do. Anyway we got some useful information, so what you grousing about?"

We certainly had. We now knew that there were enemy ski troops about, that they believed our force to be much stronger than it was, and that they were presumably concentrating around Monte Gottero. If we could draw them away from there, it might remove the danger from the partisans hiding on the summit, and we should have some fun playing "catch-as-catch-can" in the surrounding valleys.

Chapter Seventeen

Touch and Go

A pale glow in the eastern horizon gave warning that daylight was near. We hurried on to the top of the ridge and found ourselves looking into the Torpiana Valley. The plan was to lie hidden by day and see what confusion we could cause by night; at all costs we must keep clear of the villages. Apart from the fact that we were not in a position to fight a pitched battle in daylight, the enemy would welcome any excuse to burn houses and shoot the inhabitants.

We began the descent into the valley. Daylight was approaching rapidly, and it was obvious that we could not reach the bottom before full daylight was upon us. Pippo led us to a small copse of thick evergreen bushes, and, having posted sentries, we dispersed within it, to wait until dark.

The morning dragged on, and changed to afternoon. The sun appeared and warmed us for a while, and I remember envying the parachutists around me, who seemed to be sleeping as peacefully as if they were in feather beds. It was late in the afternoon that one of the sentries came creeping up to me on all fours.

"Major," he whispered. "There's a woman coming along a track at the bottom of the copse. Shall I stop her?"

I got to my knees and looked over the tops of the bushes. A peasant woman, dressed in the usual black, was approaching our hiding place, a bundle of faggots balanced on her head. I took a long look at her through my field glasses. At first sight, she was a perfectly natural adjunct to the setting – just an ordinary peasant, carrying home the wood for the evening fire. Then instinct put out its usual warning signal. I looked at her again, and noticed that while walking she kept her eyes on the copse in a fixed stare. I sent round word for everybody to keep dead still. The inquisitive visitor passed by us. When she had moved beyond the copse, she turned and looked back. Then she hastened her pace towards the village.

That was enough for me. I gave the order to move, and, making the best use of the available cover, we scuttled down into the river bed.

Hardly had we reached it, when we heard firing on the slope behind us. The river was of little use as a defensive position, so we crossed it, into a pine forest on the other side. From this we could look back on the place where we had hidden during that day. The light was beginning to fail. From our seats in the stalls, we had an excellent view of the comedy that followed and enjoyed it to the full.

Mortar shells were falling into the copse, and puffs of smoke and flames arose from the innocent bushes. Encircling them was a ring of uniformed figures gradually closing in on the ferocious enemy, their rifles at the ready. We heard an order given, and they rushed the bushes, firing wildly as they did so. We were tempted to give a cheer of encouragement. Then silence fell upon the scene. We continued to peer through the increasing gloom, and saw the attackers retreating from the copse in twos and threes. We were delighted to see one group carrying a body – apparently they had managed to cause at least one casualty among themselves which we were justified in placing to our credit. Just as darkness hid the scene, a cascina went up in flames some way from the battleground in the direction of Torpania. It could be assumed that our whereabouts was still an unsolved mystery to our irate pursuers.

When it was dark, our journey continued. The incident had acted as a tonic and the men were immensely cheered by it. Pippo, again in the lead, was anxious to take us to his village of Sero, where he was sure that some of his private band of brigands would be available to swell our numbers; by way of additional temptation, he promised us a good meal. Avio, Spartaco, Ivan and Mazzini were particularly happy, and made rosy plans for driving the enemy out of the area altogether.

We were certainly causing them some distraction. I was later able to confirm that whenever we were reported in a certain place all other operations were called off in order that the punitive expedition could concentrate there. Time was on our side, for the enemy could not remain in the mountains for an indefinite period, and by the end of the second day were already beginning to have difficulty with their transport and communications. The mules on which they depended had a mysterious tendency to disappear in the night, as did the local guides who were obliged to lead them from place to place. In addition to this their stomachs protested at the recognised diet of chestnuts and potatoes.

We spent most of the night moving by easy stages over another mountain ridge and down into a small valley well known to Pippo. In this there was a house of a superior order, its owner having built it to escape the hot weather months in La Spezia. We reached it well after midnight, and the place was already crowded with refugees, some of them partisans. The prevailing sentiment seemed to be one of fear and despondency. We were told gloomy tales of burnings and slaughter by the enemy, and given the impression that dawn would reveal a German or Mongol behind every bush. We were quite glad to move on an hour before dawn.

Our hiding place for the fourth day was a small farm from which there was an uninterrupted view of the village of Sero and of Pippo's house. The family that owned the farm did guard duty for us, and Pippo spent the day collecting information from his friends. We saw one small enemy patrol march up to the village and stop at his house before going on towards Monte Dragnone. Pippo had seen it too. He bounced into the kitchen, which we had occupied as an observation post.

"Those sons of bitches," he said. "I'll give the missus something if she has let them drink all my wine."

From what he had to tell us, things seemed to be going nicely in our favour. The performance of the day before had caused no mean upheaval, and had done something to cheer the non-combatant inhabitants of Torpiana village. The peasantry, with their native shrewdness, had been jerked out of the fatalistic attitude created by past experience, when they had to bear the full brunt of partisan experiments in gnat-like bites at the enemy, and realised that this was a game in which they could take part. Following the Battle of the Copse, the German officer in charge of troops in the Torpiana area spent a disturbed night receiving reports from old men and women with detailed descriptions of where we had last been seen. He dared not ignore the reports, with the result that by daybreak his forces were split into numerous small patrols searching in every direction except the right one for non-existent parachutists. His men became still further discouraged. He managed to get them back to his headquarters by about midday, to find that half of his pack animals could not be accounted for, and his men were worn out. He was obliged to cease operations for a while, and ask for reinforcements.

So far, so good. It now remained to be seen whether we could recruit sufficient partisans at Sero to make it worth our while launching out into ambush operations.

That night we moved to Pippo's house. We might have been arriving in time for a Sunday Festa, for we found Mrs. Siboldi busy at the kitchen stove, and Lina, after a day hidden under chestnut leaves, preparing the table for a large dinner. We sat down to a meal of soup, roast chicken, potatoes and cheese, with unlimited quantities of Pippo's good wine, from which we gathered that there had been no need for him to vent his wrath on his long-suffering spouse. Instinct began to make signals again that this was all far too easy, and that we would suffer for it. The meal over, I asked Pippo about the security angle.

"Drink some more wine, then we move," he said. "Fellow down below, I no trust him." Further explanation revealed that Pippo had a lodger who lived in the basement, and he had a hunch that his guest might be a spy. I decided the quicker we moved the better.

My watch showed eleven o'clock as we went through the village to an underground cellar on the eastern perimeter. Sentries were posted overlooking the fields outside, and we settled down for what remained of the night.

I was awakened by Lofty, who was on the last shift.

"The sky is getting very light," he said, "It looks like dawn."

He handed me back my watch, and I noticed with horror that it had stopped at four o'clock. We made a speedy exit, to find that the world was filled with a misty light. There were no partisans to join forces with us at Sero – the next most likely place to find them would be in Dani Bucchioni's village.

There was a path well known to me which led to a spring, and would take us to the next ridge. Visibility was bad, for a thick mist had swept in from the sea, and snow clouds hung low overhead. We proceeded with caution through the slush that effectively deadened our footsteps, but the squelching of heavy boots in mud made an ominous sound in the deadly silence. Two minutes after leaving the cellar, a green Very light burst in front of us.

After our first experience, we knew that the enemy were on the alert, and very close. I led the column away from the path, across a field on our left.

We had reached the middle of the field when a voice rang out ahead of us, and a machine gun opened fire. We fell flat on our faces. Our first reaction was to return the fire, when we found that the gun nearest to hand had become jammed. Another automatic opened up behind us, and I suddenly realised that, judging by the path of the tracer bullets crossing above our heads, the enemy could not see us, but were making a fairly wild guess as to our whereabouts. It seemed stupid to lie there and wait until we could be seen. I whispered to the others to follow, and, crawling rapidly across the field, regained the path.

Both guns continued to fire at each other. We could hear orders screamed in a language that was neither German nor Italian, and presumed that it was Mongol, whatever that may be. We reached a gulley, and began to cross another field towards a clump of trees outlined on the horizon. And then we saw a soldier standing on the path to our left. He did not see us, probably because he was watching the firework display near Sero. We halted and flattened ourselves in the snow.

Gargan was beside me.

"Shall I go and get him, sir?"

"Yes, but take somebody with you, and don't shoot unless you have to."

He and Lofty disappeared into the gloom. Time stood still, and we waited for what seemed hours, before we heard a murmur, a slight t scuffle, and silence descended once again.

It looked as if our parachutists had been captured. We gripped our rifles, and doubled up the hill, prepared to give battle. At the top, four figures stood in the shadow of the trees, two of them with their hands above their heads. Just as I began to wonder which was which, Gargan called softly.

"Easy as falling off a log," he said, "We've got two – the others got away." It wasn't the first time that I sent up a silent prayer of thanks to the 2nd Battalion of the S.A.S.

As we slipped over the ridge and down into the next valley Gargan explained what had happened. The captives were a German sergeant and his orderly, belonging to a mortar team that had been ordered to open fire on Sero once the light was strong enough for them to see the target. They numbered eight altogether. When firing began, they had left the gun, and run to the top of the pass to watch, and Gargan and Lofty took them by surprise. The sergeant was slow to react, and according to Gargan, the orderly was "just dopey", but the others took to their heels at once. We had scored an important victory, for the sergeant was carrying on him the slide rule giving the ranges at which the gun could fire, and a vital part of the mechanism. The gun would therefore not be of much use that day.

And so we had two prisoners in our midst.

As we stumbled down the hillside, I summed up the situation. We had broken through the ring that surrounded Sero and, with luck, might succeed in reaching the valley of Calice. On the other hand, it was now full light, and we had the best part of a day's journey ahead of us through leafless forest, and silhouetted against the white snow. If the country in between contained enemy patrols, and we were spotted, the prisoners in our midst would cause initial confusion, and would ensure that we were not slaughtered in cold blood. But we could not afford to let them escape, as they already knew too much. They must be very carefully guarded.

As the light improved, the firing behind us increased in intensity, and we could hear rifle fire in opposition to that of the enemy. I wondered vaguely where it could be coming from. The important thing was that we were not being pursued. A blizzard began, and hid us still further from the surrounding heights. To reach the next ridge of hills we had to skirt a village, and cross the metalled road leading to it, after which we would reach a pine forest. If the blizzard continued, our chances were good.

Our column was moving in single file. Avio led the way, for he knew the terrain as well as I did. Behind him was Lofty, and then the German orderly covered by my Italian courier Mazzini. The sergeant was behind me, covered by Gargan who had a proprietary interest in his well being. The rest followed. There had not yet been an opportunity to check up our numbers.

We reached a small cliff, overhanging a mountain stream. By the time I came to it, those in front of me had climbed down and crossed to the other side. Apprehensive as I was about the guarding of our prisoners, it was somewhat disturbing to find that while Avio and Lofty had rightly gone on ahead, Mazzini was concentrating on the fact that he had got a foot wet, presumably while crossing the stream, and was fiddling with his left boot, while his prisoner the orderly was looking about him with what seemed to me acute interest in the local topography.

I shouted to the Italian.

"Watch the prisoner, you ass – don't let him escape!" and endeavoured to convey to him by signs that he should keep his Sten gun at the ready position, instead of pointing at the ground, as it was at the moment.

Mazzini was one of my most faithful henchmen. He was a young peasant lad from the Valley, timid by nature, who had never shown any desire to get himself mixed up in a battle. He fulfilled his duties as a courier admirably; he would walk for hours alone over the mountains by day and night, and would not rest until he had delivered the message he had in his charge. He was loyal to the ultimate degree, but very slow thinking.

Whether he heard what I said, or only saw my signs, I shall never know, but his immediate reaction was to raise the gun to his shoulder and shoot the German orderly through the head. It was a clean shot. The victim tremored, fell into the stream and lay still, while his blood began to mingle with the cold clean water.

Avio and Lofty, hearing the shot, turned back and stared at Mazzini in amazement. My brain went numb, and I remember turning to the other wretched prisoner behind me, and muttering somewhat inadequately in Italian, "I'm sorry, it was a mistake." Mazzini was staring stupidly at the corpse, its glazed eyes looking back at him from under the water. He was appalled by what he had done and my curses fell on deaf ears as he stood motionless, his mouth gaping.

The whole incident had happened in a matter of seconds, at a moment when the firing had stopped, and there was complete silence around us. My first coherent thought was that the shot must have been heard all over the valley. The sergeant had turned a sickly green, no doubt certain that his turn would come next. I was perhaps the only one of the party to realise that, in those seconds, our position had completely changed. If we were caught the enemy could ignore the Hague Convention, and justifiably shoot the lot of us, with the other prisoner to bear witness against us. Our only alternative was to ensure that we died fighting.

I hurried the rest of the column across the stream, trying not to think what the parachutists must feel at my having involved them in an incident completely contrary to their training and to the ethics of British warfare. Not one of them uttered a word of reproach, either then or later.

Our route lay through a small wood, beyond which was the village and the road. Presently the trees thinned. I was leading the way with Avio behind me, when the first house came in sight. Outside it two soldiers stood guard, dressed in white overalls to camouflage them against the snow. We dropped under cover; presumably they had heard the shot, and were waiting for us to cross the road. I passed a message back to the men to discard everything they carried except their firearms, and hastily pushed my compass, binoculars and the German slide rule under a clump of moss, together with the few papers that were in my pockets. Then I went off to reconnoitre a way round the village.

An hour later we crept up to the road. The blizzard had ceased, but a low mist covered the mountain slopes, and firing had started up again behind us. There were no enemy in sight. We crossed the road at the double and found ourselves among the trees once more. For two hours we stumbled up a crest, beyond which lay Calice. At last we halted, and decided to wait until nearer the hour of dusk. It was midday, but the sky remained overcast and an icy wind blew the snow off the branches of the trees down our necks. Our clothing was sodden, and we shivered as we huddled beneath a clump of rhododendron bushes.

It was the first time since leaving Sero that there was a chance of checking our numbers, and we found that Pippo, Spartaco, and Ivan the Russian were missing. According to the others they had not followed in our dash from the field at daybreak.

Lofty and I interrogated the prisoner, who looked dazed and surprised, as if wondering why he had not been shot. The only things of interest we found on him were an identity card and an Iron Cross. To his further bewilderment we handed him back the Iron Cross. The identity card showed that he belonged to a German battalion stationed in Genoa. He told us that the battalion had been called in as reinforcements and had only reached Sero before dawn that day, having been rushed along the Via Aurelia the night before. They had debussed at Borghetto, already an important target in what the S.A.S. had named "Operation Gallia". This proved Pippo's information to have been accurate. The Germans were finding the rastrellamento a much tougher consignment than they had bargained for. At least that was encouraging, but I could not help thinking bitterly how much tougher it could have been for them, had other partisan units been trained to follow our example.

During our progress after crossing the road, it had occurred to me that Avio had suddenly become extraordinarily fat. His battle-dress tunic bulged in all sorts of places, and I vaguely wondered what could be the cause. The interrogation finished, he came up to me, and put a hand inside his tunic. There was a twinkle in his eyes.

"You left these behind, Maggiore, and I thought I had better bring them along," and he drew out my compass, binoculars, the slide rule, and the other items that I had hidden under the moss. Then he added: "As long as we have you and the parachutists, nobody will catch us!" He was a good fellow, Avio – that gesture completely restored my deflated morale.

We continued the march towards Dani's kingdom, and arrived on the edge of it as dusk was falling. There was a farm located on a bare ridge overlooking Calice to the north-west, and at the end of the ridge we could see the friendly horizon formed by the outer bastions of Monte Pichiara. In our wanderings, we had nearly completed the circle back to Rossano. We did not know whether the enemy was in occupation, and placed our prisoner at the head of the column. His uniform might give the impression that we were a German patrol. Cautiously we moved towards the house.

A man scuttled out of the door, and down a nearby lane. As he disappeared from sight, we heard him shouting " Tedeschi, Tedeschi!" He must have been surprised that we did not shoot at him. It was odd to feel that we were successfully playing the part of the invaders and gaining first-hand experience of what happened when an enemy patrol arrived in our villages.

Smoke was rising from a chimney of the house, and the back door was open. We were within a few yards of it when a woman emerged carrying a bucket. She made her way to the well and on seeing us, she too, screamed " Tedeschi!" and then proceeded to fill her bucket. I led the way into the house.

The woman returned and dumped the bucket on the floor, so that the water slopped over. She put her hands on her hips, and stared at me unflinchingly.

"What do you want now?" she said in acid tones. That "now" conveyed so much that I could have embraced her. I grinned instead.

"It's all right, Signora, we are not Germans. This is a prisoner we picked up. These are the English parachutists from Rossano, and we want to find Dani."

In a moment she was transformed, and her face lit up with happiness.

"O, che gioa!" she cried. "You are the English – then you must be the Maggiore. I thought your face was familiar." She ran to the door, and shouted the good news to the surrounding countryside.

Apparently the landscape was not as deserted as we had imagined. Within a few minutes several men emerged from their hiding places. Most of them were old, but one was a courier of Dani's. There was a chattering and a bustling, and in a matter of seconds the erstwhile bare table supported quantities of chestnut bread, flasks of wine, and half of a cold chicken. We set to work with a will to appease our clamouring stomachs, while the visitors told us the news.

With sly glances at our prisoner, they told us that the enemy had occupied Calice for three days. They had killed some of the population, and set fire to the houses of Dani and his father. Dani had taken to the woods with some of his men and had passed the time picking off isolated Mongols who wandered too far afield in search of loot.

They had suddenly left the area the day before, to go to Torpiana in search of us. There was no news of the Rossano Valley.

At length we set out to find Dani. The news of our arrival had gone ahead, for he met us as we began to descend towards Calice. The sight of our prisoner, whom we had now blindfolded, gave him considerable pleasure. Avio told him of the fate of the German orderly, and Dani laughed. Under cover of darkness we reached the smouldering shell of what had been his father's home, where Ardito and I had spent Christmas Day. The column halted, while Dani explained to the German in careful Italian the meaning of the sound of crumbling masonry and the acrid smell of burning ashes.

That night, while we disposed of another enormous meal, Dani gave us news of Sero. Two of his men had spent the day near the village. The enemy had surrounded it during the night. When we broke through the circle, they concluded that we had gone to earth among the buildings, and began a house-to-house search. They failed to find us, and then learnt of the fate of the mortar section. They vented their rage by shooting at random, and killed several of the population. Their irritation was increased still further by suddenly finding themselves being sniped at from the church tower.

When we had performed our vanishing act, Pippo had run back into the village. Being the tough customer that he was, he decided to have a battle on his own. He climbed into the church tower and, having accounted for three of the enemy, managed to extricate himself before the pace got too hot. Nobody knew what happened to him after that.

Spartaco and Ivan had been wounded when the Mongols first opened fire. Spartaco managed to crawl under a bush, where he was found by Pippo's daughter Lina, and carried to a safe hiding place. Ivan remained lying in the field. The Germans found him, and seeing he was still alive, they blew his head off with a hand grenade.

Somehow after that we did not feel so bad about the German orderly. The enemy followed this up by spreading a rumour that I had been captured, and the parachutists killed.

As we still had some way to travel to reach Rossano, we handed over our prisoner to Dani that night, taking care to explain that he should be carefully guarded, as he might have some exchange value after the battle was over against any of our men who might have been taken prisoner. Not unnaturally, perhaps, Dani had different views as to what his fate should be, but he promised to keep him alive. There was still no news from the Valley, and I decided to go a stage nearer next day.

We slept well that night, protected by Dani's partisans. In spite of the hardship, the men of the S.A.S. were disappointed that our game of touch and go might be nearing its end.

Chapter Eighteen

A Man of Peace

We started late next morning, with two of Dani's men to guide us on the final stage back to the Valley. As if in welcome, the sun came out and warmed the crisp, clear air. Our march was in the nature of a triumphal progress, for the news of our adventures had spread far and wide, and the peasants came out of their houses to greet us, and press upon us gifts of cheese and wine. We marched slowly with frequent halts, enjoying to the full a sense of security that was strangely unfamiliar. We followed the mountain range to the north-west of Montereggio and towards evening reached the frontier of the Valley at the point where Dani had posted his sentries on the day that the S.A.S. dropped in to Chiesa. We could see the dropping zone and the village near it – at that distance the scene looked peaceful enough.

Our objective was the ninth village of Rossano, Casa Gaggioli. It consisted of a small group of houses clinging precariously to the steep slope of the mountain ridge where it began to fall away towards the Teglia Dam. Both in summer and winter the village was hidden from observation by overhanging rocks and its encircling woods, and it was by far the poorest of them all. According to the inhabitants, it owed its existence to one Gaggioli, who was a subject of Maria Louisa, Duchess of Parma in the early 19th century. He had been outlawed, and had fled to the woods in Rossano, where he built himself a house and raised a family. Other outlaws had joined him, and so the single house became the village that it is to-day.

Two men of the International Battalion were waiting for us on the Montereggio Pass, Carlino, who with Don Davide hatched the affair of the Fascist mules six months previously, and Aldo Pappini, a young peasant who had been enrolled in the International Battalion in the early days and who had elected himself our host for that night. They led us down the steep track to the village and the schoolroom that was to be our headquarters, while the women prepared an evening meal at Aldo's house.

It was a merry evening and had there been any doubts about the rastrellamento being over, they were finally banished when somebody produced a concertina, and singing and dancing began. Aldo could tell us little of events in the Valley, as he had spent most of the time in his village, but so far as he knew, none of the population had been shot. The enemy had searched for us for two days, and then the Rossanesi began to react as their colleagues had done in the Torpiana valley by sending the patrols on false scents in all directions. One had arrived exhausted at Casa Gaggioli on the night of the third day to find the place deserted and all stores of food well hidden. Of the two mules accompanying them, one had fallen down the mountainside complete with its load and the other had been spirited away under cover of darkness. The next morning, the patrol, cold, hungry and discouraged, made its way to the Teglia Dam and gave up the unequal contest. On the fourth day most of the enemy had been sent over Monte Picchiara to join the battle at Sero. Rossano had been evacuated the day before.

We returned to Chiesa to find Bob, Chris, and most of the S.A.S. already there. They had all rendered a good account of themselves and when we had compared notes we felt that we had justified our existence. The enemy had been thoroughly exercised in body and mind and, with the exception of Dani's houses in Calice, had had little time to burn and loot.

The people of the Valley greeted us with jubilation, and declared the day a Festa.

"They told us you were dead, Luigi!" cried old Mamma. "One of them had a walking stick and a signet ring like yours, and he said he had taken them after you had been shot at Torpiana."

We established headquarters once again with Amelia's family at Valle. Silvio was a particularly happy man, for he was now the owner of a mule, which, he said with a grin, he had "found under a tree". This was an expression coined by the partisans to explain dubious ownership of particularly valuable articles – almost anything could be "trovato sotto un albero", from English cigarettes and chocolate to the latest type of rifle and ammunition. The trees became extraordinarily prolific in the Valley after the arrival of the S.A.S.

By degrees the partisan formations reassembled, much shrunken in numbers. The Colonel, with his Chief of Staff, Colonel Grossi, and our lawyer Mario, with various others, emerged from a cave on Monte Gottero. Chris Leng had kept them company for the first day and had an amusing tale to tell of a game of poker played on a mosscovered stone, bathed periodically by drips from the roof so that the cards had to be laid down and taken up again between splashes. Conversation was carried out in whispers, as a group of Mongols had unwittingly come to roost outside. They departed in due course, whereupon Chris left the cave, preferring life in the open air to one where he had to spend his time changing position to avoid getting wet; eventually he found a group of parachutists in a hut near the Due Santi Pass. There were many prisoners among the partisans, including Richetto who was captured in the hotel at Montegroppo, in the Borgo Taro area, due to the activities of a woman spy; he managed to escape again before the column reached the enemy base. Franco had moved with his men into the 6th Zone towards Genoa, where he carried out harassing tactics on the roads leading to Sesta Godano. The Beretta Brigades split into small groups and scattered towards Parma.

Remnants of the International Battalion came back to the Valley, but there was no news of Nello and Riboncia. I sent search parties to look for them and for five days they searched in vain. On the sixth day the two couriers were found on Monte Pichiara, near the point where I had told them to join us after our retreat from Arzelata. They were both dead; Nello had two bullet holes in the back of his skull. Riboncia had evidently tried to escape, and his body lay mangled in a ditch nearby.

Two coffins were made in Chiesa of chestnut wood, and over them we draped the Union Jack and the Italian flag which had been used as signals for the pilots who brought the S.A.S. Pallbearers of the International Battalion brought them into the Valley, and the population stopped work in their fields and lined the edge of the path as the funeral cortege passed, the men bareheaded and the women weeping. They placed bunches of wild flowers on the coffins and then fell in behind until the procession of mourners stretched from Montedelama to Chiesa. The dead were placed in the chapel, and the Rossanesi passed by in homage for the rest of the day.

I felt the death of these two men very deeply, for they had been my companions throughout the most difficult time of all. Bob, good fellow that he was, must have realised this, for the S.A.S. paid them the highest tribute that can be paid to a soldier. Next morning as we took the bodies to the cemetery below Chiesa, I found Bob and Riccamini with the parachutists formed up as a guard of honour.

They fell in behind the coffins and marched in slow time into the cemetery. The grave had been prepared alongside that of the American airmen; the funeral service completed, the S.A.S. fired a last salute as the coffins were lowered into it. I was not sure that I could control my emotions and stood watching the ceremony from a distance, and, after a while, became aware that Falco, who also came from Nello's village of Valeriano, was standing beside me. He said nothing, and tears were streaming down his face. We remained there some time after the others had gone.

"Ebbene, Maggiore," he said at last. "There are not many of us left now."

I was thinking the same thing. Gone were Nello, Riboncia, Chella, Carlo, Nino, and Armanetti of the original little band who had helped to create the International Battalion. Edoardo was in hiding from the politicians; Aldo, Branco and the Poles had crossed the lines. Only Geoff, the lads from Buzzo, with Falco, Ardito, and Mazzini remained. There weren't many of us left.

The day after the funeral, the weather became worse and low clouds closed in on the Valley. Bob had restored communications with Florence – Alfonso and Bianchi had hidden their wireless sets, and were struggling to get them in order again – but before the S.A.S. could recommence operations, some equipment was urgently needed. For days we waited in vain, cursing the weather. At last a single plane piloted by an American colonel literally dropped through the clouds to within a few feet of us and flung out our most urgent needs. The plane disappeared again, and returned safely to its base. He was a brave man, that colonel, and we were glad to hear later that he had received a British decoration.

The S.A.S. went into action once more, attacking convoys on the roads, and paid another unwelcome visit to the ill-fated town of Borghetto on the Via Aurelia, in which Spitfires joined and poured gunfire into the battered target. The enemy became more worried than before. At last the day arrived when Bob received a special message of congratulation for the fine work done by the S.A.S. It said that they had disrupted enemy plans to such an extent that their troops on the Gothic Line were affected, and this had been borne out by the statements of German prisoners taken north of Florence. "Operation Gallia" could now be considered as successfully concluded, and the S.A.S. squadron was to return to base for action elsewhere. At the end of February they marched out of the Valley, cheered by the Rossanesi with whom they had formed links of friendship that will last for a generation. Their last act was to recommend my couriers Falco and Ardito for a decoration in recognition of their services.

As a result of their departure, life became colourless. The Colonel had established his headquarters once again in the Torpiana valley, but I did not join him. Rumours were circulating of an imminent offensive by the Allied Armies, with the result that the history of the past months began to repeat itself with dreary accuracy. Last minute recruits were welcomed to the ranks of Actionists and Communists, and enthusiastic political amateurs ensconced in armchairs far from the operational area proceeded to tie the Colonel's hands so that he had less chance than ever of creating that central command that he dreamed of. Some of the new partisan leaders became openly rebellious, but Colonel Fontana could not depose them without the approval of some newly constituted Liberation Committee, the latter in many cases being swamped by Communist elements who gave their support to the very men whom the Colonel wanted to remove.

Following the January rastrellamento, both the enemy and the partisans sat back to lick their wounds. Alfonso and Bianchi returned to the Valley with their radio sets, and re-opened contact with Special Force Headquarters. Franco, his command reduced to thirty men, installed himself in the village of Chioso. Sick of the political intrigue, he elected once again to become part of the garrison of the Valley. His services had been of such value to the S.A.S. that he now received regular supplies by air in daylight, and Nino Ferrari, his quartermaster, kept careful check of how the material was used. At the same time, military equipment continued to rain down upon Actionists and Communists, sent by the Americans.

I felt there was no longer need to recruit new members to the International Battalion, and limited its numbers to a squad of men from Buzzo, sent me by old John, and the men of the Valley who had served us faithfully for so long. Geoff left at the end of February to cross the lines and report on the situation. Chris, Avio and I were now the only officers. The rest of the battalion was dispersed between Dani's formation, Franco, and the Beretta and Cento Croce Brigades which, in self defence, were endeavouring to create a numerical strength equal to the political formations. Mario was still with us, and took in hand once again the duties of "Lord Chief Justice" of Rossano. There was little doubt that a political crisis was developing around us, and it was a question of time whether it would come to a head before the Allies broke through the Gothic Line. Aerial bombardment increased in the Magra valley, and on lines of communication leading to the Front, but I had an uneasy feeling that we were back where we had been two months before. In spite of its temporary occupation by the enemy, the Valley still remained by comparison the most prosperous territory in the 4th Partisan Zone, and greedy eyes were concentrated on it once again.

One morning I was standing in the small paved courtyard outside Amelia's house in Valle, where the radio operator of the American Mission Wala Wala had sent the message that had meant so much to me. A squad of men from Buzzo, led by young "Jock" Sartori, were trying their hand at assembling a light machine gun spread out on a blanket on the ground. Jock's real name was Angelo, but he had earned his nickname by the fact that he had lived most of his life in Cupar, Fife, and spoke both English and Italian with a broad Scots accent.

"Maggiore," he said suddenly. "We've got visitors."

I looked in the direction in which he was pointing. Coming up the hill from the next village were two priests, the leading one, a tall impressive figure of six foot or more, wearing a round clerical hat with a green band and tassel. The other I recognised as the village priest.

"Struth!" said Jock a moment later. "It's His Excellency himself – the Bishop of Pontremoli."

The men stopped what they were doing to stare open-mouthed. They looked a bloodthirsty crew, most of them wearing beards, their battle-dress uniforms grease-stained, and their hands grubby with oil. Some were sitting, some lying around the gun. Before I could do anything to introduce a more disciplined touch to the setting, the Bishop was upon us. Hurriedly I saluted.

He walked across the yard and stopped in front of me. Giovanni Sismondo, Bishop of Pontremoli, and a Prince of the Vatican State, was approaching his seventieth year. His hair was grey, and his clearly-drawn features and ruddy complexion gave an impression of great kindliness and strength of character. He looked at me for a moment through shrewd grey eyes, and then he smiled.

"I am looking for the English Major," he said. "Would that be you, by any chance?"

"Yes, Your Excellency." We shook hands.

"And these are your men?"

Some of my stalwarts had recovered from their confusion, and struggled to their feet. I was about to make excuses for their appearance, when one of them stepped forward, dropped on one knee, and kissed the ring on the Bishop's right hand.

"Bless you, my son," he said. This encouraged the others to follow suit, and then they stood round him in a shy semi-circle.

"Well," said the Bishop, his eyes twinkling, "You are putting in a little practice I see. Bravo. Bravo!" and he looked at the dismantled gun, and then at the men.

Feeling that perhaps I should have kissed his ring as well, and, as a Protestant, resenting the idea, I endeavoured to cover up my embarrassment with conversation.

"I have to keep them busy somehow, Your Excellency, otherwise they might get lazy."

"Quite right," he said. "That would never do, particularly if certain people got to hear of it with whom I understand you have recently had rather intimate relations. But if you have a moment to spare, Signor Maggiore, I would like to have a word with you alone. And then, perhaps, I could speak to some of the partisan leaders?"

I told Jock to collect as many as he could find and take them to the priest's house as quickly as possible, and then led the way into Amelia's house. Her mother was there, bending over the smoking stove. On seeing her distinguished guest she gave a startled cry and agitatedly removed a sack of potatoes from one of the wooden benches, after which she kissed the Bishop's ring. He gave her his blessing, and she bustled into another room as we sat down.

"Well, Maggiore, I have heard a great deal about you from time to time. I understand that you met Don Grigoletti of Adelana the day before his death?"

"Yes," I replied. "And I also knew Don Quiligotti of Colloretta. Both of them helped me, and other escaped prisoners, and I feel partly responsible for their deaths."

He remained silent for a moment.

"The responsibility was not yours – it was the will of God that they should leave this troubled world when they did. They were brave sons of the Church, and are now reaping their just reward; probably they are laughing together at the foolish manner in which we allow ourselves to be upset by our futile material problems. So please rule any idea of responsibility out of your mind. There is another matter regarding which I would like to enlist your help

He looked at me, waiting for an answer.

"Yes, Your Excellency?"

"As you are doubtless aware, Maggiore, Allied bombardment of the Magra valley is becoming intensified. The cities of Aulla and Villafranca have been razed to the ground, and now only Pontremoli remains comparatively unscathed. I beg of you, Maggiore, to intercede with the Allies not to treat Pontremoli as they have treated the other towns. I know that I am asking a great deal, and I would like you to give me a frank answer."

"I will have to think about that for a moment," I replied.

I took out my pipe and proceeded to fill it. Had anybody else asked me that question, the answer would have been brutally short. Coming from the Bishop it was different, for I knew sufficient about him already to realise that I was dealing with a man of profound wisdom, whose every action was guided by truly Christian principles. On the other hand, I had grave doubts as to whether I would be able to alter the course of events, for he was right in thinking that bombs might rain down on Pontremoli at any moment. Had he been a Fascist envoy who was pleading for mercy now that the moment of reckoning had come, my answer would have been that the Rossanesi had had their houses destroyed, and had suffered every possible hardship through eighteen long months, and I therefore did not care what happened to the comfortable city dwellers. But I could not give that answer to the Bishop, for he had suffered as greatly as the rest of us.

"Eccellenza," I said at last, "I have no control over the plans of the Allied High Command. As you must realise, Pontremoli has been an important assembly point for the enemy forces over many months. From the church tower at Arzelata, I myself have seen their transport parked under the trees beside the church of Annunziata, and I know that their garrisons are sheltered in the city. The Allies are justified in taking any action they can to weaken resistance on the Gothic Line and consequently to save Allied lives there."

"There is no disputing your argument, Maggiore, but you speak as a soldier; I am a man of peace. There are other things in Pontremoli more important to the human race than a few German soldiers. The church of Annunziata is an ancient monument dating from the XIIth century, and you know what happened to Cassino. There is also the cathedral, a large convent of nuns, a Franciscan monastery, the best equipped hospital in the Magra valley, an orphanage, and several schools. Must all these be destroyed because you want to exterminate your enemies?"

A cloud of acrid smoke belched from the stove while the Bishop waited for me to reply.

"There is one way," I said slowly, "in which I might be able to help. I can send a message to my Command in Florence, but I cannot guarantee that it will reach them in time or, if it does, that they will be able to prevent the bombardment. If I send that message, however, I must have detailed information as to exactly where the enemy are billeted. How can I obtain that information?"

The Bishop looked at me for a moment in silence. "That, Maggiore, is information that I cannot give you. As a leader of the Church I would be betraying my faith if I helped you to kill others who, after all, are God's creatures. But I understand perfectly what the position is, and your answer gives me confidence that, if you could, you would do your best to help me."

"It is not a very satisfactory answer, Eccellenza – as you see, there is little that I can do at the moment."

"God will find a solution," he replied, "I shall ask Him for guidance at prayer this evening. Thank you for having been so frank with me – I shall not forget it. Now shall we talk to the partisans? I have something to discuss with them that concerns you deeply."

We were about to stand up when we heard the clucking of an angry hen, and realised that it came from the bench on which we were sitting. The seat formed the lid of a wooden chest in which I knew that various household stores were kept. I lifted the lid and the enraged bird jumped out and scuttled across the room squawking loudly enough to waken the dead.

The Bishop chuckled. "Maggiore, we have been overheard."

Old Signora Sperinde hurried into the room, and chased the hen which came to rest at the Bishop's feet. With cries of "che brutta bestia" she picked it up and was overcome by confusion.

The Bishop smiled at her. "It's a very fine bird," he said, "and it must have been very tired of our chatter. Look after it well, Signora, and it will produce good eggs. My chickens in Pontremoli are not as fat as that."

We went out into the sunshine. A small crowd had collected in front of the priest's house, and they bowed to the Bishop as we passed through the courtyard. By now Jock had managed to find a few of the partisan leaders and they were waiting for us round a table in the living-room. Among them were Chris, Franco and Nino, Ferrari, Ermano, Avio and Mario. We sat down and the Bishop opened the proceedings.

"Figlioli, you must regard me for the moment not as your Bishop, but as a special Envoy sent on a Christian mission. I have come to-day at the request of the German High Command in Pontremoli to arrange for an exchange of prisoners."

There was a gasp of amazement, for such a thing had never happened to us before. A triumphant expression lit up Franco's face, while Mario – as was to be expected – began to stroke his beard. The others leant forward, their gleaming eyes fixed intently on the speaker.

"The Germans have instructed me to open negotiations on a basis of two partisans to be exchanged for each German prisoner in your hands. This offer is subject to certain conditions."

"Conditions?" remarked Franco.

Ermano intervened. "Two partisans to one German? No, more like six would be the answer. The prison in Pontremoli is full, isn't it, Eccellenza?"

"Now wait, Figlioli, and don't excite yourselves. You must not get exaggerated ideas into your heads. This is a delicate matter and the Germans are not going to consider wild and thoughtless suggestions. I have mentioned certain conditions. I have a note here to be given to the Maggiore Inglese – when he has read it we will continue the discussion." He handed me a piece of flimsy paper, on which a few lines were typewritten in English.

"Pontremoli,
3rd March, 1945.

I hereby wish to inform you that the German Command in Pontremoli is prepared to negotiate with the Head of the British Mission in the Rossano Valley for an exchange of prisoners, time, place and date to be arranged by bearer.

Heil Hitler
Signed Herman Muller
(Captain)."

"Well I'll be damned," I said in English.

"I beg your pardon?" said the Bishop. I felt that a literal translation was not essential to the cause.

"Eccellenza, this is from a Captain Muller who says he commands the German garrison in Pontremoli. Is that correct?"

"Yes," said the Bishop. "Quite correct."

"He states that he is prepared to negotiate an exchange of prisoners with me as Head of the British Mission."

"Well, Maggiore?"

"Before we go any further, I must point out that I am not prepared to meet Captain Muller over this. If an exchange is to take place, he must address his request to Colonel Fontana as commander of the 4th Partisan Zone and representative of the legal Italian Government. Technically, my mission is only attached to his command for liaison duties."

"Bravo, Maggiore," said Ermano, the first to realise the implications. "It's no good the Germans trying to hide behind the Allies."

Mario took up the argument.

"Dunque – the Maggiore is right, but it would be as well to start making preparations for an exchange all the same. Have we any idea how many partisans the Germans hold? Perhaps His Excellency can tell us?"

The Bishop drew a notebook from an inside pocket.

"The day before yesterday there were twenty-four in the Pontremoli gaol. Of these, ten are likely to receive sentences of imprisonment. The remaining fourteen are due to be shot in the near future."

"Those under sentence of death are the ones who should be exchanged," said Franco.

"How many German prisoners do you hold?" asked the Bishop.

There fell an embarrassed silence. I heard Franco murmur into his beard, "I had two, but I sent them to chop wood," and Nino kicked him violently under the table. "Tagliare la legna" was another partisan phrase meaning that the victims had been shot. Franco was a wise and just commander, and I knew that if he had shot prisoners they had richly deserved it, but they would now have been much more use to us alive. I thought of our German sergeant languishing in Dani's stronghold – his rank ought to be worth at least three partisans. At length we arrived at the magic figure of seven. Ermano thought that the Colonel had a few tucked away somewhere, and it was decided to refer the matter to him before we sent an official reply.

"Are they interested in Fascist prisoners?" asked Franco rather wistfully. It was a matter dear to his heart, for he had made a hobby of plucking them out of the fields and hedgerows near most of the towns on the edge of the zone. Recently he had added to his collection the brother of the Prefect of Pontremoli, and his chief secretary.

"No," replied the Bishop. "But the Prefect is, poor man."

Mario spoke again.

"Might we suggest, Eccellenza, that we exchange on the basis of three partisans to one German? They can't have it all their own way. We might also suggest two partisans for one Fascist."

The Bishop's eyes twinkled.

"The trouble is," he said, "nobody seems to want Fascists any more now. But I will do what I can, once the Colonel has expressed his opinion."

The discussion ended, the Bishop said that he had to return to Pontremoli that night. He had come all the way on foot – a strenuous climb of over four hours that would have tried a much younger man – and he had to walk back again. I offered him an escort, but this he politely refused.

"I am used to it, Maggiore," he said, "and an escort might make a bad impression. I trust the people of my diocese, particularly the Rossanesi. I doubt if there are any people in the world who have so few possessions as the people of this Valley, but their hearts are made of gold. Not that they are always obedient," he added with a smile,

"I gather from their Priest that church attendance is poor – but perhaps it is that they live their religion instead of paying it lip service."

I accompanied him to the frontier, and said good-bye near the point where the memorial now stands. "I shall not forget your remarks about a message to the Allies," he said, "God bless you, and may we meet again soon in happier surroundings." With that he went on his way towards Arzelato.

Twenty-four hours later, one of Franco's men came to find me in Valle. He, like many of the others, came from the Pontremoli suburb of Annunziata, and knew the city well. Chris was with me when he handed over a bulky envelope. On opening it, I found a long report written with great care by one who was obviously not accustomed to writing anything, for the message included many spelling mistakes. It contained details of all the places in and around the city where the enemy garrison was lodged, and a description of their daily routine. "Where did you get this?" I asked the messenger.

He grinned at me.

"Maggiore," he said, "I found it under a tree."

"I see," I replied, taking the hint. "Thank you, it is most useful. Will you tell the tree when you next see it that I am sending a message to the Allied Command to-night?"

Chris and I worked on the message, for he knew more about these things than I did, and it was duly sent to Special Force headquarters with a plea that, if Pontremoli was to be bombed, every effort should be made to spare those buildings in which the enemy was not lodged. We had little hope that it would be considered by the Higher Command, harassed as they were by more important considerations, but we had done our best.

Rumours of an Allied offensive grew increasingly persistent, with resulting complications in the 4th Partisan Zone, but in spite of several requests for some kind of briefing for the future, we could obtain no confirmation of the rumours. Special Force headquarters seemed to shut up like a clam. I came to the reluctant conclusion that we had better go to Florence and find out what part the Blundell Mission was to play when the big attack began. Jock and Falco were sent on in advance, for I would have need of them if we were to return, and a visit to headquarters would do wonders for their prestige. Special Force agreed to the proposal that I should leave the Valley for a while and sent an officer to replace me – at least Chris and I had the satisfaction of knowing that our stamping ground had now become of some importance to the Allies, largely due to the activities of the S.A.S. Bob was busy arranging for the parachutists to be dropped into a Special Force Mission near Reggio Emilia, and asked that Franco and his men should join them. It was a great honour and one that so far as we knew had not been bestowed on partisans anywhere else in Italy. Franco was keen to go but the Colonel, anxious as he was, preferred to keep him in the Valley, for which decision he could hardly be blamed. In due course, another squadron of the S.A.S. was sent in to my successor, and so the Valley was protected until the end from invasion by the political formations.

A few days before our departure, Avio brought news from Pontremoli that there had been an air attack on the city. Three Spitfires shot out of the sky and machine-gunned all the targets that had been indicated in our message. None of the civilian institutions had been damaged – except for a few broken windows at the Nunnery – and the enemy, alarmed by the accuracy of the attack, moved most of their garrison into the surrounding woods. "Now, Maggiore," said a jubilant Avio, "they know what it is like to be hunted." How Special Force achieved the miracle I was never able to discover, but it had a far more profound effect on the population then wholesale bombardment would have done. I wondered whether the people of Pontremoli realised how much they owed to their Bishop.

Part IV

Liberation

Chapter Nineteen

Through the Enemy Lines

We left the Valley on the morning of March the 15th, a small party consisting of Chris, Avio, Ardito the courier, myself, and Colonel Grossi. The colonel accompanied us at the request of Fontana, with the forlorn hope of inducing the Government of Marshal Badoglio to restrain the politicians before it was too late. Franco provided us with an escort as far as Dani's kingdom. We passed through Montereggio where the partisan commander Tigre paraded his men and a detachment of the International Battalion for my final inspection, and then cheered us on our way. Dani prepared a farewell feast at Calice, and he and some of the International Battalion who now served under him escorted us to the boundary of the 4th Partisan Zone, above the valley of the Magra river. A special guide had been sent to take us south, one Pietro Giampetri, who came from the village of Crespiano high up in the mountains behind Carrara. That night I shaved off my beard – the recognised insignia of the partisan – and sent it with an appropriate farewell message to Mario. He tells me he still has it to this day.

Pietro was an excellent guide, and steered us safely through the mountains for three days, when we were handed over to a Special Force guide sent to conduct us through the enemy lines. The journey took ten days in all, and not a shot was fired at us. At dawn on the 25th we threaded our way through a minefield sown in the woods, and came upon the outskirts of Barga.

The town had been damaged in successive air raids by both sides. The enemy still held observation posts overlooking it to the north, and the daily strafe began shortly before we reached it, but the guns were now located at a greater distance than they had been for months and the shells fell among the already battered houses on the perimeter of the town.

Our column had swelled in numbers on the way, for we could not avoid other refugees attaching themselves to it, so that we now numbered more than fifteen. We entered the town and then saw our first Allied soldier, an American negro, leaning against the doorway of a house warmed by the rising sun, and enjoying a cigarette.

"Can you direct me to the Military Police Headquarters?" I asked him.

"Sure," he drawled without changing position. "Straight along the road, through the square, first turning right, and the house is the third on your right."

Chris and I went on, followed by Colonel Grossi, Avio and Ardito, the rest of the column, through force of habit, in single file behind them. Somehow our arrival seemed rather an anti-climax. As we crossed the square, Chris laughed.

"You know," he said, "I have an idea that the next hour or two might be quite exciting. Not a sentry has challenged us, and here we are in the middle of the town. Something tells me that the local Brigade Major will not be amused."

We reached the house – a luxurious villa set in its own garden – and walked through the gate, the column following. There was something ridiculously incongruous about ringing the front door bell. We told the others to wait outside while Chris and I were admitted by a uniformed servant. The officer on duty was at breakfast, but we insisted on presenting ourselves and came upon him eating porridge surrounded by all the appurtenances of a civilised breakfast table. After our ten days' march we neither of us looked exactly elegant, which may partly have accounted for the storm that followed.

It was disgraceful, perfectly disgraceful, that we should be there at all, for it was impossible for anybody to enter Barga without being stopped by a patrol, therefore we were probably enemy spies. Furthermore we had committed the outrage of having arrived at the officer's private residence accompanied by a crowd of other suspicious characters. We had no identification papers and could not prove that we were who we said we were. Why had no message been received to say that we would be arriving that morning? Why did our uniforms look so scruffy – didn't we know how to turn out on parade? And so it went on. In the middle of the explosion – the officer concerned being my junior in rank – Chris and I sat down and proceeded to join in the breakfast, and that did nothing to improve the atmosphere. Threats flew round the room; taking my cue from Chris, I said nothing and concentrated on enjoying to the full the almost forgotten taste of crisp toast, butter, and marmalade. At last our enraged host ran out of breath and Chris leapt into the breach.

"Of course, you could telephone to Florence," he said, his mouth full of cornflakes.

"Do you know the number?"

"Mm," he said, and gave it to him.

"Then why the hell didn't you say so before?"

"Hadn't much chance," and he gulped down a cup of coffee.

As luck would have it, the line was out of order, so we were shown to a couple of bedrooms upstairs, when it was explained to us that we were under open arrest, and on no account could leave the building. That did not worry us. There were hot baths available, and we spent the morning bathing and sleeping, revelling in a sense of security, and happy to let the wheels of bureaucracy grind in their own slow way. Colonel Grossi, Avio, and Ardito were less fortunate, and were obliged to spend their time in a concentration camp rubbing shoulders with representatives of the enemy they had been fighting for the past eighteen months, until we were able to bail them out.

By the afternoon, contact was established with Florence, and then things happened with amazing speed. Orderlies rushed hither and thither to obey our slightest whim. Cigarettes and beer were pressed upon us – "you know, old boy, we have to obey regulations; no ill feelings, I hope?" – and a car arrived from Florence to take us to Special Force Headquarters. We arrived at the villa in Via delle Forbici that night.

Preparations were in full swing for the coming offensive against the Gothic Line, and the place was humming with activity. Geoff was waiting for me, and we spent some busy days producing a long report on the Blundell Mission and filling in gaps on operational maps. Avio was rushed further south to carry out brief training as a parachutist and was then dropped in again to the Valley to command the International Battalion. Ardito, Falco and Jock returned through the lines on foot. I was briefed for further operations by the Special Force staff.

Activity in the 4th Partisan Zone flared up again. Following their last series of punitive expeditions the enemy concentrated on reinforcing their front line and the partisans attacked their transport columns without respite. Reports came in of bridges destroyed, lorry loads of enemy troops blown up on mines sown in the roads, attacks on barracks and ammunition dumps, and a ship moored at the quayside in Spezia harbour loaded for transfer to Genoa sank mysteriously during the night. During the first week in April, the Psychological Warfare Branch transmitted a broadcast for me to the Valley. It stated that the final day of reckoning with the enemy was at hand, and I sent personal greetings to the partisan commanders – the Colonel, Richetto, Dani, Mario, Franco, and Ermano. The message was picked up in the Valley, and passed on by word of mouth.

That night a group of partisans were climbing laboriously up into the mountains from the Via Aurelia, carrying a heavy burden on their shoulders. Shortly after midnight they reached a village and were told of the broadcast. Gently they laid the body of their dead commander at the foot of a chestnut tree. Moonlight filtered through the branches and fell upon the pale drawn features of Ermano and what remained of his shattered body. He had been killed a few hours before with two of his comrades while attacking a convoy of German vehicles near Borghetto. Like so many of the best, he had died in action against those who had ruined his country – he would not see the results of the long months of endurance, nor enjoy the fruits of the victory that had been so hardly won.

Within ten days I set off once again towards the north, provided with a jeep and a British driver, Harry Lewis. My instructions were to join the American 5th Army who were preparing to advance on the Viareggio front and, when opportunity offered, to break through the line and spur the partisans of the 4th Zone into descending on the naval port of La Spezia.

The offensive began badly; for a while we were stuck at Viareggio and then by slow degrees moved forward to the famous marble city of Carrara. I made contact with the local partisans, and set up a courier service to cover the Magra valley. Two of the most outstanding of these couriers were Paolo Buonaguidi, a young Army lieutenant who came from Sarzana, a town halfway between Carrara and La Spezia, and a certain Elio who had been born and bred in Venezia Giulia, and regarded mountain territory as his natural heritage. Elio struck up a friendship with Lewis, and they would disappear at night for what they described as "reconnaissance" trips into the front line, and never failed to return without a sinister trophy. Then there was Major Contri of the Italian Army who had created a force of partisans some time before among the marble quarries. He came to receive orders, and carried back mule loads of badly needed ammunition and supplies. Others came from the mountains of the Garfagnana which overlooked the right flank of the 5th Army, and returned to prepare their forces for the final attack.

The Carrara front was a difficult one to break. Several times it wavered, and then hardened again, but at long last the day came when Sarzana remained the only large town between us and my ultimate objective of La Spezia.

Chapter Twenty

The Road to La Spezia

Sarzana lies in a dusty plain at the mouth of the river Magra. It is one of those cities where the advent of Fascism had been hotly opposed, and it had its martyrs many years before the outbreak of war – martyrs whose memory is kept fresh to-day by a marble tablet set in a wall of the town hall in the main square. Partisans were numerous in the foothills to the east and had suffered heavily from enemy reprisals. Giorgio, their leader, was a young artisan who had been employed in a factory in Sarzana until he took to the hills. He had worked with other Allied missions and had served them well. The role that I assigned him was not easy. At a given moment his force was to attack the city in collaboration with the advancing Allied troops, so as to create a diversion and make the enemy disperse their forces in all directions. If the garrison withdrew, he was to assume control of the town until the American commander arrived. He was warned to keep the partisans clear of the approaches to the city until a pre-arranged Allied artillery barrage had been completed. Giorgio's only comment was to express a hope that the shells of his collaborators would not hit the main hotel, as he was looking forward to making it his headquarters.

The operation began, and for a while all went well. As usual, however, the Germans were prepared for it; they commenced an intensive bombardment of the route along which the 5th Army were advancing, using heavy batteries that had been established long before in an impregnable position at Punto Bianco, where the waters of the River Magra join the Mediterranean. Before the day was out, the advance came to a standstill. The partisans entered the outskirts of the city but were obliged to withdraw again when enemy reinforcements arrived from Aulla to the north-east. The stalemate lasted for a day. Orders went out to the partisan formations in the mountains calling on them to attack the lines of communication at three widely dispersed points at the same time. One of these points was on the road between Aulla and Sarzana, and the partisans responded with such effect that the Germans panicked. Under cover of darkness they blew up the coastal batteries that had delayed the advance and began to withdraw, some towards Pontremoli and the dangerous Cisa Pass, and some along the Via Aurelia through La Spezia. The 5th Army swung to the north-east in pursuit, and advanced along the valley of the Magra. The long drawn out war of Liberation was nearing its end, and its final stages had cost the partisans of Sarzana more than ninety men in casualties.

On the day that the enemy front collapsed, I moved forward to the ancient castle in the village of Castelnuovo Magra, together with a British Artillery lieutenant who was laying down harassing fire on the retreating enemy columns. Watching from the ramparts, we saw the railway bridge over the river dissolve in a cloud of dust as the Germans destroyed it. Below us lay Sarzana, where we could hear sporadic bursts of rifle fire. The partisan Elio had gone ahead to explore in the hope of making contact with some of Dani's men on the far side of the river. Throughout the morning we watched the American infantry units moving slowly forward.

I got into the jeep and we moved along the road towards the city. Progress was slow, for the road was pitted with shell holes and the bridges over the many canals had been destroyed. On the outskirts, trees bordering the road had been cut down to form tank obstacles. We reached the town square, which was littered with rubble from the surrounding houses. Sarzana was a dead city, and the smell of blistered iron and stonework filled the air.

Giorgio was waiting for me near the town hall and Elio was with him. The partisan commander grinned happily.

"They haven't hit the hotel, Maggiore," he said. "Come and have a drink with me to celebrate the Liberation; there is still some good wine left."

We walked across the square and sat down in the deserted hotel bar. Elio, unshaven and dishevelled after many hours of walking, did not speak until the first bottle was empty. Then he lit a cigarette and told me the result of his wanderings.

He had crossed the river that morning and had made contact with a group of partisans on the other side. From them he learnt that Dani and his men were engaged in battle further along the valley, but they did not know exactly where he was. There was still an enemy detachment in La Spezia – or at least there had been the evening before – and Colonel Fontana with the partisans of the 4th Zone was preparing to block their retreat along the Via Aurelia to Genoa. All enemy craft had left the port, but there was sniping going on in the city. He did not know whether any of the main buildings had been mined with booby traps.

"In any case, Maggiore," he concluded, "The road should be clear as far as La Spezia – shall we go and have a look at it?"

Harry Lewis took his place at the wheel of the jeep, with a look of happy anticipation on his face, and we wound our way out of the town towards the river. The battle raged on our right now, for the artillery had moved forward and was concentrating on the outer defences of Aulla. We followed a rough cart track, traversing fields where the wheat was already high; I felt a peculiar satisfaction in knowing that the harvest would not be stolen by the enemy this time. We arrived at the river bed, and began to cross it, keeping close under cover of the ruined bridge. We were halfway across when rifle shots rang out from the opposite bank and figures emerged from the railway tunnel. Elio recognised them as the partisans whom he had met that morning, and shouted,

"Va bene, ragazzi, we are Allies."

They were waiting by the water when we reached the opposite bank. They explained that the ground between the river and the road was sown with mines, and they guided us safely through them. Once on the main road, they pointed the way to La Spezia.

"Good luck. Look out for the Brigata Nera – they may have hidden snipers in the houses." We left them standing looking rather wistfully at our disappearing jeep.

It was a fantastic journey that followed. The afternoon was drawing to a close and the sun hung low in the sky, ready to sink from view behind a tree-covered ridge that ended abruptly in the cliffs of Punto Bianco We reached a place where a mass of stones blocked the roadway from a fallen wall, and a squad of civilians was working feverishly to clear a passage. Lewis was shown a way round, and we bumped across a ploughed field until we reached the asphalt again near the suburb of Migliarina. News of our coming had preceded us in the mysterious way that such news travels in the mountains, and we found the road into the city lined with spectators. As we sped past, people clapped enthusiastically and flowers were showered upon us until the jeep was covered. Elio sat at the back, his face expressionless, clasping his Sten gun, and watching for a sign of hostility, for without doubt many of those spectators had been dressed in army uniform only a short while before. The crowd broke into cheers. I stood up and saluted.

"I wouldn't have missed this for anything, sir," said Harry. "You wait until I tell the folks at home about it – they have never seen anything like this in Wales, and I will be given free beer for a week, I will."

"They probably won't believe you," I said.

We steered a stately course along the sea front, and then turned into the Piazza Verdi. There was a dense crowd in the square, so dense that at last we were obliged to stop altogether. I stood up on the bonnet of the jeep, and shouted to make myself heard above the roar of cheering "civilians".

"Where is the acting Prefect? Will somebody ask him to come here, please."

At this the excitement increased. There were cries of "Inglesi! Inglesi!" and still more flowers were showered upon us. Men jumped on to the vehicle and wrung our hands, while women embraced us hysterically. There was something theatrical about the scene – the half-light of approaching night, the sea of upturned faces, the flowers, the noise, and the majestic building of the Prefettura looming overhead. It only lacked Verdi's music to complete the opera. At length a tall figure could be seen struggling through the crowd.

"I am the acting Prefect," shouted the newcomer. "Welcome, welcome!"

He was dressed in the white uniform of a commander of the Italian Navy, and his name was Bussalino. Somehow he managed to clear a way to the door of the building in which the Prefect's apartments were situated, and called somebody to guard the jeep. Then he took us to the office of the Chief of Police, which I was surprised to find plentifully furnished with armchairs and a large mahogany desk covered with stationery in such disorder that the previous occupant had obviously departed in haste not long before.

A miscellaneous crowd of happy townsfolk followed us into the room until it could hold no more and somebody closed the doors. It was quite dark by now and an empty bottle was produced with a lighted candle wedged in its neck. Commandante Bussalino drew the heavy curtains across the windows, and we sat down to consider what to do next.

Most of those present had escaped from the prisons a few days before, when the main body of the enemy garrison had left the city to establish positions on the Via Aurelia to cover their retreat towards Genoa. Their last act had been to shoot hostages in the suburbs. At Le Grazie alone seven youngsters had been murdered by the Brigata Nera. An attempt had been made to destroy the lighting and water supplies, but with only partial success, and I was told that it would be possible to get the trams running, and the lighting repaired in the main streets, within twenty-four hours. There were some pockets of resistance in the city, especially near the barracks in the northern suburb of La Chiappa. None of the buildings had been mined.

While all this was being explained to me, Elio and Harry were wandering about the room peering into cupboards on the hunt for souvenirs. They found a collection of photographs, apparently those of hostages and people who had fallen under suspicion, for some of the citizens present recognised friends among them. On a shelf in one of the cupboards was a pile of bayonets, and these were quickly distributed Then Elio tired of the game and came over to the desk.

"Maggiore, these people say that there are more than thirty Fascists and Germans shut up in a house near here – may we go and have a look at them?"

"They are said to be only lightly armed," Harry joined in. "I think we ought to have a little talk with them, sir."

An expectant hush fell upon the spectators. I accepted a cigarette from the Commandant, and lit it from the spluttering candle, which threw wavering shadows against the walls, creating a macabre atmosphere that was certainly appropriate.

"There's no need to run your heads into danger," I said. "You'd better wait until the partisans arrive."

"We'll be careful, sir," the driver pleaded, and added with a grin, It would be a shame to let them feel that they had been forgotten. Besides there are some people outside to keep us company."

"All right, but no funny business. If there are any Germans, they are to be brought here." I saw a steely glint in Elio's eyes. "Alive," I added. His expression changed to one of acute disappointment. They left the room followed by several eager citizens.

Information about the partisans of the 4th Zone was vague. They were known to be in position ready to ambush the enemy's retreating columns but nobody could say exactly where. There was a small formation of clandestine saboteurs in La Spezia, but they were not strong enough to resist a German counter-attack. Commandante Bussalino said that we must do our best to prevent alarm spreading among the population, and he hoped that the main bulk of the 5th Army would arrive soon. I thought it kinder not to break the news to him that the 5th Army were at that moment in full pursuit of the enemy along the Magra valley. My wireless set was still at Castelnuovo Magra, for when we had left that afternoon I hardly expected to find myself within a few hours the uneasy possessor of one of Italy's most important naval bases, complete with its unarmed population. If the Germans did put in a counter attack against the unprotected left flank of the 5th Army, the resulting chaos would not be pleasant. Some of the local underground workers had reported by this time, and I sent two of them off with appropriate messages to the Americans.

Shortly after midnight, enemy shells fell in the northern suburb of La Chiappa, killing a woman. They were believed to come from a vessel outside the harbour, for parts of the coast were patrolled by speed-boats sent from Genoa to look for disbanded units that might attempt to escape by sea. Throughout the night messengers arrived at the Prefettura, bringing wildly exaggerated reports of German troops posted in different parts of the city. Eventually Harry and Elio returned with five hungry, bedraggled and utterly demoralised German prisoners, whom they swore were all that they could find. I handed them over to be lodged in the notorious prison at Villa Andraini, where so many partisans, and probably our men of the S.A.S., had been shot in the course of the past year.

By dawn a number of partisans had drifted in from the outlying districts, and they were organised into sentries and a makeshift police force. Bussalino took over the ex-Prefect's office, and I settled down in a chair to snatch a few hours' sleep.

I was suddenly awakened in the middle of the morning by the sound of running feet in the street outside the window. The curtains were still drawn; I pulled them aside and looked out on to the square An angry roar began and grew louder and louder as a crowd converged on the Piazza Verdi from all directions, surrounding a man in civilian clothing whom they had recognised as a member of the Brigata Nera. I saw what was about to happen, and could do nothing to prevent it. The miserable wretch screamed as the crowd closed in on him, and then disappeared under their feet. As suddenly as it had begun, the yelling ceased. The crowd melted away, as if ashamed of what they had done, dazed by the fact that, after twenty years of despotism, they had the power to do it. A gory mess of human flesh lay in the square, bathed in the bright spring sunshine, and I turned away from the window duly sobered by my first taste of mob violence. By the time the American advanced guard arrived that evening, the Piazza Verdi was clean again.

*   *   *

As might have been expected, Franco and his men were the first to answer my call – they arrived in La Spezia shortly before the Americans. I was proud of them that day, for their appearance was smart and they did much to restore the confidence of the population. Franco was quick to appreciate the atmosphere and sent out patrols to find the mythical pockets of resistance. He had brought with him a few men from Pontremoli – Lupo, Elio, Edmundo and Lino – and his quartermaster, Nino Ferrari, who lived in the village of Vezzano Ligure in the mountains overlooking the bay of Lerici. Nino refused to part with his beard, and wears it still as a permanent reminder of his life as a partisan. Franco told me that an exchange of prisoners had taken place after I left the Valley, and all those under sentence of death had been retrieved from the prison. Falco, Ardito and Jock turned up, so that once more I had with me men of the International Battalion.

Contact was re-established with Special Force and I received orders to remain in La Spezia to supervise the rehabilitation of my partisans. The administration was to be handed over to the Allied Military Government, but for two days its representatives, sent hurriedly from Massa, showed a marked reluctance to establish themselves in such dangerous surroundings. There was in fact little danger, but rumours continued to circulate of enemy rearguard actions on the Via Aurelia, and distant sounds of battle floated into the city on the prevailing wind. The 5th Army eventually sent a force along the coast road to liberate the port of Genoa and the fighting died down. On the 24th of April, I went out to the heights above La Chiappa, and waited on the bend of the road where it begins to climb towards the pass that takes it to Borghetto.

Presently I heard the tramp of marching feet, and the songs of the partisans began to echo round the hills. Then a lone figure came into view round the next bend. It was Colonel Fontana, leading the men of the 4th Zone into their liberated capital. I saluted as he reached me and we shook hands, repeating in miniature the Wellington and Blucher touch. As we marched down the hill, crowds lined the pavements and cheered frantically. Flowers were showered upon us, and printed leaflets floated down from the rooftops welcoming the partisans, acclaiming them the new "Garibaldini". The column made an impressive sight winding through the close packed streets, the men singing and calling to their friends, the red scarves that so many of them were wearing adding a further patch of colour to the sunshine, the flowers, and the carpets and curtains fluttering from the windows in our honour. Women ran from doorways to embrace us, and shopkeepers along the route thrust sweets, cakes and wine into our hands. The column halted in the Piazza Verdi, where I was asked to inspect the partisans for the last time, and they were officially disbanded. Then followed three days of festivity when good-will abounded and all thoughts were turned upon the Allied Military Government that had come to right all wrongs.

The Government at last settled in to the Prefettura and I began my task of dismantling the machine that Special Force had so effectively helped to construct. It was a bitter experience.

Mario and Avio marched in with the others; Mario left us to continue with his interrupted career, and his resonant "Dunque" began once again to echo round the Spezia Law Courts. Avio returned to service with the Italian Air Force. With Falco, Ardito and Jock, I toured the area, trying to help my partisans in their return to civilian life.

Dani had ended the war fighting at Aulla, preparing the way for the 5th Army. The small town is dominated by the Fortezza della Brunella, a fine mediaeval fortress that had been requisitioned from its English owner, Aubrey Waterfield, by a Fascist regiment, the Xa Flottilla M.A.S. In ancient days it had played an important part in local history. Dani managed to contain the enemy within its walls until the American artillery reached it, when Aulla was liberated and the garrison fled, leaving behind the usual legacy of ruin and desolation.

The Beretta brothers and Richetto, with their brigades, were among those who marched triumphantly into the city of Parma, and occupied it before the arrival of the British and Italian armies. Communist formations were in the majority, for their leaders had trebled their numbers a month before the end hoping thereby to influence the elections in their favour when the time came. Guglielmo, Gino, and Richetto returned in disgust to their mountains, and their men had no part in the murder and looting that took place before the arrival of the Allied Military Government. Events in the plains of Emilia – particularly the atrocities committed in the city of Bologna – did much to influence the opinions of Allied Military Governors against the partisans, and, my mission in La Spezia being what it was, I soon began to feel the repercussions.

I was my own free agent, attached to the Government as Liaison Officer for Partisan Affairs, which meant that I could go where I liked in the province. Harry Lewis and a partisan courier accompanied me, and we visited all the towns on the gulf of La Spezia, from Pontovenere to Lerici; we toured the "Cinque Terre" where we found "Bacciccia", the railway worker at Vernazza, who told us of his adventures with the "A" Force Missions. At Levanto I met a lady who had helped several British escaped prisoners, one of them a colonel whom she hid in her house for six weeks and nursed through a serious illness, in spite of the fact that half of the villa had been commandeered by the Germans, who were in residence there. She was a very brave woman, the Baronness Massola Taliacarne, and the people of Levanto loved her for it. At Varese Ligure we met Richetto and his two chaplains, Don Bordigoni and Don Luigi, who had returned to their respective parishes in the mountains, saddened by the course that events were taking. We went back to Torpiana and Calice, to find men of the International Battalion who had returned to their homes, to till the fields and raise families, puzzled and disillusioned by the stories that reached them of "Partisans" turned bandits and causing trouble to the Government authorities. I visited the prisons and interceded for men who had been sentenced for carrying firearms after they had been ordered to surrender them, and I called on innumerable Italian Government officials and business men, to seek employment for partisans who were out of work; they had been received with cynical smiles and cold looks, and turned away with evasive answers. It was small wonder that the A.M.G. officials, knowing nothing of partisans during their slow journey from Sicily to the north, should be influenced by the opinions of the opportunists and sycophants who surrounded them, most of whom had spent the war hidden safely far from the sound of battle. Gradually it became painfully obvious to me that I could do little for the partisans, and I grew irritable and longed for England.

The climax came quite suddenly.

One day, with Falco, I went to the fishing village of Fezzano on the gulf of Spezia to find the de Santo family, whose only son Riboncia had been killed with Nello in January. It was a harrowing interview, for the aged parents were heartbroken, and there was little I could do to comfort them. To make it worse, the sister of Riboncia was there as well, and insisted on hearing all the details of his death and of his funeral, and collapsed into hysterics at the end of it. Falco and I slunk out of the house, feeling like damned souls, the girl's screams of "Vigliacchi Fascisti!" ringing in our ears.

We were silent as we walked along the water front, and turned towards the road where Harry Lewis was to pick us up in the jeep. Coming down the steps from the roadway was an A.M.G. captain. I was in uniform as usual; on seeing me, he asked me to have a drink with him.

"Thanks," I said. "I could do with one now."

He had some business or other in the area, and had billeted himself in a requisitioned house nearby. I was shown into a small living-room, and Falco, ever the loyal partisan escort, followed me in. On the table was a bottle of whisky and two glasses.

"Not a bad joint, this," said the captain, "if it wasn't for the natives. They are always wanting something and they yell throughout the God-darned day."

"Do you understand the language?" I asked, my hackles rising.

I knew that Falco could not understand, so his feelings could not, be offended by anything that might follow, but I suddenly realised that mine could. It was almost funny to realise how sensitive I had become on behalf of the Italian peasants and partisans.

"No," he replied. "No need to – no object in learning their bloody language when you've got an interpreter, is there? Have a whisky?" He half filled one of the glasses. "I reckon your chap here wants one too – they generally do." He poured some into the other glass, then turned towards the open door.

"Maria! " he yelled. "Portare another bicchiere and make it pronto."

There was a muffled reply. A moment later a girl came in and set the glass down on the table. She was young and very pretty, with an attractive figure, and she smiled at the captain, who responded by slapping her on the bottom. I was looking at her, my senses responding to her attraction, when my partisan instincts flashed a warning signal. It was only then that I took in the fact that she was wearing a scarf bound round her head, turban fashion. At the same moment she looked at Falco, and the laughter died on her lips. Something passed between them, and I saw Falco clench his fists.

Our host, quite oblivious, went on talking.

"Good girl, Maria, you know how to look after me. Sit down now, and have one yourself." He passed the glasses round; Falco refused his.

"Now, Major, you see Maria – don't you think she's wonderful? As pretty as you can find. You wouldn't think anybody would want to hurt her, would you?"

I said nothing.

"And yet they did. I found her in Leghorn, and those god-darned sons of bitches of partisans had shaved off all her hair. Can you imagine it? A sweet little thing like that, who couldn't hurt a fly. Jesus, if I catch any of those bloody partisans, I'll cut their throats."

Before my eyes flashed the vision of Violetta, screaming with hysteria a few doors away. I swallowed the whisky in one gulp.

"Thanks for the drink," I said, "Andiamo, Falco," and we walked out of the house, followed by a surprised shout of "Hi, what's the matter? Have another drink!"

Fortunately Harry was waiting with the jeep. We both climbed in front beside him, and he looked at me as if to speak, and changed his mind. We had been through a good deal of this kind of thing together during the three weeks since we had arrived in La Spezia, and he knew the signs. He drove back to the city.

It was Falco who spoke first.

"That woman," he said. "She was a spy."

"I know, I know," I replied wearily. "Shut up, can't you?"

He relapsed into silence, an angry flush on his face. After a while I began to feel that I had behaved like what the captain would have described as "one of the natives", but I had good reason. The incident was the last of a series in which I had heard the partisans reviled and slandered by people who knew nothing whatever about them – it was not for this that so many of the youth of the country had given their lives in the War of Liberation. Probably the captain didn't know about his girl friend. The punishment meted out to women who had betrayed their country and informed against the partisans was that of having their heads shaved, so that they could not hide their crime before the general public. In France or Yugoslavia they would have been shot. It was an education to see how many women wearing turbans arrived in the wake of the Allied Military Government, and they were getting away with it, adding their little drops of poison to the general mixture. I decided that it was high time that I left La Spezia.

Next morning I went to see the Military Governor, one of the wisest and most efficient administrators that A.M.G. produced in the whole of Italy. He heard me out patiently, then told me to sit down, and offered me a cigarette. Then he lectured me like a father. At the end of it he smiled.

"All the same," he said, "I can well understand your feelings – you know more about the partisans than any of us – but I don't think you fully appreciate our difficulties. You tell me that you want to leave La Spezia at once. Come back to-morrow, and if you are of the same mind, I will give you my answer."

I saluted and returned to my room in the Albergo Firenze.

The following morning I reported at the Prefettura and found the Colonel waiting for me.

"Well?" he said.

"I still want to go, sir, and would like to leave to-day."

"I thought you would, as you are the obstinate type," he said, his eyes twinkling. "Very well, then. I have been in touch with Special Force, and they have lent you to A.M.G. for another six weeks."

"Six weeks, sir?" My voice must have sounded like one condemned to death.

"You are to report for orders to the Allied Military Governor of Massa, and the sooner you leave the better." He stood up.

We shook hands and I saluted; as I reached the door, he added:

"I think you will find the new job more in your line. Thank you for all you have done here, and good luck."

Chapter Twenty-One

His Excellency

"Your tea, Excellency – it is 7 o'clock."

The voice spoke from a vast distance, and dragged me back to consciousness from a dream in which the Valley figured, and a cascina with a leaking roof and bare boards on which I was trying to sleep, while sheep bleated in the stall below.

I opened my eyes and could not remember where I was.

Bright sunlight poured through the high windows, on to the damask curtains, to fall in golden patches on the marble floor. Above me stretched a painted ceiling depicting overfed warriors on overfed horses riding through clouds. I lay between soft sheets in a large State bed, and saw myself reflected in the mirrors that stretched from floor to ceiling against the walls. There was not a chestnut leaf to be seen anywhere. My uniform, carefully brushed and pressed, lay across a Louis XIV gilded chair, a pair of brightly polished shoes beneath it. I blinked, and looked at them again, faintly surprised that they should belong to me.

My tea, steaming in a porcelain teapot, stood on a silver tray on the table beside the bed.

"What time would Your Excellency care to take breakfast?"

"At eight o'clock."

The servant glided through the long panelled doors, closing them silently behind him.

I shaved and dressed, and at five minutes to eight, walked into the corridor. Marble busts on pedestals glared reproachfully as I traversed it, to descend the broad staircase leading down to the entrance hall. Two uniformed Carabinieri stood on duty at each side of the main doors. As I arrived on the last step, they drew themselves up, and saluted.

"Buon giorno," I greeted them.

"Buon giorno, Eccellenza."

I entered the banqueting hall. At the far end of a long mahogany table, a place was laid for one, another servant standing behind the high armchair.

Deferentially, he waited for me to be seated, placed a snow white table napkin across my knees, and then brought me a dish on which eggs and bacon sizzled. Mechanically I watched him pour hot coffee from a silver coffee pot. Equally mechanically, I disposed of the bacon and eggs, and sipped the coffee, then fingered the white roll on the side plate.

"I suppose there isn't any chestnut bread?" I asked.

The waiter looked startled. "Chestnut bread, Excellency?" he repeated – and his tone implied that I had caused him serious offence.

"It doesn't matter. You may go now."

The man bowed and withdrew.

The splendour and glitter of the banqueting hall was overpowering, as if the room resented my presence and compared it with the crowded assemblies that it had looked down upon throughout the centuries. I suddenly felt very lonely.

A clock on the mantelpiece chimed the half hour. I rose from the breakfast table and walked slowly into the entrance hall, and again the Carabinieri saluted. On the opposite side, beyond the high doors, was my office, and I wondered what I should find there.

I began to cross the hall. One of the ceremonial guard guessed my intention and hurried forward. So I could not even open a door. This task performed, he saluted once again and returned to his post.

I found myself in a long ante-room. Heavy crimson curtains were drawn back from the windows and upright gilt chairs lined both the walls, as if in preparation for a ball. Another pair of doors faced me at the far end. I opened these unaided and found myself in my office.

Facing the door was a long mahogany desk, its top covered in crimson leather, behind it a high backed armchair. There was a telephone beside a series of bell pushes, beneath each of which was a tablet bearing the name of some functionary. I sat down in the chair and looked at the room.

Expensive rugs covered parts of the marble floor and more gilt chairs added to the furniture. On the walls hung portraits of distinguished governors and aristocrats dressed in various fashions. I concentrated on one who had ruled the city in the days of the Duchess of Parma. I wonder, I thought, if things have changed very much since you were here? The portrait stared back unblinkingly, but somehow I felt that its ghost was my friend. The others looked definitely hostile.

I lit my pipe – feeling that I should ask permission from the Duchess' representative – and endeavoured to restore my shattered sense of proportion.

The figure sitting in this chair could not possibly be me – and yet it was. The Allied Military Governor in the province of Massa Carrara had asked me to assist him by performing the duties of Governor in the City of Pontremoli. It was not a very important city, said he (that, of course, was a matter of opinion) but it controlled what was known as a *circondario*, consisting of six Communes, and was therefore of some value as an administrative centre. There was trouble with the partisans – awful cutthroats these partisans, and all Communists – and it would be as well to have somebody there to represent A.M.G. It would help to sort out billeting arrangements when necessary, for Administrative Units of the American Fifth Army were moving to Parma, and would have to pass that way to cross the Cisa Pass. So he had borrowed me for the job as he understood that I knew a little about the area – due to a visit before the war, perhaps? – and I spoke Italian. A car was at my disposal and the sooner I left the better.

The car was a vast Alfa Romeo limousine, complete with a Roman chauffeur. I still had my Special Force jeep, and decided that had better come too, partly because I knew the roads around Pontremoli to be quite unsuited to such a luxurious vehicle as the Alfa Romeo, and partly because I sensed that the friendly face of Driver Harry Lewis would be a consolation in time of trouble.

We neared Annunziata, the southern suburb of the city, as dusk was falling. News of my arrival had gone ahead. It was pouring with rain but a motor cycle escort had been sent to meet me, and we proceeded in state to the town hall. Various city dignitaries were presented and a great many people made a great many speeches. At length I was escorted to the "Governor's" Villa and left in peace.

So here I was, and in a minute I would have to begin my first day's work. I looked at the various bells. Apparently I had a formidable staff at my command. Somewhat apprehensively I pressed the bell marked "Secretary", and sat back to watch the effect.

Somebody must have been waiting with ears glued to the bell, for at once there was the clip-crop of high heels on marble as a pair of feet crossed the ante-room. The door opened.

A young lady entered, a fixed smile on her face.

"Good morning, Your Excellency," she said, in English. "I am Signorina Rossi, your secretary."

"Good morning," I said. "Please sit down."

She drew up one of the chairs from the wall, while I studied her.

She wore a clinging grey dress, cut very low at the neck. There were rings on her fingers, a heavy gold bracelet flashed on one wrist, a scarlet belt round her slim waist, bare legs and crimson sandals, the nails of her toes painted to match. Heavy gilt ear-rings distorted her ears, and her peroxide blonde hair was swept back behind them. She was pretty enough but her eyes were as hard as nails. I had a feeling that Signorina Rossi and I were not going to get on very well together. She sat on the edge of the chair dose to my desk, knees crossed, leaning slightly forward, a notebook open on her lap.

"Well, Signorina, it is a pleasure to meet you. Do you live in Pontremoli?"

"Oh, no, I come from Naples, Excellency." A flashing smile revealed strong white teeth between two ridges of carmine. "I have only been lent to A.M.G. for a few months."

"I am only on loan too," I replied, "but we will manage somehow." I smiled at her. "How do we start?"

"I have the list of engagements here, your Excellency. At nine-thirty there is an interview with the head of one of the local banks. At ten a.m., His Excellency the Bishop of Pontremoli will call; at ten-thirty, an interview requested by the Commandant of Carabinieri; at eleven a.m., the Mayor of Scorcetoli; at eleven-thirty, the Director of the local cement factory would like to see you; at twelve noon, the head of the Pontremoli hospital will call. At twelve-thirty, there is an official lunch given by the municipal council in your honour. I have not made any appointments for the afternoon as I thought you would prefer to rest. At six-thirty there is to be a reception given by the Mayor of one of the Communes, followed by a dinner at the house of a leading business man. And that is all for to-day."

"I see. If necessary, you can make some appointments after three-thirty, as we should have finished lunch by then."

"Very well," she said, "although there is nothing else of importance at the moment."

"Then let us begin; it is nearly nine-thirty."

She leant over the desk, rang a bell marked "Security Guard", and then moved slowly to the door. There was the sound of footsteps crossing the ante-room again, followed by a scuffle, and I heard one of the Carabinieri shouting, "Now then, one at a time, there is plenty of room for everybody." The door opened and the bank manager entered. For a moment I caught a glimpse of the chairs outside, and realised that they were rapidly becoming occupied.

The bank manager stayed his full half hour and I found myself involved in a long discussion concerning blocked sterling and currency restrictions. It was a relief when he went. Once more I caught sight of the ante-room, packed with humanity, who rose to their feet as the Bishop entered.

He came into the office, a smile of welcome on his face. "How pleased I am to see you, your Excellency."

It was the form of address that struck me more than anything. He wore his crimson ceremonial robes, which matched the splendour of my surroundings. Could this be the same man who had toiled up into the Valley to see me? The smile was the same, and I could see by the twinkle in his eyes that he was enjoying the situation even if I was not. Our conversation consisted of an exchange of meaningless platitudes. Whether he sensed that I was not comfortable in my new surroundings it was hard to tell. However that may be, I knew that he had been taking stock of my efficient secretary, as his final remark confirmed.

He had said good-bye to me, and had reached the door that Signorina Rossi had opened for him. In full hearing of the crowded ante-room, he remarked to the secretary:

"You are fortunate to be working for His Excellency, Signorina – he is a very brave partisan, and it is due to him that the city of Pontremoli is not in ruins. Everybody in Pontremoli wishes him well, and knows that from him we will receive nothing but justice and sympathy," and with that he departed.

Signorina Rossi looked a bit flustered, but before she could say anything, the Commander of the Carabinieri was shown in.

By the end of the morning I found myself wishing that Mario was with me, for although most of the visits had been in the nature of courtesy calls, I foresaw trouble in the future. Signorina Rossi reminded me of the luncheon appointment and said that she had arranged for the car to be ready at a quarter to one. I got up from my desk, and passed through the door into the ante-room.

Occupied with the interviews, I had forgotten about the crowd outside. I called the Secretary.

"Are you sure you have no appointments for this afternoon? There are a great many people waiting here, I could see some of them. "

"Oh no," she said hastily, flashing another bright smile. "They are only here out of curiosity. There are others who would like to see you this afternoon and I have now made appointments for them."

I took her at her word and walked through the ante-room, at the end of which one of the Carabinieri had taken up his post to keep the "curious" under observation.

The lunch was a very formal affair, but dragged on to an end at last. I returned to my office at 4 o'clock, to find the ante-room still crowded. There followed a further series of interviews. It was at six o'clock that one of the Carabinieri guards brought me a pencilled note from the Bishop, in which he said that there was some trouble in the nearby village of Scorcetoli and that the policeman could explain.

The enemy had been driven out of Pontremoli by the Beretta Brigades and Guglielmo had then done his best to restore order before returning to Borgo Taro, of which he was now the virtual ruler. On his departure, a mob of Communist pseudo- "partisans", a formation hastily raised by the politicians only a month or so before the end of hostilities, descended on various outlying villages and began to terrorise the population. One of the leaders had gone too far and had declared a curfew in the village of Scorcetoli that night because the inhabitants had made unflattering remarks about his men. He well knew that I had arrived in Pontremoli, and that the village concerned was henceforth under Allied Military Government. So there was to be a final trial of strength between us.

It was a tricky situation, but one that I felt more capable of dealing with than explaining exchange control regulations to the bank manager. There were two courses of action. I could have the man arrested, thus playing into Communist hands by giving them added fuel for their campaign against A.M.G. to the detriment of the' partisans as a whole, or I could ignore the incident and thus lose the confidence of the Pontremolesi and give the Communists an opportunity of spreading a rumour that I was frightened of them. I decided to adopt a middle course.

I called for Driver Lewis.

"Harry, take the jeep and collect Lupo and Lino, of Franco's old squad. You will find them in the suburb of Annunziata. See that you carry arms. I then want you to go to the village of Scorcetoli and bring the partisan leader here. I will give you a written note to prove that the order is official. Remember that unless he shows signs of truculence, it is an invitation, but I expect to see him here within an hour."

"One of the Carabinieri should go as well," intervened Signorina Rossi.

"No, thank you, Signorina," I replied. "This is a matter between myself and the partisans." This met with a frown of disapproval but she said no more.

Harry departed, delighted at the idea of action. An hour later he returned, and with Lupo and Lino escorted the "Dictator" into my office.

The boy wore the usual red handkerchief round his neck, and was obviously embarrassed. For ten minutes I talked to him, by which time he was blushing profusely.

"You know," I concluded, "that this area is now under the ,Military Government, which has the support of the legal Italian Government in Rome. I am empowered to arrest and imprison anybody who acts against law and order, and that includes you."

"But the people of Scorcetoli spoke insultingly about the partisans," he said.

"From what I have heard, they were perfectly justified in condemning your crowd. Unless you have left the village by ten o'clock to-morrow morning, I will have the lot of you arrested."

"Oh, so you will use Carabinieri against the partisans who fought for their country?"

"No," I replied, "I shall use partisans who did fight for their country against a mob of hooligans who have never done anything but loot, and cause trouble to the villagers. The Carabinieri have orders to see that the curfew is not applied to-night, that is all. If it is, they will report to me. You have been warned. Now you can walk back to your village, and I hope we will not meet in the morning."

The interview had taken place in the presence of his escort, for I wanted to be sure of having reliable witnesses. The culprit sullenly turned and walked out. There was no more trouble of that kind.

Next morning I purposely arrived late in my office. The ante-room was full and I recognised faces I had seen there the day before. A suspicion was forming in the back of my mind, as I took my place at the desk. Signorina Rossi was already there, her diary open at the page for that day.

"When you are ready, Excellency," she said, "we can begin the interviews. At nine-thirty – that is in five minutes – there is a representative of the Carrara marble industry, at ten o'clock, a shipping magnate from Genoa, at ten-thirty, the head of the Spezia Tourist Bureau would like to see you, at eleven o'clock ..." Before she completed her monotonous recital, I rang the bell marked "Security Guard".

The Carabiniere posted at the door of the ante-room answered the call. He saluted smartly.

"Who are all those people outside?" I asked him.

"Some are from the mountains and some are from Pontremoli, Excellency," he replied, standing stiffly to attention. "They are hoping to speak to you, when your Excellency has time."

I looked at my secretary, who had blushed a delicate pink.

"I understood from you, Signorina Rossi, that they were only here out of curiosity." I looked at the Carabiniere. "You say they want to see me?"

He made no answer, and remained at attention, his eyes fixed on an undefined point above my head. His silence spoke volumes.

"Signorina, kindly be so good as to cancel all the appointments that you have made this morning. I will spend the day interviewing the people in the ante-room."

She looked at me in dismay.

"But, your Excellency, they are of no importance whatsoever – they are only peasants, or partisans."

She could not have made a more unfortunate remark. Its immediate effect was to make me see red. Never before had I felt really mad with rage as I did then. She, poor girl, could not realise what significance the words "peasants" and "partisans" had for me. The diary had been placed open on the desk at my right elbow. I tore out the page on which she had drawn up the programme for the day and, reducing it to shreds, threw it in the gilded west. paper basket. Then I stood up with such violence that the armchair fell over with a resounding crash.

"You may go, Signorina – I no longer require your services, and will inform the Governor of Massa accordingly."

She looked at me as if about to say something, then changed her mind, and with a shrug of her shoulders, walked out of the room. The guard remained motionless.

"Stand at ease, Carabiniere. I want you to help me interview those outside and make a note of their names and addresses in this diary."

"Si, Eccellenza."

I walked to the door, while he picked up the chair, and took the diary and a pencil from the desk.

That morning I began to get acquainted for the first time with the people of Pontremoli, and for the first time began to feel the full weight of responsibility. They came in singly and in couples; they were by no means all "peasants and partisans", but represented those classes who had suffered most from the war. There was the lawyer who wanted to set up practice again after years of internment by the Fascists, and requested a written recommendation; there was the Jewish doctor whose possessions had been looted and who requested employment in an Allied hospital, the Marquis who was being hounded by the Communists because he was an aristocrat and asked for Allied protection, the schoolmaster who begged for equipment for his school, the landowner who begged for a loan with which to pay his labourers, the father whose only child was dying and who begged for a supply of penicillin to save him, and the mothers whose sons were imprisoned in camps all over Europe, and who begged for news of them. In one brief day I learnt the tragic history of wartime Italy and thanked God that England had never had to endure occupation by a ruthless enemy. There was no time for lunch and I remained in my office guiltily aware that somewhere in the city a banquet awaited me.

At five o'clock there was a momentary lull, and I went to the door and looked into the ante-room. The Carabiniere saluted.

"I don't think I can see many more to-day," I said. "Let them come in until seven o'clock, and then tell those that are left to come back to-morrow."

"Si Eccellenza."

I looked past him at the far end of the long room, trying to estimate how many petitioners remained. Every chair was occupied and I had counted up to fifty, when suddenly I saw Tarquinio's mother sitting very upright in the far corner, Tarquinio and Amelia on each side of her.

"Carabiniere, you see those three people over there – bring them in next."

I re-entered the office and waited. Mamma was the first to enter. She was wearing her best black dress and her hair was drawn back and collected in a tight bun. Her old lined face wore an awed expression and her eyes looked sad. Amelia walked demurely behind her, also dressed in black. Tarquinio looked the most nervous of the three. His thinning fair hair was ruffled and, as always in moments of excitement, his Adam's apple kept bobbing up and down as if he had violent hiccoughs.

"Mammina, what are you doing here?" I said, and went forward to embrace her as I was accustomed to do. She baffled me by stooping and kissing my hand. Before I could recover, Amelia followed suit.

"We have come to pay our respects, Eccellenza," she said.

Mamma fumbled with her dress, and produced a small bundle wrapped in a piece of silk parachute. "I have brought this, Eccellenza, we thought you might need it," and I knew that the bundle contained two eggs, a cheese, and some chestnut bread.

"Thank you, Mammina, but please don't call me Eccellenza – my real name is the one you gave me – Luigi."

At that they looked more embarrassed than ever and for a moment there was silence in the room.

"How are things in Rossano?" I said at last, in a desperate attempt to restore the situation to normal.

"Well enough," Tarquino spoke for all three. "We hoped that you would return to us, but now –" Words failed him and he looked down at his boots.

" Now, what?"

"You will not want to come up there any more, Eccellenza" Amelia spoke unemotionally, as if it was a foregone conclusion. "The Rossanesi send you their good wishes, and will always remember you. We must go now, as we have disturbed you for too long." Hastily I put my hands behind my back. I would have given anything to stop them going – to sit them down in chairs with a flask of wine, and talk far into the night about the past, but it was no good. I knew only too well that when my Rossanesi got an idea into their heads, it would take much more than a flask of wine to remove it. The women bowed, and all three filed silently out of the room.

I looked at the silk bundle that I was still holding, and felt a mad desire to escape to the mountains again, to throw myself upon the hospitality of the people of the Valley, and find that friendship that now seemed so far away. For a moment I hated the Governor's Palace and all that it represented.

That evening, I called on the Bishop. He must have known that I would come to him in due course for advice, as all my Italian and German predecessors had done over the past thirty years, for he led me into his study, a small, intimate room that had about it the air of the Confessional. His desk and chair were on a dais, the wall behind lined with glass-fronted bookshelves; in front were two rows of chairs for the use of his many petitioners, and I sat down before him in the middle of the front row. I noticed a well-thumbed copy of the Laws of the Vatican State close to his right hand, and it was easy to imagine how carefully he had studied it during the German occupation

Our meeting in the Valley had removed all barriers between us, and I spoke to him as freely as I had spoken to the Military Governor of La Spezia. We spent two hours together, and at the end of it I knew a great deal about the problems that beset Pontremoli. Never before or since have I met a man of such profound wisdom as Giovanni Sismondo. When we parted, I felt that my task would be much easier in the future.

Chapter Twenty-Two

The Freedom of the City

The moment I awoke in my State bed next morning, I realised that great changes had taken place in Government House overnight. The servant who called me gave me a cheery grin.

"Time to get up, Maggiore, you can't sleep all day," and I recognised Ardito, partisan of the International Battalion.

"How did you get here?"

"Orders, Maggiore – I found them under a tree."

"Oh, I see, those kind of orders. What is there for breakfast?"

"Two eggs and a bit of patona," he said. "What time do you want it?"

On going down to breakfast in the banqueting hall, I found Ardito standing by my chair.

"Thought I'd better bring in the breakfast myself, Maggiore," he said. "Though I didn't cook it. They are special eggs – the ones old Mamma brought." There were eggs and bacon, and on a priceless and-painted dish made in Faenza reposed a solitary piece of chestnut bread.

After breakfast, when I crossed the hall to the office, the Carabinieri looked much happier than I had ever seen them, and gave a knowing grin with their salute. Once behind my desk, I rang the bell marked Secretary, wondering what would happen. I need not have worried.

My new secretary was a very charming lady from the nearby town of Bagnone, who spoke fluent English and French, and whose husband was a partisan. We understood each other from the first moment. During the morning, Harry Lewis came in to say that the Roman chauffeur had "disappeared" and in his place to drive the official car was a partisan, one Paride, from the mountain village of Cargalla below the Cisa Pass, and an excellent driver he proved to be. The business of "governing" Pontremoli became a much more pleasant occupation after that day.

The aftermath of the war in Italy brought two consequences that seemed to find the Italian and Allied Governments equally unprepared. One was the return of thousands of prisoners of war, released from concentration camps all over the continent of Europe. The majority of them were from those Italian army units who had given inspiration to the resistance movement in the early days. Throughout the six months following the armistice of September 1943, they had fought in the mountains north of Genoa with such success that for a time the frontier zone round Domodossola was declared an independent Republic. The Allied Command in North Africa was slow to learn of it, and before they could appreciate its value to the war effort, the enemy invaded the territory and overcame the defenders; those who were not shot were transported to prison camps in Germany. Others were civilian workers who had been deported, and who had refused to collaborate with their foreign overlords. At the end of hostilities, the one desire of these unfortunates was to return to their mother country, and they crossed the frontiers on foot to find their way to their homes. During the month of May the road leading to Pontremoli from the Cisa Pass was full of them – men who were emaciated and hungry, their bleeding feet bound up with rags, and only kept alive by the overruling desire to see their families again. I could hear the continual shuffle of dragging feet all night, as they passed through Pontremoli to towns further along the Magra valley.

The other development was a growing discontent among the partisans, who felt that they had earned the right to a greater share in directing their country's affairs. This belief was aggravated by the fact that the auxiliary police which the country so badly needed were brought up from southern Italy, when use might have been made of the more disciplined partisan formations. They felt that they were being deliberately ignored by their Government, and were not sufficiently tolerant to understand the difficult task that Italy's elder statesmen had to deal with far away in Rome. Thus many partisans who were not politically minded when the war ended became easy victims of Communist oratory and were swept into the maelstrom of political intrigue.

In Pontremoli, public order remained undisturbed, and the Carabinieri, as the police force responsible for upholding the law, had a comparatively easy time. But the city had a tragedy of its own to contend with. Before their retreat the Germans had sown mines among the wheat crops and along the river banks in places where only the peasants and their women and children were likely to walk A group of partisans, including Lupo, Edmundo, and Elio Fantoni of Franco's squad, set to work to remove the mines with their bare hands. There were many casualties. Mirko, whose father Gianello was the leader of the underground movement in Pontremoli, was killed outright. Luciano Bracelli and his uncle had their legs blown off while clearing the ground in an orchard at Annunziata. Casualties happened daily among the peasant families, and yet the work went on. I tried to get mine detectors from the Allied armies, but there were none to be spared, for the same thing was happening in many towns in northern Italy.

There were other problems much easier to handle. One day I had returned from a tour of inspection to the outlying Communes, travelling in the official car, and as we neared the railway station, a despatch rider stopped Paride and handed me a note. It was from my secretary, and said that a detachment of American coloured troops had arrived in Pontremoli that afternoon, and the officer in charge, not having found me at the villa, had billeted them in the first large building he could find and then gone on to Parma, leaving the men in charge of a sergeant. All might have been well, were it not for the fact that the building chosen happened to be the convent. The Mother Superior, alarmed for the fate of the nuns, called upon me for help – would I please have the unwelcome troops removed?

We drove over the bridge to the convent, and arrived at the same time as the Bishop, who had been summoned from his palace. Fearing the worst, we walked together into the entrance hall where the Mother Superior awaited us. Behind her stood one of the nuns and a silent and abashed negro sergeant.

It seemed that the troops had requisitioned one wing of the building, the holy ladies having shut themselves up in the other. The Mother Superior was greatly distressed and begged me to restore the status quo as soon as possible, and anyway before nightfall. The Bishop tried to put her fears at rest, but she was adamant, and presently we all three fell silent, while I considered the most tactful way of dealing with the situation.

Suddenly girlish laughter broke out behind us. The Mother Superior raised her eyebrows in horror on seeing that the nun and the sergeant had retreated into a corner and were chatting amiably together. She came forward bubbling over with excitement, and explained that the sergeant was from dear old Texas, and that she had been in Texas many years ago. The sergeant joined in.

"Yes, Ma'am," he said. "We know all the same places," and his white teeth flashing in a happy smile, he turned his attention again to the nun. The Mother Superior looked relieved, so did I, so did the Bishop. She said that after all, perhaps the situation was not very serious as the language difficulty had been solved. The Bishop agreed, and we hurriedly left the building in case the Mother Superior might change her mind. As we went down the steps to our respective cars, the Bishop said quietly,

"You see, Maggiore, the Almighty sometimes has His own way of solving our problems!"

The American soldiers only stayed for two days, and went on their way laden with gifts bestowed upon them by the nuns, who probably had to do penance afterwards, but the incident undoubtedly served to strengthen international relations.

I learnt a great deal about the area from Paride. Among other places he took me to the little hamlets of Bratto and Braia, perched on hills overlooking the city to the north-east. These two hamlets regard St. George as their patron saint, and most of the male population are named "Giorgio". St. George is also said to have had something to do with the fact that, at the end of the last century, half the population emigrated to the United Kingdom and became British subjects. Their descendants return every year, in expensive cars carrying British number plates, and sit about outside the cafes in Pontremoli talking with broad cockney and Scots accents of London and Edinburgh. One day, Paride took me to his village of Cargalla, where I met his uncle.

Oriole Santino was a farmer, and one of a large colony of emigrants who had returned to the country of their birth, while proudly retaining their new nationality. Oriole had acquired American citizenship many years before, and had served in the American Army in the 1914-18 war. In spite of threats and intimidation by the Fascists, he had clung to his American passport throughout. His village is dangerously near to the arterial road that crosses the Cisa Pass to Parma, and every time the partisans carried out an ambush on it – which they did frequently – Cargalla was invaded by the infuriated Huns and Fascists on the lookout for hostages, whom they carted off to prison. Somehow Oriole always managed to return home, to carry on his self-imposed task of passing escaped prisoners of war through the lines. Many a hunted partisan sought refuge in his house, and was hidden beneath the leaves in the cattle stall under the living-room. Oriole had seen a good deal of the world during his lifetime and he exerted a valuable influence on the partisans of Pontremoli in those hard days after the war. We became firm friends, and I found his advice on partisan affairs of inestimable value.

I met others who taught me much about the people of Pontremoli. Guglielmo Gianello, father of the dead Mirko, whose infectious optimism brightened any company that he was in; Bruno Necchi, a retired captain of the Army who had turned partisan in Yugoslavia and had returned to his pre-war profession of schoolmaster; Mario Polverini, a quiet serious-minded fellow who was struggling to keep the local partisan association out of the political turmoil; Doctor Buttini, who owned a chemist's shop near the town hall and performed the arduous task of first Mayor of Pontremoli after the liberation; Avio's family, whose fortunes had crashed with the Fascist regime, and who were struggling to earn enough money to keep their home together; Professor Don Marco Mori, a learned divine who ran the local seminary; Aldo Bertolini and his family, who owned the most popular bar in the city and who had been leading figures in the Pontremoli underground movement – and countless others, professors, lawyers, doctors and members of the clergy too numerous to mention. I met parliamentary deputies preparing for the forthcoming elections, who helped me to judge the political struggle in its correct perspective, and to appreciate the difficulties that the elder statesmen had to overcome. They all accepted me as one of themselves, and before my term as Governor ended, the people of Pontremoli paid me the highest honour that they could bestow upon a foreigner.

Every year a festival is held in Pontremoli; it dates from the 2nd of July 1622, when the Madonna performed a miracle in the city and saved the population from annihilation by an outbreak of bubonic plague. As a sign of gratitude, a ceremony is held in the cathedral on this day, at which the Mayor and the city dignitaries present to the Madonna twelve pounds in weight of wax candles, which are laid upon the altar. They burn in honour of the Madonna throughout the year. It is the common belief that, should this ceremony not take place, the plague will return. It is predominantly a religious function, and culminates in a procession led by the Bishop, accompanied by the city dignitaries and the municipal band.

On the appointed day, I was invited to the Town Hall, where I found His Excellency awaiting me, flanked by the Mayor and the municipal council. After a speech outlining my activities as a partisan, in which tribute was paid to the people of the Valley, I was presented with an illuminated parchment declaring me a free citizen of Pontremoli. The Mayor explained that, according to tradition, this honour carried with it certain responsibilities, and it had never before been bestowed upon a foreigner. In the event of the city being besieged it would be my duty to bring my private army to its assistance, to man the city walls (which, incidentally, no longer exist), each man to wear my coat of arms, and to be provided with rations, forage for his horse, and an aquebus. In return, I was entitled to hang my coat of arms in the city Council Chamber. I also had one special privilege which, said the Mayor with a twinkle in his eye, was very important as I was a partisan. If, at any time, I found myself on the wrong side of the law, provided I could make my way to the cathedral and lay my hands upon the doors, it was the duty of my fellow citizens to protect me, and I could not be arrested within the confines of the city. Fortunately it has not yet been necessary to exercise this privilege, but so that all may be in order when the day comes my coat of arms now hangs in the Council Chamber.

The procession took place in the evening. It was a hot day, and the sun beat down mercilessly out of a clear sky. We formed up in the cathedral square, a municipal guard leading, followed by the Bishop and his retainers. I was stationed in the place of honour behind him, uncomfortably conspicuous in my army uniform. Behind me came the Mayor and corporation followed by the choir and then the band. After a while, Avio fell in beside me, having obtained a few days' leave for the occasion. We threaded our way to the north gate of the city, while hymns were sung and the band played alternately, then round the perimeter and down to the suburb of Annunziata and back again. Carpets and curtains were hung from the windows to brighten the scene and my fellow citizens stood at the windows and on the pavements watching. Eventually the procession began to file into the cathedral.

I looked round wildly for a means of escape, but it was not to be. Don Marco seized me by the arm and led me inside and almost up to the altar steps – the cathedral was packed with a dense crowd of worshippers, and I was the only "heathen" among them. It was an impressive spectacle that I saw.

The magnificent silver altar, saved by the Bishop from the predatory hands of the enemy, glistened in the light created by fifteen candelabra suspended from the vaulted ceiling above it; one could see, dimly outlined, the glass-fronted niche high up above the chancel in which stands the statue of the Madonna. Sunlight poured down from the great white dome above the nave and threw into relief the religious paintings in their frames which take the place of stained glass windows. On each side of us were brilliantly lighted chapels, with statues of the saints in their niches. The air was heavy with burning incense and vibrated with the strains of Gounod's immortal Ave Maria, beautifully played on the cathedral organ.

Presently the Bishop spoke to the congregation from his throne and, to my further embarrassment, his sermon dealt mainly with their latest citizen. The ceremony completed at last, we returned to the main square, and the rest of the day was given over to feasting and dancing. Since then, there has been an addition to the procedure, for every year, the Colours of the International Battalion are taken from their case in the Council Chamber and paraded through the city in the procession, carried by one of the partisans of Pontremoli.

A few days later, the office of Governor was closed down and Special Force sent orders for me to return to Siena and then to proceed to Naples for embarkation. Three days before leaving, I went into the mountains to bid farewell to the Valley.

The Rossanesi were too preoccupied with their own affairs to take much interest in what was happening in the rest of Italy. To them, Pontremoli was just a city, what little interest they took in it being influenced by the facts that their Bishop had his palace there and it provided a market for their grain and chestnut flour. Their energies were devoted to tilling the fields and taking their cattle to graze on the mountain slopes. The people of the Valley had the practical outlook of countrymen of all nations – let the past and the future take care of themselves, it is the present that matters. Fortunately, through the co-operation of an organisation known as UNRRA-CASAS, I was able to arrange for the rebuilding of the burnt houses in Rossano and Zeri, and the work was already well under way.

I had prepared them for my visit. Harry was driving the jeep and as we climbed over the frontier beyond Arzelato where the memorial now stands, we saw a tattered Union Jack fluttering from the church tower in Chiesa. Old Mamma was the first to greet us and I realised that our relations were restored, for she ran to me with cries of "Luigi, Luigi, you have come back to us," and allowed me to embrace her. We had to visit house after house and consume vast quantities of wine; in the evening there was a dance in the cow stall at Valle that served as ballroom, and I took part in the Rossanesi jig, while the "orchestra" churned out the rhythm, the hole in the base of the 'cello having been enlarged to hold two flasks of wine instead of one. For a while we relived the past, and spoke of the dead. When I left the Valley at last, the car was loaded with little white bundles and straw-covered fiascos, the final tribute from the people to whom I owed so much.

There were more farewells in Pontremoli and then we started south, away from that strange little world where so many terrible and wonderful things had happened. They had become a page of history, but one that I, at least, could never forget. It would have been a sad moment, were it not that after seven long years, I was bound for England and the girl who was shortly to become my wife.

Epilogue

I

The Bishop of Pontremoli unveiled the memorial on the 6th of June 1946. It had been designed for me by one of the city architects and was erected at the highest point beside the road where it crosses the frontier of the Valley from Arzelato. The Bishop was assisted in the ceremony by his warrior priest Don Pietro from the nearby village of Pozzo; Pontremoli was represented by officials, citizens and partisans and from the Valley came the Rossanesi. Many speeches were made, and the Colours of the International Battalion fluttered overhead in a strong summer breeze. The rest of the day was declared a Festa which now takes place there every year.

After the ceremony, the partisans began to sing the marching song of Franco the Sardinian, which the International Battalion had adopted as its own. The words rang out in the still air and were taken up by the crowd until it became a mighty roar, rolling down the mountain side to startle the sheep grazing placidly in the terraced fields below:

> "Sul suolo della Spezia
> Un di noi scenderemo
> Nel nome dei caduti,
> Noi li vendicheremo
> È la Compagnia Arditi
> Arditi e nulla piu
> È Franco che comanda,
> Andiamo giu, andiamo giu, andiamo giu."

Many legends will grow up in those mountains and be recounted from father to son as the years pass – when the cramped stone houses have been replaced and the fires no longer burn on the kitchen floor, leaving the smoke to escape as best it can, when the women no longer carry water from the wells in earthenware vessels balanced on their heads. There will be ghosts flitting among the chestnut trees to stir up memories of a glorious past, when a group of sturdy peasants proved their worth as members of the human race, and gave Italy a new name with which to emblazon another page of her history, in the Valley of Rossano.

II

And what of the partisans?

There is no happy ending to their part in the story.

The British Italian Society sponsored a visit by Dani and Avio to London two years ago, and invited Aldo, Nino Ferrari, and Captain Gambarotta (who brought the miraculous bottle of whisky to Torpiana) to the Coronation Festivities in 1953. Of the others, Colonel Fontana, Ardito, and old John of Buzzo died after the war; some have made progress in their various careers, some have emigrated, some have swelled the ranks of the unemployed, and some are in prison. Nello's family have never received the medal which he so bravely won. Very few of those who remain like it to be known that they were partisans. I found this attitude hard to understand, until I discovered the reason.

In 1950 I visited the city of Parma at the invitation of Gianni, the Bersagliere sentry from my prison camp at Veano, for the official celebrations that take place on the 25th April each year, the anniversary of the end of the war in Italy. The main event was a march past by partisans. I noticed that they were very numerous, all wore red scarves about their necks, and not one familiar face did I see.

The parade over, I was standing beneath the bronze statue of Garibaldi – its shirt and cap painted red for the occasion – in the main square, when I saw a partisan in front of me who had taken part.

"Buon giorno, Partigiano," I said. "Did you enjoy the parade?"

He looked suspiciously at my civilian clothes.

"Si, Signore," he said at last.

To break the ice, I offered him a drink at a nearby cafe, and while we disposed of a Vermouth, he became more amiable.

"There are a great many partisans in Parma," I said. "What formation do you belong to?"

"Garibaldini," he replied.

He could not have been more than eighteen years old, and a rapid calculation produced the answer that he must have been about thirteen when the war ended.

"I have heard a lot about them. Were you with them during the war?"

"Oh no," he said. "I was only twelve when the war ended."

We finished our drinks, and went into the square again.

"I became a partisan after the war," he added "You see I am a Partisan of Peace."

"I see." I stopped on the edge of the pavement and looked at him.

"Viva Stalin," I said, with what was intended to be irony.

"Viva Stalin, Compangno," he replied, eyes flashing as he gave me the Communist clenched fist salute. We parted company.

Now I understood why my old companions in arms do not like to be referred to as "partisans". We have been forgotton, and our places taken by the rank and file of the Communist party who are making political profit out of our good name. There is not very much we can do about it.

Ormont House.
15th October 1954.